VIRAL SPIRAL

ALSO BY DAVID BOLLIER

Brand Name Bullies

Silent Theft

Aiming Higher

Sophisticated Sabotage
(with co-authors Thomas O. McGarity
and Sidney Shapiro)

The Great Hartford Circus Fire
(with co-author Henry S. Cohn)

Freedom from Harm
(with co-author Joan Claybrook)

VIRAL SPIRAL

How the Commoners Built a
Digital Republic of Their Own

David Bollier

THE NEW PRESS

NEW YORK
LONDON

To Norman Lear,
dear friend
and intrepid explorer of the frontiers
of democratic practice

Published in the United States by The New Press, New York, 2008
Distributed by W. W. Norton & Company, Inc., New York

ISBN 978-1-59558-396-3 (hc.)
CIP data available

The New Press was established in 1990 as a not-for-profit alternative to the large, commercial publishing houses currently dominating the book publishing industry. The New Press operates in the public interest rather than for private gain, and is committed to publishing, in innovative ways, works of educational, cultural, and community value that are often deemed insufficiently profitable.

www.thenewpress.com

A Caravan book.
For more information, visit www.caravanbooks.org.

Composition by dix!
This book was set in Bembo

Printed in the United States of America

10 9 8 7 6 5 4 3 2 1

CONTENTS

ACKNOWLEDGMENTS

In this book, as with any book, dozens of barely visible means of support conspired to help me. It has been hard work, but any author with sufficient honesty and self-awareness realizes the extent to which he or she is a lens that refracts the experiences, insights, and writings of others. It is a pleasure to pay tribute to those who have been helpful to me.

I am grateful to Larry Lessig, a singular visionary in developing the commons as a new paradigm, for helping to make this book possible. He submitted to several interviews, facilitated my research within the Creative Commons community, and, despite our shared involvements in various projects over the years, scrupulously respected my independence. It is also a pleasure to thank the Rockefeller Foundation for generously helping to cover my research, reporting, and travel expenses.

I interviewed or consulted with more than one hundred people in the course of writing this book. I want to thank each of them for carving out some time to speak with me and openly sharing their thoughts. The Creative Commons and iCommons staff were particularly helpful in making time for me, pointing me toward useful documents and Web sites and sharing their expertise. I must single out Glenn Otis Brown, Mia Garlick, Joichi Ito, Heather Ford, Tomislav Medak, Ronaldo Lemos, and Hal Abelson for their special assistance.

Since writing a book resembles parachuting into a forest and then trying to find one's way out, I was pleased to have many friends who recommended some useful paths to follow. After reading some or all of my manuscript, the following friends and colleagues offered many invaluable suggestions and criticisms: Charles Schweik, Elliot E. Maxwell, John Seely Brown, Emily Levine, Peter Suber, Julie

Ristau, Jay Walljasper, Jonathan Rowe, Kathryn Milun, Laurie Racine, and Gigi Sohn. It hardly requires saying that none of these astute readers bears any responsibility for the choices that I ultimately made.

For the past seven years, the Tomales Bay Institute, recently renamed On the Commons, has nurtured my thinking and commitment to the commons. (On the Commons has no formal affiliation to the Creative Commons world, but it enthusiastically shares its commitments to the commons.) I am grateful to my colleagues Peter Barnes, Harriet Barlow, and Julie Ristau for their unflagging support of my book over the past three years, even when it impinged on my other responsibilities.

In the early stages of this book, Elaine Pagels was unusually generous in offering her help, and my conversations with Nick Bromell helped pry loose some important insights used in my conclusion. Cherry Alvarado was of extraordinary help to me as she transcribed scores of interviews with unfailing good humor and precision. I also wish to thank Andrew Ryder for resourceful assistance in the early stages of my research.

I have dedicated this book to my dear friend and mentor Norman Lear. The zeal, imagination, and grace that he brings to the simple imperatives of citizenship have been more instructive and inspirational than he perhaps realizes. He has also been of incalculable support to me in my headstrong explorations of the commons.

Finally, at the end of the day, when I emerge from my writer's lair or return from yet another research and reporting trip, it is Ellen and my sons Sam and Tom who indulge my absences, mental and physical, and reacquaint me with the things that matter most. I could not wish for more.

David Bollier
Amherst, Massachusetts
May 1, 2008

INTRODUCTION

It started with that great leap forward in human history the Internet, which gave rise to free software in the 1980s and then the World Wide Web in the early 1990s. The shockingly open Internet, fortified by these tools, began empowering a brash new culture of rank amateurs—you and me. And this began to reverse the fierce tide of twentieth-century media. Ordinary people went online, if only to escape the incessant blare of television and radio, the intrusive ads and the narrow spectrum of expression. People started to discover their own voices . . . and their own capabilities . . . and one another.

As the commoners began to take charge of their lives, they discovered anew that traditional markets, governments, and laws were often not serving their needs very well. And so some pioneers had the audacity to invent an infrastructure to host new alternatives: free and open-source software. Private licenses to enable sharing and bypass the oppressive complications of copyright law. A crazy quilt of Web applications. And new types of companies that thrive on servicing social communities on open platforms.

At the dawn of the twenty-first century, the commoners began to make some headway. More people were shifting their attention away from commercial media to homegrown genres—listservs, Web sites, chat rooms, instant messaging, and later, blogs, podcasts, and wikis. A swirling mass of artists, legal scholars, techies, activists, and even scientists and businesses began to create their own online commons. They self-organized themselves into a loosely coordinated movement dedicated to "free culture."

The viral spiral was under way.

Viral spiral? *Viral,* a term borrowed from medical science, refers to the way in which new ideas and innovations on the Internet can proliferate with astonishing speed. A video clip, a blog post, an advertisement released on the Internet tumbles into other people's consciousness in unexpected ways and becomes the raw feedstock for new creativity and culture. This is one reason the Internet is so powerful—it virally propagates creativity. A novel idea that is openly released in the networked environment can often find its way to a distant person or improbable project that can really benefit from it. This recombinative capacity—efficiently coordinated through search engines, Web logs, informal social networks, and other means— radically accelerates the process of innovation. It enlivens democratic culture by hosting egalitarian encounters among strangers and voluntary associations of citizens. Alexis de Tocqueville would be proud.

The *spiral* of *viral spiral* refers to the way in which the innovation of one Internet cohort rapidly becomes a platform used by later generations to build their own follow-on innovations. It is a corkscrew paradigm of change: *viral* networking feeds an upward *spiral* of innovation. The cutting-edge thread achieves one twist of change, positioning a later thread to leverage another twist, which leverages yet another. Place these spirals in the context of an open Internet, where they can sweep across vast domains of life and cat-alyze new principles of order and social practice, and you begin to get a sense of the transformative power of viral spirals.

The term *viral spiral* is apt, additionally, because it suggests a process of change that is anything but clean, direct, and mechanical. In the networked environment, there is rarely a direct cause-and-effect. Things happen in messy, irregular, indeterminate, serendipi-tous ways. Life on the Internet does not take place on a stable Cartesian grid—orderly, timeless, universal—but on a constantly pulsating, dynamic, and labyrinthine *web* of finely interconnected threads radiating through countless nodes. Here the context is as rich and generative as any individual. *Viral spiral* calls attention to the holistic and historical dynamics of life on the Web, which has a very different metaphysical feel than the world of twentieth-century media.

The viral spiral began with free software (code that is free to use, not code at no cost) and later produced the Web. Once these open platforms had sufficiently matured, tech wizards realized that soft-ware's great promise is not as a stand-alone tool on PCs, but as a social platform for Web-based sharing and collaboration. The commoners could then begin to imagine: How might these tools be used to overcome the arbitrary and confusing limitations of copyright law? One answer, the Creative Commons (CC) licenses, a free set of public licenses for sharing content, helped mitigate the legal risks of sharing of works under copyright law. This innovation, in turn, helped unleash a massive wave of follow-on innovations.

Web 2.0 applications flourished, many of them relying upon sharing made legal through CC licenses. By avoiding the costly overhead of centralized production and marketing, and tapping into the social vitality of a commons, Web 2.0 platforms have enabled ordinary people to share photos (Flickr), favorite browser bookmarks (del.icio.us), favorite news stories (Digg, Reddit), and homemade videos (YouTube). They let people access user-created archives (Wikipedia, Internet Archive, Ourmedia.org), collaborate in news gathering (OhmyNews, Assignment Zero), participate in immersive communities (Second Life), and build open-business models (Magnatune, Revver, Jamendo).

This book seeks to trace the long arc of change wrought by a kaleidoscopic swarm of commoners besieged by oppressive copyright laws, empowered by digital technologies, and possessed of a vision for a more open, democratic society. Their movement has been fired by the rhetoric of freedom and actualized by digital technologies connected by the Internet. These systems have made it extremely cheap and easy for ordinary people to copy and share things, and to collaborate and organize. They have democratized creativity on a global scale, challenging the legitimacy and power of all sorts of centralized, hierarchical institutions.

This larger story has rarely been told in its larger scope. It is at base a story of visionary individuals determined to protect the shared code, content, and social community that they have collectively generated. Richard Stallman pioneered the development of free software; Lawrence Lessig waged challenges against excessive copyright protection and led the development of the Creative Commons licenses; citizen-archivist Eric Eldred fought to preserve his online body of public-domain literature and the community that grew up around it. These are simply the better-known leaders of a movement that has attracted thousands of commoners who are building legally defensible commons into which to pour their creative energies and live their lives.

The commons—a hazy concept to many people—is a new paradigm for creating value and organizing a community of shared interest. It is a vehicle by which new sorts of self-organized publics can gather together and exercise new types of citizenship. The commons can even serve as a viable alternative to markets that have grown stodgy, manipulative, and coercive. A commons arises whenever a given community decides that it wishes to manage a resource in a collective manner, with special regard for equitable access, use, and sustainability. The commons is a means by which individuals can band together with like-minded souls and express a sovereignty of their own.

Self-styled commoners can now be found in dozens of nations around the world. They are locally rooted but internationally aware citizens of the Internet. They don't just tolerate diversity (ethnic, cultural, aesthetic, intellectual), they celebrate it. Although commoners may have their personal affinities—free software, open-access publishing, remix music, or countless others—they tend to see themselves as part of a larger movement. They share an enthusiasm for innovation and change that burbles up from the bottom, and are known to roll their eyes at the thickheadedness of the mainstream media, which always seem to be a few steps behind.

If there is an element of self-congratulatory elitism at times, it stems from the freedom of commoners to negotiate their own rules and the pleasure of outmaneuvering conventional institutions. The commoners know how to plug into the specialized Web sites and practitioner communities that can provide just-in-time, highly specialized expertise. As Herbert Simon, the computer-oriented social scientist, once put it, "The meaning of 'knowing' today has shifted from being able to remember and repeat information to being able to find and use it."[1] Commoners realize that this other way of being, outside hierarchical institutions, in the open space where viral spirals of innovation are free to materialize, is an important source of their insurgent power.

It is perilous to generalize about a movement that has so many disparate parts pushing and pulling and innovating in so many different directions at once. Yet it is safe to say that the commoners— a digital embodiment of *e pluribus unum*—share a common goal. They wish to transcend the limitations of copyright law in order to build their own online communities. It's not as if the commoners are necessarily hostile to copyright law, markets, or centralized institutions. Indeed, many of them work for large corporations and universities; many rely on copyright to earn a livelihood; many are entrepreneurs.

Yet the people who are inventing new commons have some deeper aspirations and allegiances. They glimpse the liberating potential of the Internet, and they worry about the totalizing inclinations of large corporations and the state, especially their tendency to standardize and coerce behavior. They object as well to processes that are not transparent. They dislike the impediments to direct access and participation, the limitations of credentialed expertise and arbitrary curbs on people's freedom.

One of the first major gatherings of international commoners occurred in June 2006, when several hundred people from fifty nations converged on Rio de Janeiro, Brazil, for the iCommons Summit. The people of this multinational, eclectic vanguard blend the sophistication of the establishment in matters of power and politics with the bravado and playfulness of Beat poets. There were indie musicians who can deconstruct the terms of a record company licensing agreement with Talmudic precision. There were Web designers who understand the political implications of arcane rules made by the World Wide Web Consortium, a technical standards body. The lawyers and law professors who discourse about Section 114 of the Copyright Act are likely to groove on the remix career of Danger Mouse and the appropriationist antics of Negativland, a sound-collage band. James Boyle and Jennifer Jenkins, two law scholars at Duke Law School, even published a superhero comic book, *Down by Law!*, which demystifies the vagaries of the "fair use doctrine" through a filmmaker character resembling video game heroine Lara Croft.[2] (Fair use is a provision of copyright law that makes it legal to excerpt portions of a copyrighted work for non-commercial, educational, and personal purposes.)

The Rise of Socially Created Value

The salience of electronic commerce has, at times, obscured an important fact—that the commons is one of the most potent forces driving innovation in our time. Individuals working with one another via social networks are a growing force in our economy and society. This phenomenon has many manifestations, and goes by many names—"peer production," "social production," "smart mobs," the "wisdom of crowds," "crowdsourcing," and "the commons."[3] The basic point is that *socially created value* is increasingly competing with conventional markets, as GNU/Linux has famously shown. Through an open, accessible commons, one can efficiently tap into the "wisdom of the crowd," nurture experimentation, accelerate innovation, and foster new forms of democratic practice.

This is why so many ordinary people—without necessarily having degrees, institutional affiliations, or wealth—are embarking upon projects that, in big and small ways, are building a new order of culture and commerce. It is an emerging universe of economic, social, and cultural activity animated by self-directed amateurs, citizens, artists, entrepreneurs, and irregulars.

Hugh McGuire, a Montreal-based writer and Web designer, is one. In 2005, he started LibriVox, a digital library of free public-domain audio books that are read and recorded by volunteers. More than ten thousand people a day visit the Web site to download audio files of Twain, Kafka, Shakespeare, Dostoyevsky, and others, in nearly a dozen languages.[4] The Faulkes Telescope Project in Australia lets high school students connect with other students, and with professional astronomers, to scan the skies with robotic, online telescopes.[5] In a similar type of learning commons, the Bugscope project in the

United States enables students to operate a scanning electronic microscope in real time, using a simple Web browser on a classroom computer connected to the Internet.[6]

Thousands of individual authors, musicians, and filmmakers are using Web tools and Creative Commons licenses to transform markets for creative works—or, more accurately, to blend the market and commons into integrated hybrids. A nonprofit humanitarian group dedicated to doing reconstructive surgery for children in poor countries, Interplast, produced an Oscar-winning film, *A Story of Healing*, in 1997. Ten years later, it released the film under a Creative Commons license as a way to publicize Interplast's work while retaining ownership of the film: a benefit for both film buffs and Interplast.[7]

Scoopt, a Glasgow, Scotland–based photography agency, acts as a broker to help bloggers and amateurs sell newsworthy photos and videos to the commercial media.[8] The Boston band Two Ton Shoe released its music on the Web for free to market its concerts. Out of the blue, a South Korean record label called one day to say it loved the band and could it come over to Seoul, all expenses paid, to perform four concerts? Each one sold out.[9] Boing Boing blogger and cyberactivist Cory Doctorow released his 2003 science-fiction novel, *Down and Out in the Magic Kingdom*, under a CC license, reaping a whirlwind of worldwide exposure.[10]

The Commoners Build a Digital Republic of Their Own

The profusion of commons on the Internet may appear to be a spontaneous and natural development. In fact, it is a hard-won achievement. An infrastructure of software, legal rights, practical expertise, and social ethics had to be imagined, built, and defended. In a sense, the commoners had to invent themselves as commoners. They had to learn to recognize their own distinct interests—in how to control their creative works, how to organize their communities, and how to engage with market players without being co-opted. They have, in fact, invented a new sort of democratic polity within the edifice of the conventional nation-state.

The commoners differ from most of their corporate brethren in their enthusiasm for sharing. They prefer to freely distribute their writing, music, and videos. As a general rule, they don't like to encase their work in airtight bubbles of property rights reinforced by technological locks. They envision cyberspace more as a peaceable, sociable kingdom than as a take-no-prisoners market. They honor the individual while respecting community norms. They are enthusiastic about sharing while respecting the utility of markets. Idealistic yet pragmatic, they share a commitment to open platforms, social cooperation, and elemental human freedoms.

It is all very well to spout such lofty goals. But how to actualize them? That is the story that the following pages recount. It has been the work of a generation, some visionary leaders, and countless individuals to articulate a loosely shared vision, build the infrastructure, and develop the social practices and norms. This project has not been animated by a grand political ideology, but rather is the result of countless initiatives, grand and incremental, of an extended global family of hackers, lawyers, bloggers, artists, and other supporters of free culture.

And yet, despite its focus on culture and its aversion to conventional politics, the growth of this movement is starting to have political implications. In an influential 2003 essay, James F. Moore announced the arrival of "an emerging second superpower."[11] It was not a nation, but the coalescence of people from around the world who were asserting common values, and forming new public identities, via online networks. The people of this emerging "superpower," Moore said, are concerned with improving the environment, public health, human rights, and social development. He cited as early examples the international campaign to ban land mines and the Seattle protests against the World Trade Organization in 1999. The power and legitimacy of this "second superpower" do not derive from the constitutional framework of a nation-state, but from its ability to capture and project people's everyday feelings, social values, and creativity onto the world stage. Never in history has the individual had such cheap, unfettered access to global audiences, big and small.

The awakening superpower described in *Viral Spiral* is not a conventional political or ideological movement that focuses on legislation and a clutch of "issues." While commoners do not dismiss these activities as unimportant, most are focused on the freedom of their peer communities to create, communicate, and share. When defending these freedoms requires wading into conventional politics and law, they are prepared to go there. But otherwise, the commoners are more intent on building a kind of parallel social order, inscribed within the regnant political economy but animated by their own values. Even now, the political/cultural sensibilities of this order are only vaguely understood by governments, politicians, and corporate leaders. The idea of "freedom without anarchy, control without government, consensus without power"—as Lawrence Lessig put it in 1999 [12]—is just too counterintuitive for the conventionally minded to take seriously.

Very early on, the commoners identified copyright law as a major impediment to their vision of a "sharing economy." It is not that they revile copyright law as such; indeed, many commoners defend the importance of copyright law to creative endeavor. The problem, they insist, is that large corporations with vast inventories of copyrighted works—film studios, record labels, book publishers, software companies—have used their political power unfairly to extend the scope and term of copyright privileges. A limited monopoly granted by the U.S. Constitution has morphed into an expansive, near-perpetual monopoly, enforced by intrusive technologies and draconian penalties.

The resulting curbs on citizen freedom, as large entertainment and media corporations gain legal privileges at the expense of the public, is a complicated issue that I return to in chapter 2. But it is worth noting briefly why copyright law has been particularly harmful to the commons in the digital age. When Congress enacted a major revision of U.S. copyright law in 1976, it eliminated a long-standing requirement that works had to be formally registered in order to receive copyright protection. [13] Under the new law, *everything* became automatically copyrighted upon creation. This meant that all information and artistic work created after 1978 (when the law took effect) has been born into an invisible envelope of property rights. It sounds appealing to eliminate bureaucratic formalities like registration. But the shift to automatic copyright has meant that every digital scribble is born with a © branded on its side. *Culture = private property.*

The various industries that rely on copyrights have welcomed this development because it helps them portray their ownership rights as all-encompassing. They can cast the public's right to use works without permission or payment—traditionally guaranteed under the fair use doctrine and the public domain—as exceptions to the general rule of absolute property rights. "What could be wrong with enclosing works in ever-stronger packages of property rights?" the music and film industries argue. "That's how new economic wealth is created." The media oligopolies that control most of television, film, music, and news gathering naturally want to protect their commercial content. It is the fruit of a vast system of fixed investment—equipment, high-priced stars, lawyers, distribution channels, advertising, etc.—and copyright law is an important tool for protecting that value.

The Internet has profoundly disrupted this model of market production, however. The Internet is a distributed media system of low-cost capital (your personal computer) strung together with inexpensive transmission and software. Instead of being run by a centralized corporation that relies upon professionals and experts above all else, the Internet is a noncommercial infrastructure that empowers amateurs, citizens, and ordinary individuals in all their quirky, authentic variety. The mass media have long regarded people as a commodifiable audience to be sold to advertisers in tidy demographic units.

Now, thanks to the Internet, "the people formerly known as the audience" (in Jay Rosen's wonderful phrase) are morphing into a differentiated organism of flesh-and-blood, idiosyncratic individuals, as if awakening from a spell. Newly empowered to speak as they wish, in their own distinctive, personal voices to a global public of whoever cares to listen, people are creating their own transnational tribes. They are reclaiming culture from the tyranny of mass-media economics and national boundaries. In Lessig's words, Internet users are overthrowing the "read only" culture that characterized the "weirdly totalitarian" communications of the twentieth century. In its place they are installing the "read/write" culture that invites everyone to be a creator, as well as a consumer and sharer, of culture.[14] A new online citizenry is arising, one that regards its socially negotiated rules and norms as at least as legitimate as those established by conventional law.

Two profoundly incommensurate media systems are locked in a struggle for survival or supremacy, depending upon your perspective or, perhaps, mutual accommodation. For the moment, we live in a confusing interregnum—a transition that pits the dwindling power and often desperate strategies of Centralized Media against the callow, experimental vigor of Internet-based media. This much is clear, however: a world organized around centralized control, strict intellectual property rights, and hierarchies of credentialed experts is under siege. A radically different order of society based on open access, decentralized creativity, collaborative intelligence, and cheap and easy sharing is ascendant. Or to put it more precisely, we are stumbling into a strange hybrid order that combines both worlds—mass media and online networks—on terms that have yet to be negotiated.

The Rise of the Commoners

But who shall do the negotiating? Who will set forth a compelling alternative to centralized media, and build it? That task has fallen to a loosely coordinated global federation of digital tribes—the free software and open-source hackers, the Wikipedians, the bloggers and citizen-journalists, the remix musicians and filmmakers, the avant-garde artists and political dissidents, the educators and scientists, and many others. It is a spontaneous folk-tech conspiracy that belongs to everyone and no one.

As we will see in chapter 1, Richard Stallman, the legendary hacker, played an indispensable first-mover role by creating a sovereign domain from which to negotiate with commercial players: free software. The software commons and later digital commons inspired by it owe an incalculable debt to Stallman's ingenious legal innovation, the General Public License, or GPL, launched in 1989. The GPL is a license for authorizing anyone to use a copyrighted software program so long as any copies or derivative versions are also made available on the same terms. This fairly simple license enables programmers to contribute code to a common pool without fear that someone might privatize and destroy the commons.

As the computer revolution continued through the 1980s and the Internet went wide in the 1990s, the antisocial, antidemocratic implications of copyright law in networked spaces became more evident. As we will see in chapter 2, a growing community of progressive legal scholars blew the whistle on some nasty developments in copyright law that were shrinking the public's fair use rights and the public domain. Scholars such as James Boyle, Pamela Samuelson, Jessica Litman, Yochai Benkler, Lawrence Lessig, Jonathan Zittrain, and Peter Jaszi provided invaluable legal analyses about the imperiled democratic polity of cyberspace.

By the late 1990s, this legal scholarship was in full flower, Internet usage was soaring, and the free software movement produced its first significant free operating system, GNU/Linux. The commoners were ready to take practical action. Lessig, then a professor at Harvard Law School, engineered a major constitutional test case, *Eldred v. Reno* (later *Eldred v. Ashcroft*), to try to strike down a twenty-year extension of copyright terms—a case that reached the U.S. Supreme Court in 2002. At the same time, Lessig and a number of his colleagues, including MIT computer scientist Hal Abelson, Duke law professor James Boyle, and Villanova law professor Michael W. Carroll, came together to explore innovative ways to protect the public domain. It was a rare moment in history in which an ad hoc salon of brilliant, civic-minded thinkers from diverse fields of endeavor found one another, gave themselves the freedom to dream big thoughts, and embarked upon practical plans to make them real.

The immediate upshot of their legal and techno ingenuity, as we will see in chapters 3 and 4, was the drafting of the Creative Commons licenses and the organization that would promote them. The purpose of these free, standardized public licenses was, and is, to get beyond the binary choice imposed by copyright law. Why must a work be considered either a chunk of privately owned property or a kind of nonproperty completely open to anyone without constraint ("in the public domain")? The CC licenses overcome this stifling either/or logic by articulating a new middle ground of ownership that sanctions sharing and collaboration under specified terms. To stress its difference from copyright law, which declares "All Rights Reserved," the Creative Commons licenses bear the tagline "Some Rights Reserved."

Like free software, the CC licenses paradoxically rely upon copyright law to legally protect the commons. The licenses use the rights of ownership granted by copyright law not to exclude others, but to invite them to share. The licenses recognize authors' interests in owning and controlling their work—but they also recognize that new creativity owes many social and intergenerational debts. Creativity is not something that emanates solely from the mind of the "romantic author," as copyright mythology has it; it also derives from artistic communities and previous generations of authors and artists. The CC licenses provide a legal means to allow works to circulate so that people can create something new. *Share, reuse, and remix, legally,* as Creative Commons puts it.

After the licenses were introduced in December 2002, they proliferated throughout the Internet and dozens of nations as if by spontaneous combustion. It turns out that the licenses have been more than a legal fix for the limitations of copyright law. They are a powerful form of social signaling. The licenses have proven to be a flag for commoners to advertise their identities as members of a culturally insurgent sharing economy—an aesthetic/political underground, one might say. Attaching the CC logo to one's blog, video, MP3 file, or laptop case became a way to proclaim one's support for free culture. Suddenly, all sorts of participatory projects could be seen as elements of a larger movement. By 2007, authors had applied one or more of six CC licenses to 90 million works, by one conservative estimate, or more than 220 million works by another estimate. Collectively, CC-licensed works constitute a class of cultural works that are "born free" to be legally shared and reused with few impediments.

A great deal of the Creative Commons story revolves around its founder, the cerebral yet passionate Larry Lessig, a constitutional law professor at Harvard in the mid-1990s until a move to Stanford Law School in 2000. As a scholar with a sophisticated grasp of digital technologies, Lessig was one of the first to recognize that as computers became the infrastructure for society, software code was acquiring the force of law. His 1999 classic, *Code and Other Laws of Cyberspace*, is renowned for offering a deep theoretical framework for understanding how politics, law, technology, and social norms shape the character of cyberspace—and in turn, any society.

In popularizing this message, it didn't hurt that Lessig, an experienced classroom lecturer, is a poised and spellbinding performer. On the tech and copyright circuit, in fact, he has become something of a rock star. With his expansive forehead and wire glasses, Lessig looks every bit the professor he is. Yet in his signature black jeans and sport jacket, delivering punchy one-liners punctuated by arresting visuals projected on a big screen behind him, Lessig makes a powerful impression. He's a geek-chic techie, intellectual, legal activist, and showman all rolled into one.

From the beginning, Lessig and his colleagues wondered, How far can the sharing ethic be engineered? Just how far can the idea of free culture extend? As it turns out, quite far. At first, of course, the free culture project was applied mostly to Web-based text and music. But as we see in chapters 5 through 12, the technologies and ethic of free culture have rapidly taken root in many creative sectors of society—video, music, books, science, education—and even business and international arts and culture.

Remix culture. Thanks to digital technologies, musicians can sample verbatim snippets of other musicians' work in their own works, producing "remixes" that blend sounds from a number of copyrighted songs. It's all patently illegal, of course, unless you're wealthy enough to pay for the rights to use a sample. But that hasn't stopped artists.

In fact, the underground remix scene has become so robust that even established artists feel obliged to engage with it to bolster their street cred. With a wink and a nudge from record labels, major rap stars like Jay-Z and Eminem have released instrumental tracks of their records in the hope and expectation that remix *auteurs* will recycle the tracks. Record labels have quietly relied on mixtapes—personalized compilations of tracks—to gain exposure and credibility.[15] To help an illegal social art go legit, many artists are using Creative Commons licenses and public-domain sound clips to build a legal body of remix works.

In the video world, too, the remix impulse has found expression in its own form of derivative creativity, the mashup. From underground remakes of *Star Wars* films to parodies of celebrities, citizen-amateurs are taking original video clips and mixing them with other images, pop music tracks, and their own narrations. When Alaska senator Ted Stevens compared the Internet to a "series of tubes," video clips of his rambling speech were mashed up and set to a techno dance beat. Beyond this playful subculture, serious film-makers are using CC licenses on their works to develop innovative distribution systems that attract large audiences and earn money. Machinima animations—a filmmaking technique that uses computer game action sequences, shot with in-game cameras and then edited together—are pioneering a new market niche, in part through their free distribution under a CC license.

Open business. One of the most surprising recent developments has been the rise of "open business" models. Unlike traditional businesses that depend upon proprietary technology or content, a new breed of businesses see lucrative opportunities in exploiting open, participatory networks. The pioneer in this strategy was IBM, which in 2000 embraced GNU/Linux, the open-source computer operating system, as the centerpiece of its service and consulting business.[16] Dozens of small, Internet-based companies are now exploiting open networks to build more flexible, sustainable enterprises.

The key insight about many open-platform businesses is that

they no longer look to copyright or patent law as tools to assert market control. Their goal is not to exclude others, but to amass large communities. Open businesses understand that exclusive property rights can stifle the value creation that comes with mass participation, and so they strive to find ways to "honor the commons" while making money in socially acceptable forms of advertising, subscriptions, or consulting services. The brave new economics of "peer production" is enabling forward-thinking businesses to use social collaboration among thousands, or even millions, of people to create social communities that are the foundation for significant profits. *BusinessWeek* heralded this development in a major cover story in 2005, "The Power of Us," and called sharing "the net's next disruption." [17]

Science as a commons. The world of scientific research has long depended on open sharing and collaboration. But increasingly, copyrights, patents, and university rules are limiting the flow of scientific knowledge. The resulting gridlock of rights in knowledge is impeding new discoveries and innovation. Because of copyright restrictions and software incompatibilities, scientists studying genetics, proteins, and marine biology often cannot access databases containing vital research. Or they cannot easily share physical samples of lab samples. When the maker of Golden Rice, a vitamin-enhanced bioengineered rice, tried to distribute its seeds to millions of people in poor countries, it first had to get permissions from seventy patent holders and obtain six Material Transfer Agreements (which govern the sharing of biomedical research substances). [18]

The problem of acquiring, organizing, and sharing scientific knowledge is becoming more acute, paradoxically enough, as more scientific disciplines become dependent on computers and the networked sharing of data. To help deal with some of these issues, the Creative Commons in 2005 launched a new project known as the Science Commons to try to redesign the information infrastructure for scientific research. The basic idea is to "break down barriers to sharing that are hindering innovation in the sciences," says John

Wilbanks, executive director of Science Commons. Working with the National Academy of Sciences and other research bodies, Wilbanks is collaborating with astronomers, archaeologists, microbiologists, and medical researchers to develop better ways to make vast scientific literatures more computer-friendly, and databases technically compatible, so that they can be searched, organized, and used more effectively.

Open education and learning. A new class of knowledge commons is poised to join free and open-source software, the Creative Commons and Wikipedia as a coherent social movement. The new groundswell goes by the awkward name "Open Educational Resources," or OER.[19] One of the earlier pioneers of the movement was the Massachusetts Institute of Technology which has put virtually all of its course materials on the Web, for free, through its OpenCourseWare initiative. The practice has now spread to scores of colleges and universities around the world, and inspired a broader set of OER initiatives: digital repositories for articles, reports, and data; open-access scholarly journals that bypass expensive commercial publishers; and collaborative Web sites for developing teaching materials. There are wikis for students and scholars working together, sites to share multimedia presentations, and much more.

The OER movement has particular importance for people who want to learn but don't have the money or resources—scholars in developing countries, students struggling to pay for their educations, people in remote or rural locations, people with specialized learning needs. OER is based on the proposition that it will not only be cheaper or perhaps free if teachers and students can share their materials through the Web, it will also enable more effective types of learning. So the OER movement is dedicated to making learning tools cheaper and more accessible. The revolutionary idea behind OER is to transform traditional education—teachers imparting information to passive students—into a more learner-driven process facilitated by teachers. Self-directed, socially driven learning supplants formal, hierarchical modes of teaching.

The international sharing economy. Shortly after the first CC licenses were released in 2002, dozens of exceptionally capable volunteers—from Japan, Finland, Brazil, South Africa, and other countries—came knocking on the door of CC. How can we adapt the American CC licenses to our respective national legal systems? they asked. This unexpected turn prompted the Creative Commons to inaugurate Creative Commons International, based in Berlin, Germany, to supervise the complicated task of "porting" the U.S. licenses to other legal jurisdictions. To date, CC affiliates in forty-seven nations have adapted the U.S. licenses to their legal systems, and another seventeen have porting projects under way.

The volunteers include avant-garde artists in Croatia, free software programmers in the Netherlands, South Korean judges, Italian law professors, South African musicians, Malaysian citizen-journalists, Bulgarian filmmakers, and Taiwanese songwriters. The passionate international licensing movement has even been embraced by the Brazilian government, which has proclaimed itself the first Free Culture Nation. As usage of the licenses spreads, they are effectively becoming the default international legal structure of the sharing economy.

A New Type of Emergent Democracy?

Peter Suber, a leading champion of open-access scholarly publishing, once explained to me why a disparate, rambunctious crowd of commoners spread around the globe might wish to work together to do something about their plight. "People are taking back their culture," Peter said. "People who have not been served by the current law have quietly endured it until they saw that they didn't have to." [20] The Creative Commons has become both a symbol and a tool for people to reclaim creativity and culture from the mass-media leviathans. The licenses and the organization have become instruments to advance a participatory, sharing economy and culture.

How far can it go? Will it significantly affect conventional politics and government? Can it bring market forces and social needs into a more positive alignment?

This book is about the struggle to imagine this new world and push it as far as it can go. It is, in one sense, a history, but "history" suggests that the story is over and done. The truth is that the commons movement is tremendously robust and expansive right now. The early history about free software, the public domain, and the Creative Commons is simply a necessary foundation for understanding the propulsive logic of what is happening.

The story told in these pages is not entirely new; it has been told in fragments and through the restless lens of journalism. But it has not been told in its larger conceptual and historical sweep. That's partly because most of its players are usually seen in isolation from one another, and not put in the context of the larger open-platform revolution. It's also because the free culture movement, nothwithstanding its vigor, is generally eclipsed by the big-money corporate developments that are ostensibly more important. But that is precisely the problem: conventional economics does not understand the actual significance of open platforms and the commons. We need to understand what the online commons represent: a powerful sociotechnological paradigm that is reordering some basic dynamics of creative practice, culture, politics, and everyday life.

I am no bystander in this story, it must be said, but a commoner who has grappled with the quandaries of copyright law and the public domain for nearly twenty years. In 2001, after co-founding Public Knowledge, a Washington advocacy group to defend the public's stake in copyright and Internet policies, I went on to write books on the market enclosure of myriad commons and on the absurd expansions of copyright and trademark law. Over the course of this work, I discovered how a commons analysis can help us understand the digital revolution. It can help us see that it is not just about technological innovation, but about social and legal innovations. Reading Elinor Ostrom and Yochai Benkler, in particular—two leading theorists of the commons—I came to realize that social communities, and not just markets, must be recognized as powerful vehicles for creating value. I realized that many basic assumptions about property rights, as embedded in copyright law and neoclassical economics, fail to take account of the generative power of online communities.

How then shall we create the commons and protect it? That question lies at the core of this book and the history of the commoners in cyberspace. I am mostly interested in exploring how the Creative Commons has galvanized a variety of interrelated crusades to build a digital republic of, by, and for the commoners. One reason why a small licensing project has grown into a powerful global brand is that, at a time of mass-media dominance and political stalemate, free culture offers an idealistic alternative vision. Something you can *do*. A movement in which everyone can play some useful role. The free culture movement stands for reclaiming culture by making it yourself and for reviving democracy by starting in your own digital backyard. CC stands for personal authenticity and diversity in a world of stale, mass-marketed product. It stands for good fun and the joys of sharing.

Put the CC logo on your blog or music CD or video, and you too can belong to a movement that slyly sticks it to Big Media without getting into an ugly brawl. Don't get mad, the CC community seems to whisper. Just affiliate with a growing virtual nation of creative renegades. Transcend a rigged game by migrating to a commons of your own making. Build therefore your own world, in the manner of Henry David Thoreau—then imagine its embrace by many others. Imagine it radiating into conventional politics with a refreshing ethic of open accountability and earned rewards, a contempt for coercive business practices and governmental abuses, and an insistence upon transparency, participation, and the consent of the governed. You may be an entrepreneur who just wants to build a profitable business, or a scientist who just wants to find better ways to research Huntington's disease. The commons has some solutions in these areas, too. This big-tent movement is unabashedly ecumenical.

This is the vision now exploding around the world anyway. The recurring question in its earliest days, and now, remains—How can we build it out? *Can* it be built out? And how far? For the commoners, just asking the question is halfway to answering it.

PART I

Harbingers of the Sharing Economy

The rise of the sharing economy had its roots among the renegades living on the periphery of mainstream culture. At the time, they were largely invisible to one another. They had few ways of making common cause and no shared language for even naming the forces that troubled them. It was the 1990s, after all, a time of alluring mercantile fantasies about the limitless possibilities of the laissez-faire "information superhighway." Even for those who could pierce the mystifications, the new technologies were so new, powerful, and perplexing that it was difficult to understand their full implications.

The renegades, while sharing a vision of technological progress, were disturbed by many on-the-ground realities. A small network of hackers, for example, was enraged to learn that software was becoming a closed, proprietary product. Companies could prohibit interested individuals from tinkering with their own, legally purchased software. On both creative and political grounds, this development was odious to Richard Stallman, a brilliant programmer who soon hatched a dream of building a protected kingdom of "free software," the subject of chapter 1.

Meanwhile, a loose community of legal scholars and tech activists was becoming alarmed by the antisocial, anti-democratic tendencies of copyright law and digital technology. Scholars such as Lawrence Lessig, James Boyle, and Hal Abelson began to realize that copyright law and software code were acquiring unsuspected powers to redesign our political and social order. They also began to understand the ways in which the public domain is not a wasteland, as conventional minds had long supposed, but a highly generative zone of culture. This intellectual journey is described in chapter 2.

Finally, it was becoming painfully apparent to yet another amorphous band of renegades—artists, musicians, writers, scientists, educators, citizens—that copyright law and technological controls were artificially restricting their creative freedoms. With scant public attention, the music, film, and publishing industries were using their clout to protect their archaic business models at the expense of innovation and the commons. This onslaught ultimately provoked one exemplary commoner, Eric Eldred, to team up with legal scholar Lawrence Lessig to mount an unprecedented constitutional challenge to copyright law, the focus of chapter 3.

None of these surges of innovative dissent was well funded or particularly promising. For the most part, they were improvisational experiments undertaken by public-spirited individuals determined to vindicate their visions for a better society. With the benefit of hindsight, we can now see that while many of these initiatives were only partially successful, each was indispensable to the larger, later task of imagining and building a digital republic to secure basic human freedoms, the subject of Part II.

1

IN THE BEGINNING WAS FREE SOFTWARE

Richard Stallman's mythic struggle to protect the commons of code set the viral spiral in motion.

The struggle to imagine and invent the software commons, which later set in motion a viral spiral now known as free culture, began with Richard Stallman, a brilliant, eccentric MIT computer programmer. Stallman's history as a hacker and legal innovator has by now become the stuff of legend. As one of the first people to confront the deep tensions between proprietary control and the public domain in software development, Stallman has achieved that rare pinnacle in the high-tech world, the status of celebrity geek. Besides his programming prowess, he is renowned for devising the GNU General Public License, more commonly known as the GPL, an ingenious legal mechanism to protect shared software code.

Stallman—or RMS, as he likes to be called—has become an iconic figure in the history of free culture in part because he showed courageous leadership in protecting the commons well before anyone else realized that there was even a serious problem. He was a lone voice in the wilderness for at least ten years before the Internet became a mass medium, and so has earned enormous credibility as a leader on matters of free culture. He has also been reviled by some as an autocratic zealot with bad manners and strident rhetoric.

It is perhaps fitting that Stallman could be mistaken for an Old Testament prophet. He is a shaggy, intense, and fiercely stubborn guy. On his Web site, visitors can find a gag photo of him posed as Saint IGNUcius, with his hand raised in mock genuflection and his head encircled by a gold aureole (held in place by two admiring acoyltes). He has been known to deliver lectures barefoot, sleep on the couch in a borrowed office for weeks at a time, and excoriate admirers for using taboo phrases like "intellectual property" and "copyright protection." Stallman explains that "intellectual property" incorrectly conflates three distinct bodies of law—copyright, patent, and trademark—and emphasizes individual property rights over public rights. "Copyright protection" is misleading, he says, because it implies a positive, necessary act of *defending* something rather than an acquisitive, aggressive act of a monopolist. Stallman considers *content* to be a disparaging word, better replaced by "works of authorship." He has even made a list of fourteen words that he urges people to avoid because of their politically misleading valences.[1]

Even though Stallman frequently speaks to august academic and scientific gatherings, and meets with the heads of state in developing countries, he resembles a defiant hippie. Yet for his visionary role in developing free software and the free software philosophy, Stallman is treated as if he were a head of state . . . which, in a way, he is. His story has irresistible mythological resonances—the hero's journey through hardship and scorn, later vindicated by triumph and acclaim. But for many, including his most ardent admirers, Stallman's stubborn idealism can also be supremely maddening.

His first encounter with the creeping ethic of proprietary control, in the late 1970s, is an oft-told part of his story. The Xerox Corporation had donated an experimental laser printer to the MIT Artificial Intelligence Lab, where Stallman was then a graduate student. The printer was constantly jamming, causing frustration and wasting everyone's time. Stallman wanted to devise a software fix but he discovered that the source code was proprietary. Determined to find out who was responsible and force them to fix it, he tracked down a computer scientist at Carnegie Mellon University who had supposedly written the code—but the professor refused to help him; he had signed a nondisclosure agreement with Xerox prohibiting him from sharing the code.

Stallman considered Xerox's lockup of code a profound moral offense that violated the integrity of the hacker community. (Among practitioners, *hacker* is a term of respect for an ingenious, resourceful programmer, not an accusation of criminality.) Not only did it prevent people from fixing their own equipment and software, the nondisclosure agreement flouted the Golden Rule. It prohibited sharing with one's neighbor. The proprietary ethic was not just immoral, by Stallman's lights, but a barrier to developing great software.

By the late 1970s, he had developed a breakthrough text editor, Emacs, in collaboration with a large community of programmers. "Everybody and his brother was writing his own collection of rede-fined screen-editor commands, a command for everything he typi-cally liked to do," Stallman wrote. "People would pass them around and improve them, making them more powerful and more general. The collections of redefinitions gradually became system programs in their own right."[2] Emacs was one of the first software projects to demonstrate the feasibility of large-scale software collaboration and the deep well of innovative ideas that it could yield. Emacs enabled programmers to add new features with great ease, and to constantly upgrade and customize the program with the latest improvements. The Emacs experiment demonstrated that *sharing* and *interoperability* are vital principles for a flourishing online commons.

Two problems quickly emerged, however. If people did not communicate their innovations back to the group, divergent streams of incompatible code would produce a Tower of Babel effect. Sec-ond, if the code and its derivations were not shared with everyone, the usefulness of the program would slowly decline. The flow of in-novation would dissipate.

To solve these problems, Stallman invented a user contract that he called the "Emacs Commune." It declared to all users that Emacs was "distributed on a basis of communal sharing, which means that all improvements must be given back to me to be incorporated and distributed." He enforced the provisions of the contract with an iron hand. As Stallman biographer Sam Williams writes, when the administrators for the MIT Laboratory for Computer Science insti-tuted a new password system—which Stallman considered an anti-social power grab—he "initiated a software 'strike,' refusing to send lab members the latest version of Emacs until they rejected the se-curity system on the lab's computers. The move did little to improve Stallman's growing reputation as an extremist, but it got the point

across: commune members were expected to speak up for basic
hacker values."

Stallman was groping for a way to sustain the hacker ethic of
community and sharing in the face of new types of top-down control. Some programmers were beginning to install code that would
turn off access to a program unless money was paid. Others were
copyrighting programs that had been developed by the community
of programmers. Bill Gates, as an undergraduate at Harvard in the
late 1970s, was nearly expelled for using publicly funded labs to create commercial software. He was forced to put his code into the
public domain, whereupon he left the university to found an obscure Albuquerque company called Micro-Soft.

Software was simply becoming too lucrative for it to remain a
shared resource—an attitude that enraged Stallman. He was determined to preserve the integrity of what we would now call the software commons. It was an immense challenge because copyright
law makes no provisions for community ownership of creative work
beyond "joint authorship" among named individuals. Stallman
wanted to devise a way to ensure that all the talent and innovation
created by commoners would *stay* in the commons. The idea that an
outsider—a university administrator, software entrepreneur, or large
company—could intrude upon a hacker community and take its
work was an appalling injustice to Stallman.

Yet this was precisely what was happening to the hacker community at MIT's AI Lab in the early 1980s. It was slowly disintegrat-
ing as one programmer after another trooped off to join commercial
software ventures; the software itself was becoming annexed into the
marketplace. Software for personal computers, which was just then
appearing on the market, was sold as a proprietary product. This
meant that the source code—the deep design architecture of the
program that operated everything—was inaccessible.[3] Perhaps most
disturbing to Stallman at the time was that the leading mainframe
operating system, Unix, was locking up its source code. Unix had
been developed by AT&T with generous federal funding, and had
been generally available for free within academic computing circles.
At the time, most mainframe software was given away to encourage

buyers to purchase the computer hardware. But when the Department of Justice broke up AT&T in 1984 to spur competition, it also enabled AT&T to enter other lines of business. Naturally, the company was eager to maximize its profits, so in 1985 it began to charge a licensing fee for Unix.

Stallman grieved at the disintegration of the hacker community at the AI Lab as closed software programs inexorably became the norm. As he wrote at the time:

> The people remaining at the lab were the professors, students, and non-hacker researchers, who did not know how to maintain the system, or the hardware, or want to know. Machines began to break and never be fixed; sometimes they just got thrown out. Needed changes in software could not be made. The non-hackers reacted to this by turning to commercial systems, bringing with them fascism and license agreements. I used to wander through the lab, through the rooms so empty at night where they used to be full, and think, "Oh my poor AI lab! You are dying and I can't save you."

Stallman compared himself to Ishi, "the last survivor of a dead [Native American] culture. And I don't really belong in the world anymore. And in some ways I feel I ought to be dead."

Stallman decided to leave MIT—why stay?—but with a brash plan: to develop a free software operating system that would be compatible with Unix. It would be his brave, determined effort to preserve the hacker ethic. He dubbed his initiative the GNU Project, with "GNU" standing for "GNU's Not Unix"—a recursive hacker's pun. He also started, in 1985, the Free Software Foundation to help develop GNU software projects and distribute them for free to anyone. (The foundation now occupies a fifth-floor office on a narrow commercial street in downtown Boston.)

The Emacs Commune experience had taught Stallman about the limits of informal social norms in protecting the software commons. It also revealed the difficulties of being the central coordinator of all code changes. This time, in developing a set of software programs for his GNU Project, Stallman came up with a better idea—a legally enforceable license. The goal was to ensure that people could have free access to all derivative works and share and reuse software. The licensing rights were based on the rights of ownership conferred by copyright law.

Stallman called his license the GNU General Public License, or GPL. He puckishly referred to it as "copyleft," and illustrated it with a reverse copyright symbol (a backward *c* in a circle). Just as programmers pride themselves on coming up with ingenious hacks to solve a software problem, so the GPL is regarded as a world-class hack around copyright law. Copyright law has no provisions for protecting works developed by a large community of creators. Nor does it offer a way to prevent works from being made proprietary. Indeed, that's the point of copyright law—to create private property rights.

The GPL bypasses these structural limitations of copyright law by carving out a new zone of collective ownership. A work licensed under the GPL permits users to run any program, copy it, modify it, and distribute it in any modified form. The only limitation is that any derivative work must also be licensed under the GPL. This provision of the GPL means that the license is *automatically* applied to any derivative work, and to any derivative of a derivative, and so on—hence its viral nature.* The GPL ensures that the value created by a given group of commoners shall stay within the commons. To guarantee the viral power of the license, users of GPL'd works cannot modify the licensing terms. No one has to pay to use a GPL'd work—but as a condition for using it, people are legally obliged to license any derivative versions under the GPL. In this way, a GPL'd work is born and forever protected as "shareable."

Version 1.0 of the GPL was first published in 1989. It was significant, writes Sam Williams, because it "demonstrated the intellec-

---

* Stallman told me he considers it "a common calumny to compare the GNU GPL to a virus. That is not only insulting (I have a virus infection in my throat right now and it is no fun), it is also inaccurate, because the GPL does not spread like a virus. It spreads like a spider plant: if you cut off a piece and plant it over here, it grows over here."

tual similarity between legal code and software code. Implicit within the GPL's preamble was a profound message: instead of viewing copyright law with suspicion, hackers should view it as yet another system begging to be hacked."[4] The GPL also served to articulate, as a matter of law, the value of collaborative work. A universe of code that might previously have been regarded as part of the "public domain"—subject to free and unrestricted access—could now be seen in a subtly different light.

A GPL'd work is not part of the public domain, because the public domain has no rules constraining how a work may be used. Works in the public domain are open to anyone. The GPL is similar, but with one very important restriction: no private appropriation is allowed. Any follow-on uses must remain free for others to use (a provision that some property rights libertarians regard as "coercive"). Works in the public domain, by contrast, are vulnerable to privatization because someone need only add a smidgen of "originality" to the work and she would own a copyright in the resulting work. A GPL'd work and its derivatives stay free forever—because anyone who tries to privatize a GPL'd work is infringing on the license.

For Stallman, the GPL became the symbol and tool for enacting his distinct political vision of "freedom." The license rests on four kinds of freedoms for users of software (which he lists using computer protocols):

Freedom 0: The freedom to run the program for any purpose;

Freedom 1: The freedom to study how the program works, and to adapt it to your needs. (Access to the source code is a precondition for this);

Freedom 2: The freedom to redistribute copies so you can help your neighbor; and

Freedom 3: The freedom to improve the program, and release your improvements to the public, so that the whole community benefits. (Access to the source code is a precondition for this.)

Stallman has become an evangelist for the idea of freedom embodied in all the GNU programs. He refuses to use any software programs that are not "free," and he has refused to allow his appearances to be Webcast if the software being used was not "free." "If I am to be an honest advocate for free software," said Stallman, "I can hardly go around giving speeches, then put pressure on people to use nonfree software. I'd be undermining my own cause. And if I don't show that I take my principles seriously, I can't expect anybody else to take them seriously." [5]

Stallman has no problems with people making money off software. He just wants to guarantee that a person can legally use, copy, modify, and distribute the source code. There is thus an important distinction between software that is commercial (possibly free) and software that is proprietary (never free). Stallman tries to explain the distinction in a catchphrase that has become something of a mantra in free software circles: *"free as in 'free speech,' not as in 'free beer.' "* The point is that code must be freely accessible, not that it should be free of charge. (This is why "freeware" is not the same as free software. Freeware may be free of charge, but it does not necessarily make its source code accessible.)

Eben Moglen, a professor of law at Columbia University and general counsel for the Free Software Foundation since 1994, calls the provisions of the GPL "elegant and simple. They respond to the proposition that when the marginal cost of goods is zero, any non-zero cost of barbed wire is too high. That's a fact about the twenty-first century, and everybody had better get used to it. Yet as you know, there are enormous cultural enterprises profoundly committed to the proposition that more and more barbed wire is necessary. And their basic strategy is to get that barbed wire paid for by the public everywhere." [6]

The GPL truly was something new under the sun: a legally enforceable tool to vouchsafe a commons of software code. The license is based on copyright law yet it cleverly turns copyright law against itself, limiting its reach and carving out a legally protected zone to build and protect the public domain. In the larger scheme of things, the GPL was an outgrowth of the "gift economy" ethic that has governed academic life for centuries and computer science for decades. What made the GPL different from these (abridgeable) social norms was its legal enforceability.

The GPL might well have remained an interesting but arcane curiosity of the software world but for two related developments: the rise of the Internet in the 1990s and software's growing role as core infrastructure in modern society. As the computer and Internet revolutions have transformed countless aspects of daily life, it has become evident that software is not just another product. Its design architecture is seminally important to our civic freedoms and democratic culture. Or as Lawrence Lessig famously put it in his 1999 book *Code*, "code is law." Software can affect how a business can function, how information is organized and presented, and how individuals can think, connect with one another, and collaborate. Code invisibly structures people's relationships, and thus serves as a kind of digital constitutional order. As an economic force, software has become as critical as steel or transportation in previous eras: a building block for the basic activities of the economy, businesses, households, and personal life.

Stallman's atavistic zeal to preserve the hacker community, embodied in the GPL, did not immediately inspire others. In fact, most of the tech world was focused on how to convert software into a marketable product. Initially, the GPL functioned like a spore lying dormant, waiting until a more hospitable climate could activate its full potential. Outside of the tech world, few people knew about the GPL, or cared.* And even most techies were oblivious to the political implications of free software.

Working under the banner of the Free Software Foundation, Stallman continued through the 1980s and 1990s to write a wide number of programs needed to build a completely free operating

---

* The GPL is not the only software license around, of course, although it was, and remains, the most demanding in terms of protecting the commons of code. Other popular open-source licenses include the MIT, BSD, and Apache licenses, but each of these permit, but do not require, that the source code of derivative works also be freely available. The GPL, however, became the license used for Linux, a quirk of history that has had far-reaching implications.

system. But just as Lennon's music was better after finding McCartney, Stallman's free software needed to find Linus Torvalds's kernel for a Unix-like operating system. (A kernel is the core element of an operating system that controls how the various applications and utilities that comprise the system will run.)

In 1991, Torvalds was a twenty-one-year-old computer science student at the University of Helsinki, in Finland. Frustrated by the expense and complexity of Unix, and its inability to work on personal computers, Torvalds set out to build a Unix-like operating system on his IBM AT, which had a 33-megahertz processor and four megabytes of memory. Torvalds released a primitive version of his program to an online newsgroup and was astonished when a hundred hackers responded within a few months to offer suggestions and additions. Over the next few years, hundreds of additional programmers joined the project, which he named "Linux" by combining his first name, "Linus," with "Unix." The first official release of his program came in 1994.[7]

The Linux kernel, when combined with the GNU programs developed by Stallman and his free software colleagues, constituted a complete computer operating system—an astonishing and unexpected achievement. Even wizened computer scientists could hardly believe that something as complex as an operating system could be developed by thousands of strangers dispersed around the globe, cooperating via the Internet. Everyone assumed that a software program had to be organized by a fairly small group of leaders actively supervising the work of subordinates through a hierarchical authority system—that is, by a single corporation. Yet here was a virtual community of hackers, with no payroll or corporate structure, coming together in a loose, voluntary, quasi-egalitarian way, led by leaders who had earned the trust and respect of some highly talented programmers.

The real innovation of Linux, writes Eric S. Raymond, a leading analyst of the technology, was "not technical, but sociological":

> Linux was rather casually hacked on by huge numbers of volunteers coordinating only through the Internet. Quality

was maintained not by rigid standards or autocracy but by the naively simple strategy of releasing every week and getting feedback from hundreds of users within days, creating a sort of rapid Darwinian selection on the mutations introduced by developers. To the amazement of almost everyone, this worked quite well.[8]

The Free Software Foundation had a nominal project to develop a kernel, but it was not progressing very quickly. The Linux kernel, while primitive, "was running and ready for experimentation," writes Steven Weber in his book *The Success of Open Source*: "Its crude functionality was interesting enough to make people believe that it could, with work, evolve into something important. That promise was critical and drove the broader development process from early on."[9]

There were other powerful forces driving the development of Linux. Throughout the 1990s, Microsoft continued to leverage its monopoly grip over the operating system of personal computers, eventually attracting the attention of the U.S. Department of Justice, which filed an antitrust lawsuit against the company. Software competitors such as Hewlett-Packard, Sun Microsystems, and IBM found that rallying behind an open-source alternative—one that was legally protected against being taken private by anyone else— offered a terrific way to compete against Microsoft.

Meanwhile, the once-free Unix software program was becoming a fragmented mess. So many different versions of Unix were being sold that users were frustrated by the proliferation of incompatible proprietary versions. In the words of a Sun Microsystems executive at the time, users were unhappy with the "duplication of effort around different implementations, leading to high prices; poor compatibility; and worst of all, slower development as each separate Unix vendor had to solve the same kinds of problems independently. Unix has become stagnant. . . ."[10]

Given these problems, there was great appeal in a Unix-like operating system with freely available source code. Linux helped address the fragmentation of Unix implementations and the difficulties of competing against the Microsoft monopoly. Knowing that Linux was GPL'd, hackers, academics, and software companies could all contribute to its development without fear that someone might take it private, squander their contributions, or use it in hostile ways. A commons of software code offered a highly pragmatic solution to a market dysfunction.

Stallman's GNU Project and Torvalds's Linux software were clearly synergistic, but they represented very different styles. The GNU Project was a slower, more centrally run project compared to the "release early and often" developmental approach used by the Linux community. In addition, Stallman and Torvalds had temperamental and leadership differences. Stallman has tended to be more overbearing and directive than Torvalds, who does not bring a political analysis to the table and is said to be more tolerant of diverse talents.[11]

So despite their natural affinities, the Free Software Community and the Linux community never found their way to a grand merger. Stallman has applauded Linux's success, but he has also resented the eclipse of GNU programs used in the operating system by the Linux name. This prompted Stallman to rechristen the program "GNU/Linux," a formulation that many people now choose to honor.

Yet many hackers, annoyed at Stallman's political crusades and crusty personal style, committed their own linguistic raid by renaming "free software" as "open source software," with a twist. As GNU/Linux became more widely used in the 1990s, and more corporations began to seriously consider using it, the word *free* in "free software" was increasingly seen as a problem. The "free as in free speech, not as in free beer" slogan never quite dispelled popular misconceptions about the intended sense of the word *free*. Corporate information technology (IT) managers were highly wary about putting mission-critical corporate systems in the hands of software that could be had for *free*. Imagine telling the boss that you put the company's fate in the hands of a program you downloaded from the Internet for free!

Many corporate executives clearly recognized the practical

value of free software; they just had no interest in joining Stallman's ideological crusade or being publicly associated with him. They did not necessarily want to become champions of the "four freedoms" or the political vision implicit in free software. They simply wanted code that works well. As Eric Raymond wrote: "It seemed clear to us in retrospect that the term 'free software' had done our movement tremendous damage over the years. Part of this stemmed from the well-known 'free speech/free beer' ambiguity. Most of it came from something worse—the strong association of the term 'free software' with hostility to intellectual property rights, communism, and other ideas hardly likely to endear themselves to an MIS [management information systems] manager." [12]

One response to this issue was the rebranding of free software as "open-source" software. A number of leading free software programmers, most notably Bruce Perens, launched an initiative to set forth a consensus definition of software that would be called "open-source." At the time, Perens was deeply involved with a community of hackers in developing a version of Linux known as the Debian GNU/Linux distribution. Perens and other leading hackers not only wanted to shed the off-putting political dimensions of "free software," they wanted to help people deal with the confusing proliferation of licenses. A lot of software claimed to be free, but who could really tell what that meant when the terms were so complicated and legalistic?

The Open Source Initiative, begun in 1998, helped solve this problem by enumerating criteria that it considered significant in judging a program to be "open." [13] Its criteria, drawn from the Debian community, helped standardize and stabilize the definition of open-source software. Unlike the GPL, permissive software licenses such as BSD and MIT *allow* a program to be freely copied, modified, and distributed but don't *require* it. A programmer can choose to make a proprietary derivative without violating the license.

The Open Source Initiative has focused more on the practical, technical merits of software than on the moral or political concerns that have consumed Stallman. Free software, as Stallman conceived it, is about building a cohesive moral community of programmers dedicated to "freedom." The backers of open-source software are not necessarily hostile to those ideals but are more interested in building reliable, marketable software and improving business performance. As Elliot Maxwell described the free software/open source schism:

> [S]upporters of the Open Source Initiative were willing to acknowledge a role for proprietary software and unwilling to ban any link between open-source software and proprietary software. Richard Stallman aptly characterized the differences: "We disagree on the basic principles but agree more or less on the practical recommendations. So we can and do work together on many specific projects."[14]

The philosophical rift between free software and open-source software amounts to a "friendly schism," a set of divergent approaches that has been bridged in some respects by language.[15] Observers often use the acronym FOSS to refer to both free software and open-source software, or sometimes FLOSS—the *L* stands for the French word *libre,* which avoids the double meaning of the English word *free.* Whatever term is used, free and open-source software has become a critical tool for making online marketplaces more competitive, and for creating open, accessible spaces for experimentation. In his classic essay, "The Cathedral and the Bazaar," Eric Raymond explains how the licenses help elicit important noneconomic, personal energies:

> The Linux world behaves in many respects like a free market or an ecology, a collection of selfish agents attempting to maximize utility which in the process produces a self-correcting spontaneous order more elaborate and efficient than any amount of central planning could have achieved. . . . The utility function Linux hackers are maximizing is not classically economic, but is the intangible of their own ego satisfaction and reputation among other hackers.[16]

It turns out that an accessible collaborative process, FOSS, can elicit passions and creativity that entrenched markets often cannot. In this respect, FOSS is more than a type of freely usable software; it reunites two vectors of human behavior that economists have long considered separate, and points to the need for new, more integrated theories of economic and social behavior.

FOSS represents a new breed of "social production," one that draws upon social energies that neoclassical economists have long discounted or ignored. It mobilizes the personal passions and moral idealism of individuals, going beyond the overt economic incentives that economists consider indispensable to wealth creation. The eighteenth-century economist Adam Smith would be pleased. He realized, in his 1776 book *The Wealth of Nations*, that people are naturally given to "truck, barter and exchange"—but he also recognized, in his earlier *The Theory of Moral Sentiments*, written in 1759, that people are motivated by deep impulses of human sympathy and morality. Neoclassical economists have long segregated these as two divergent classes of human behavior, regarding altruism and social sympathies as subordinate to the rational, utility-maximizing, self-serving behavior. FOSS embodies a new synthesis—and a challenge to economists to rethink their crude model of human behavior, *Homo economicus*. Free software may have started as mere software, but it has become an existence proof that individual and collective goals, and the marketplace and the commons, are not such distinct arenas.[17] They are tightly intertwined, but in ways we do not fully understand. This is a golden thread that will reappear in later chapters.

Red Hat, a company founded in 1993 by Robert Young, was the first to recognize the potential of selling a custom version (or "distribution") of GNU/Linux as a branded product, along with technical support. A few years later, IBM became one of the first large corporations to recognize the social realities of GNU/Linux and its larger strategic and competitive implications in the networked environment. In 1998 IBM presciently saw that the new software development ecosystem was becoming far too variegated and robust for any single company to dominate. It understood that its proprietary mainframe software could not dominate the burgeoning, diversified Internet-driven marketplace, and so the company adopted the open-source Apache Web server program in its new line of Web-Sphere business software.

It was a daring move that began to bring the corporate and open-source worlds closer together. Two years later, in 2000, IBM announced that it would spend $1 billion to help develop GNU/Linux for its customer base. IBM shrewdly realized that its customers wanted to slash costs, overcome system incompatibilities, and avoid expensive technology "lock-ins" to single vendors. GNU/Linux filled this need well. IBM also realized that GNU/Linux could help it compete against Microsoft. By assigning its property rights to the commons, IBM could eliminate expensive property rights litigation, entice other companies to help it improve the code (they could be confident that IBM could not take the code private), and unleash a worldwide torrent of creative energy focused on GNU/Linux. Way ahead of the curve, IBM decided to reposition itself for the emerging networked marketplace by making money through tech service and support, rather than through proprietary software alone.[18]

It was not long before other large tech companies realized the benefits of going open source. Amazon and eBay both saw that they could not affordably expand their large computer infrastructures without converting to GNU/Linux. GNU/Linux is now used in everything from Motorola cell phones to NASA supercomputers to laptop computers. In 2005, *Business Week* magazine wrote, "Linux may bring about the greatest power shift in the computer industry since the birth of the PC, because it lets companies replace expensive proprietary systems with cheap commodity servers."[19] As many as one-third of the programmers working on open-source projects are corporate employees, according to a 2002 survey.[20]

With faster computing speeds and cost savings of 50 percent or more on hardware and 20 percent on software, GNU/Linux has demonstrated the value proposition of the commons. Open source demonstrated that it can be cheaper and more efficacious to collaborate in the production of a shared resource based on common standards than to strictly buy and own it as private property.

But how does open source work without a conventional market apparatus? The past few years have seen a proliferation of sociological and economic theories about how open-source communities create value. One formulation, by Rishab Ghosh, compares free software development to a "cooking pot," in which you can give a little to the pot yet take a lot—with no one else being the poorer. "Value" is not measured economically at the point of transaction, as in a market, but in the nonmonetary *flow* of value that a project elicits (via volunteers) and generates (through shared software).[21] Another important formulation, which we will revisit later, comes from Harvard law professor Yochai Benkler, who has written that the Internet makes it cheap and easy to access expertise anywhere on the network, rendering conventional forms of corporate organization costly and cumbersome for many functions. Communities based on social trust and reciprocity are capable of mobilizing creativity and commitment in ways that market incentives often cannot—and this can have profound economic implications.[22] Benkler's analysis helps explain how a global corps of volunteers could create an operating system that, in many respects, outperforms software created by a well-paid army of Microsoft employees.

A funny thing happened to free and open-source software as it matured. It became hip. It acquired a cultural cachet that extends well beyond the cloistered precincts of computing. "Open source" has become a universal signifier for any activity that is participatory, collaborative, democratic, and accountable. Innovators within filmmaking, politics, education, biological research, and drug development, among other fields, have embraced the term to describe their own attempts to transform hidebound, hierarchical systems into open, accessible, and distributed meritocracies. Open source has become so much of a cultural meme—a self-replicating symbol and idea—that when the Bikram yoga franchise sought to shut down unlicensed uses of its yoga techniques, dissident yoga teachers organized themselves into a nonprofit that they called Open Source Yoga Unity. To tweak the supremacy of Coca-Cola and Pepsi, culture jammers even developed nonproprietary recipes for a cola drink and beer called "open source cola" and "open source beer."[23]

Stallman's radical acts of dissent in the 1980s, regarded with bemusement and incredulity at the time, have become, twenty-five years later, a widely embraced ideal. Small-*d* democrats everywhere invoke open source to lambaste closed and corrupt political systems and to express their aspirations for political transcendence. People invoke open source to express a vision of life free from overcommercialization and corporate manipulation. The term enables one to champion bracing democratic ideals without seeming naïve or flaky because, after all, free software is solid stuff. Moreover, despite its image as the software of choice for granola-loving hippies, free and open-source software is entirely compatible with the commercial marketplace. How suspect can open source be when it has been embraced by the likes of IBM, Hewlett-Packard, and Sun Microsystems?

The appeal of "openness" has become so great that it is sometimes difficult to recognize that *limits* on openness are not only necessary but desirable. The dark side of openness is the spam that clogs the Internet, the ability to commit fraud and identity theft, and the opportunities for disturbed adults to prey sexually upon children. Still, the virtues of an open environment are undeniable; what is more difficult is negotiating the proper levels of openness for a given realm of online life.

Nearly twenty years after the introduction of the GPL, free software has expanded phenomenally. It has given rise to countless FOSS software applications, many of which are major viral hits such as Thunderbird (e-mail), Firefox (Web browser), Ubuntu (desktop GNU/Linux), and Asterisk (Internet telephony). FOSS has set in motion, directly or indirectly, some powerful viral spirals such as the Creative Commons licenses, the iCommons/free culture movement, the Science Commons project, the open educational resource movement, and a new breed of open-business ventures. Yet Richard Stallman sees little connection between these various "open" movements and free software; he regards "open" projects as too vaguely defined to guarantee that their work is truly "free" in the free software sense of the term. "Openness and freedom are not the same thing," said Stallman, who takes pains to differentiate free software from open-source software, emphasizing the political freedoms that lie at the heart of the former.[24]

Any revolution is not just about new tools and social practices, however. It is also about developing new ways of understanding the world. People must begin to *see* things in a new perspective and *talk* with a new vocabulary. In the 1990s, as Disney, Time Warner, Viacom, and other media giants realized how disruptive the Internet might be, the public was generally oblivious that it might have a direct stake in the outcome of Internet and copyright policy battles. Big Media was flexing its muscles to institute all sorts of self-serving, protectionist fixes—copy-protection technologies, broader copyright privileges, one-sided software and Web licenses, and much more—and most public-interest groups and civic organizations were nowhere to be seen.

Fortunately, a small but fierce and keenly intelligent corps of progressive copyright scholars were beginning to discover one another in the 1990s. Just as the hacker community had had to recognize the enclosure of its commons of software code, and embrace the GPL and other licenses as defensive remedies, so progressive copyright scholars and tech activists were grappling with how to defend against a related set of enclosures. The relentless expansion of copyright law was eroding huge swaths of the public domain and fair use doctrine. Tackling this problem required asking a question that few in the legal or political establishments considered worth anyone's time—namely, What's so valuable about the public domain, anyway?

2

THE DISCOVERY OF THE PUBLIC DOMAIN

How a band of irregulars demonstrated that the public domain is enormously valuable after all.

For decades, the public domain was regarded as something of a wasteland, a place where old books, faded posters, loopy music from the early twentieth century, and boring government reports go to die. It was a dump on the outskirts of respectable culture. If anything in the public domain had any value, someone would sell it for money. Or so goes the customary conception of the public domain.

Jack Valenti, the longtime head of the Motion Picture Association of America, once put it this way: "A public domain work is an orphan. No one is responsible for its life. But everyone exploits its use, until that time certain when it becomes soiled and haggard, barren of its previous virtues. Who, then, will invest the funds to renovate and nourish its future life when no one owns it?"[1] (Valenti was arguing that longer copyright terms would give film studios the incentive to digitize old celluloid films that would otherwise enter the public domain and physically disintegrate.)

One of the great, unexplained mysteries of copyright law is how a raffish beggar grew up to be King Midas. How did a virtually ignored realm of culture—little studied and undertheorized—become a subject of intense scholarly interest and great practical importance to commoners and businesses alike? How did the actual value of the public domain become known? The idea that the public domain might be valuable in its own right—and therefore be worth protecting—was a fringe idea in the 1990s and before. So how did a transformation of legal and cultural meaning occur?

Unlike Richard Stallman's crusade to create a sustainable public domain of code,* the discovery of the public domain for cultural works was not led by a single protagonist or group. It emerged over time through a loose network of legal scholars, techies, activists, and some businesses, who were increasingly concerned about worrisome expansions of copyright and patent law. Slowly, a conversation that was occurring in a variety of academic and tech communities began to intensify, and then coalesce into a more coherent story.

Scholarship about copyright law is not exactly gripping stuff. But it has played an important role in the viral spiral. Before anyone could begin to imagine how an online commons could be structured and protected, someone needed to explain how intellectual property law had become "uncontrolled to the point of recklessness"—as law professor David Lange put it in 1981, well before the proprietarian explosion of the late 1980s and 1990s.

Fortunately, a new breed of public-spirited professors was reaching a critical mass just as the Internet was becoming culturally important. These professors, collaborating with programmers and activists, were among the first to understand the ways in which copyright law, historically an arcane backwater of law, was starting to pose serious threats to democracy-loving citizens and Internet users. The full complexity of this legal literature over the past generation cannot be unpacked here, but it is important to understand how progressive copyright scholarship played a critical role in identifying dangerous trends in law and technology—and in constructing a new narrative for what copyright law should be.

This legal scholarship reconceptualized the public domain—then a vague notion of nonproperty—and developed it into an affirmative theory. It gave the public domain sharper definition and empirical grounding. Thinkers like Yochai Benkler (Harvard Law

---

* Free software constitutes a "sustainable public domain" because the General Public License protects the code and its derivatives from private appropriation yet otherwise makes the code free for anyone to use. The public domain, by contrast, is vulnerable to private appropriation in practice if a company has sufficient market power (e.g., Disney's appropriation of fairy tales) or if it uses the public domain to make derivative works and then copyrights them (e.g., vendors who mix government data with proprietary enhancements).

School), Lawrence Lessig (Stanford Law), and James Boyle (Duke Law) developed bracing new theories that recognize the power of social communities, and not just the individual, in the creative process. Others, such as Julie Cohen (Georgetown Law Center) and Pamela Samuelson (Boalt Hall), have respectively explored the need to develop a new social theory of creative practice[2] and the theoretical challenges of "mapping" the public domain.[3] All of this thinking, mostly confined to scholarly workshops, law reviews, and tech journals, served as a vital platform for imagining the commons in general and the Creative Commons in particular.

The Elusive Quest for "Balance"

Historically, copyright has been regarded as a "bargain" between the public and authors. The public gives authors a set of monopoly rights to help them sell their works and earn rewards for their hard work. In return, the public gets the marketable output of creators—books, films, music—and certain rights of free access and use. The primary justification of copyright law is not to protect the fortunes of authors; it is to promote new creative works and innovation. By giving authors a property right in their works—and so helping them to sell those works in the marketplace—copyright law aims to promote the "progress of human knowledge."

That's the author's side of the bargain. The public's stake is to have certain limited rights to use copyrighted works. Under the "fair use" doctrine (or "fair dealing" in some countries), people are entitled to excerpt copyrighted works for noncommercial purposes such as journalism, scholarship, reviews, and personal use. People are also entitled to resell the physical copies of copyrighted works such as books and videos. (This right is granted under the "first sale doctrine," which enables libraries and DVD rental stores to exist.) The public also has the right to use copyrighted works for free after the term of a copyright has expired—that is, after a work has "entered the public domain." This general scheme is said to establish a balance in copyright law between the private rights of authors and the needs of the public and future authors.

This "balance" has been more rhetorical than real, however. For decades, critics have complained that the public's side of the copyright bargain is being abridged. Content industries have steadily expanded their rights under copyright law at the expense of the public's modest access rights.

What is notable about the long history of seeking "balance" in copyright law is the singular failure of critics to make much headway (until recently) in redressing the problem. The public's interests in copyright law—and those of authors'—have never been given that much attention or respect. From the authors of eighteenth-century England, whose formal rights were in practice controlled by booksellers, to the rhythm-and-blues singers of the 1940s whose music was exploited for a pittance by record labels, to academics whose copyrights must often be ceded to commercial journals, authors have generally gotten the short end of the stick. No surprise here. Business practices and copyright policy have usually been crafted by the wealthiest, most politically connected players: book publishers, film studios, record labels, broadcasters, cable operators, news organizations. The public's lack of organized political power was reflected in its lack of a coherent language for even describing its own interests in copyright law.

For most of the twentieth century, the forging of copyright law was essentially an insider contest among various copyright-dependent industries for market advantage. Congress hosted a process to oversee the squabbling and negotiation, and nudged the players now and again. This is what happened in the fifteen-year run-up to congressional enactment of the Copyright Act of 1976, for example. For the most part, Congress has preferred to ratify the compromises that industry players hammer out among themselves. The unorganized public has been treated as an ignorant bystander.

Naturally, this has strengthened the hand of commercial interests. Copyright disputes could be argued within a congenial intellectual framework and closely managed by a priesthood of lawyer-experts, industry lobbyists, and friendly politicians. The interests of citizens and consumers, blessedly absent from most debates, could be safely bracketed as marginal.

But letting industries negotiate their own solutions has its own problems, as Professor Jessica Litman has pointed out: "Each time we rely on current stakeholders to agree on a statutory scheme, they produce a scheme designed to protect themselves against the rest of us. Its rigidity leads to its breakdown; the statute's drafters have incorporated too few general principles to guide courts in effecting repairs."[4] By letting the affected industries negotiate a series of fact-specific solutions, each reflecting that moment in history, Congress has in effect let copyright law become an agglomeration of complex and irregular political compromises—or, as some might say, a philosophically incoherent mess.

Perhaps because it is so attentive to its industry benefactors, Congress has generally regarded the fair use doctrine and the public domain as a sideshow. Under the Copyright Act of 1976, for example, fair use is set forth only as an affirmative defense to accusations of copyright infringement, not as an affirmative right. Moreover, fair use is defined by four general statutory guidelines, which courts have proceeded to interpret in wildly inconsistent ways. In real life, Lawrence Lessig has quipped, fair use amounts to "the right to hire a lawyer."

Congress has shown a similarly low regard for the public domain. After extending the term of copyright law eleven times since 1961, the copyright monopoly now lasts for an author's lifetime plus seventy years (ninety-five years for corporations). For Congress, writes Professor Tyler Ochoa, "allowing works to enter the public domain was something to be condemned, or at least only grudgingly tolerated, rather than something to be celebrated."[5] Congress's most hostile act toward the public domain—and to the public's rights of access—was the elimination of the registration requirement for copyright protection.[6] Since 1978, copyright holders have not had to formally register their works in order to receive protection. Doodle on a scratch pad, record your guitar strumming, and it's automatically copyrighted.

Sounds great . . . but this provision had especially nasty consequences once the digital revolution kicked into high gear in the 1990s, because every digital byte was born, by default, as a form of property. Automatic copyright protection dramatically reversed the previous default, where most everything was born in the public domain and was free to use unless registered. Today, anyone wishing to reuse a work legally has to get permission and possibly pay a fee. To make matters worse, since there is no longer a central registry of who owns what copyrighted works, it is often impossible to locate the copyright holder. Such books, films, and images are known as "orphan works."

Thirty years ago, the idea of throwing a net of copyright over all information and culture was not alarming in the least. As Jessica Litman recalled, "When I started teaching in 1984, we were at what was about to be the crest of a high-protectionist wave. That is, if you looked at the scholarship being written then, people were writing about how we should expand copyright protection, not only to cover useful articles and fashions and semiconductor chips and computer programs, but also recombinant DNA. The Chicago School of scholarship was beginning to be quite influential. People were reconceiving copyright in Chicago Law and Economics terms, and things like fair use were seen to be 'free riding.' "[7]

Yet the effects of this protectionist surge, at least for the short term, were muted for a number of reasons. First, corporate lobbying on copyright issues was extremely low-key. "I started going to congressional hearings in 1986," said Litman, "and no one was there. There were no members of Congress; there was no press. The witnesses would come and they'd talk, and staffers would take notes. And that would be it."[8] The big-ticket lobbying—receptions, slick reports, legislative junkets, private movie screenings with Jack Valenti—did not really begin to kick in until the late 1980s and early 1990s, when trade associations for every conceivable faction stepped up their Washington advocacy. When the Internet's commercial implications became clear in the mid-1990s, copyright-dependent industries ratcheted up their campaign contributions and lobbying to another level entirely.

The protectionist surge in copyright law in the 1980s was mitigated by two stalwart public servants: Representative Robert Kastenmeier of Wisconsin, the chair of the House judiciary subcommittee that oversaw copyright legislation, and Dorothy Schrader, the longtime general counsel of the U.S. Copyright Office. Both considered it their job to protect the public from grasping copyright industries. When Kastenmeier lost his reelection bid in 1990 and Schrader retired in 1994, the film, music, broadcast, cable, and publishing industries would henceforth have staunch allies— sometimes their former lawyer-lobbyists—in key congressional staff positions and copyright policy jobs. Government officials no longer saw their jobs as protecting consumers from overbearing, revenue-hungry media industries, but as helping copyright owners chase down and prosecute "pirates." Copyright law was recast as a form of industrial policy—a way to retain American jobs and improve the U.S. balance of trade—not as an instrument that affects social equity, consumer rights, and democratic values.

Ironically, the mercantilist view of copyright was gaining ground at precisely the time when the public's stake in copyright law was growing. An explosion of consumer electronics in the 1980s was giving the public new reasons to care about their fair use rights and the public domain. The introduction of the videocassette recorder, the proliferation of cable television, personal computers, software and electronics devices, and then the introduction of the Web in 1993 all invited people to control their own creative and cultural lives. The new media meant that the baroque encrustations of copyright law that had accumulated over decades were now starting to interfere with people's daily activities.

Yet rather than negotiate a new copyright bargain to take account of the public's needs and interests, copyright industries stepped up their demands on Congress to ram through even stronger copyright, trademark, and patent privileges for themselves. Their basic goal was, and generally remains, a more perfect control over all downstream uses of works. Content industries generally do not concede that there is any presumptive "free use zone" of culture, notwithstanding the existence of the fair use doctrine. Works that citizens may regard as fair-use entitlements industry often regards as chunks of information that no one has yet figured out how to turn into marketable property.

Most content industries, then and now, do not see any "imbalance" in copyright law; they prefer to talk in different terms entirely. They liken copyrighted works to personal property or real estate, as in "and you wouldn't steal a CD or use my house without permission, would you?" A copyrighted work is analogized to a finite physical object. But the essential point about works in the digital age is that they can't be "used up" in the same way that physical objects can. They are "nondepletable" and "nonrival," as economists put it. A digital work can be reproduced and shared for virtually nothing, without depriving another person of it.

Nonetheless, a new narrative was being launched—copyrighted works as property. The idea of copyright law reflecting a policy bargain between the public and authors/corporations was being supplanted by a new story that casts copyright as property that is nearly absolute in scope and virtually perpetual in term. In hindsight, for those scholars who cared enough to see, a disquieting number of federal court cases were strengthening the hand of copyright holders at the expense of the public. James Boyle, in a much-cited essay, called this the "second enclosure movement"—the first one, of course, being the English enclosure movement of common lands in medieval times and into the nineteenth century.[9]

Enclosure took many forms. Copyright scholar Peter Jaszi recalls, "Sometime in the mid-1980s, the professoriate started getting worried about software copyright."[10] It feared that copyrights for software would squelch competition and prevent others from using existing code to innovate. This battle was lost, however. Several years later, the battle entered round two as copyright scholars and programmers sought to protect reverse-engineering as fair use. This time, they won.[11]

Then, in 1985, the U.S. Supreme Court ruled that it was not fair use for the *Nation* magazine to excerpt three hundred words from President Ford's 200,000-word memoir. The *Nation* had acquired a copy of Ford's book before its publication and published an article of highlights, including a handful of quotations. The material, derived from Ford's official duties as president, was of obvious value to the democratic process. But by a 6–3 margin the Court held that the

Nation had violated Ford's copyright.[12] The proprietary tilt of copy-right law only intensified in the following years. Companies claimed copyrights for all sorts of dubious forms of "originality"— the page numbers of federal court decisions, the names and numbers in telephone directories, and facts compiled in databases.

The Great Expansion of Intellectual Property

These expansions of proprietary control in the 1980s proved to be a prelude to much more aggressive expansions of copyright, patent, and trademark law in the 1990s. Congress and the courts were granting property rights to all sorts of things that had previously been considered unowned or unownable. The Supreme Court had opened this door in 1980 when it recognized the patentability of a genetically modified bacterium. This led to ethically and economi-cally dubious patents for genes and life-forms. Then businesses began to win patents for "business methods"—ideas and theoretical systems—that would otherwise be in the public domain. Mathe-matical algorithms, if embedded in software, could now be owned. Amazon.com's patent on "one-click shopping" on its Web site be-came the symbol of this trend. Boat manufacturers won a special *sui generis* ("in a class by itself") form of protection for the design of boat hulls in 1998. Celebrities and talent agencies prevailed upon state legislatures to extend the scope of ownership of celebrity names and likenesses, which had long been considered in the public domain.

Companies developed still other strategies to assert greater pro-prietary control over works. Software companies began to rely upon mass-market licenses—often referred to as "shrink wrap" contracts and "click-through" Web agreements—to expand their rights at the expense of consumers and the public domain. Various computer companies sought to enact a model state law that, in Samuelson's words, would "give themselves more rights than intellectual prop-erty law would do and avoid the burdens of public interest limita-tions."[13] Consumers could in effect be forced to surrender their fair use rights, the right to criticize the product or their right to sue, because of a "contract" they ostensibly agreed to.

Trademarks, originally designed to help people identify brands and prevent fraud in the marketplace, acquired a new power in 1995—the ability to control public meanings. For years, large corporations had wanted to extend the scope of their trademark protection to include "dilution"—a fuzzy concept that would prohibit the use of a trademark without permission, even for legitimate public commentary or parody, if it "dilutes" the recognized public associations and meanings of a trademark. For a decade or more, Kastenmeier had prevented antidilution legislation from moving forward. After Kastenmeier left Congress, the trademark lobby succeeded in getting Congress to enact the legislation. This made it much easier for Mattel to threaten people who did parodies of Barbie dolls. The *Village Voice* could more credibly threaten the *Cape Cod Voice* for trademark infringement. Wal-Mart could prevent others from using "its" smiley-face logo (itself taken from the cultural commons).[14]

The election of Bill Clinton as president in 1992 gave content industries new opportunities to expand their copyright privileges. The Clinton administration launched a major policy effort to build what it called the National Information Infrastructure (NII), more commonly known as the Information Superhighway. Today, of course, we call it the Internet. A task force of industry heavyweights was convened to determine what policies should be adopted to help build the NII.[15] Vice President Al Gore cast himself as a visionary futurist and laid out astonishing scenarios for what the NII could deliver: access to every book in the Library of Congress, the ability of doctors to share medical information online, new strides against inequality as everyone goes online.

The NII project was a classic case of incumbent industries trying to protect their profit centers. Executives and lobbyists associated with broadcasting, film, and music were being asked how to structure the Information Superhighway. Predictably, they came up with fantasies of digital television with five hundred channels, programs to sell products, and self-serving scenarios of even stronger copy-right protection and penalties. Few had any inkling of the trans-formative power of open networks or the power of the sharing economy—and if they did, the possibilities certainly were not ap-pealing to them.

One part of the NII campaign was a working group on intellec-tual property headed by Bruce Lehman, a former congressional staffer, lobbyist for the software industry, and commissioner of patents and trademarks. The Lehman panel spent two years devel-oping a sweeping set of copyright policies for the Information Superhighway. When the panel's report was released in September 1995, anyone who cared about open culture and democracy was livid. The White Paper, as it was called, recommended a virtual elimination of fair use rights in digital content and broader rights over any copyrighted transmissions. It called for the elimination of first-sale rights for digitally transmitted documents (which would prevent the sharing of digital files) and endorsed digital rights management systems for digital works (in order to monitor and prosecute illegal sharing). The White Paper even sought to reinter-pret existing law so that transient copies in the random-access memory of computers would be considered illegal unless they had a license—essentially outlawing Web browsing without a license. With visions of Soviet-style indoctrination, the document also rec-ommended an ambitious public education program to teach Amer-icans to properly respect copyright laws.

Litman wrote a revealing history of the misbegotten NII project in her book *Digital Copyright*. Her chapter title "Copyright Lawyers Set Out to Colonize Cyberspace" says it all.[16] Samuelson alerted the readers of *Wired* about the outrageous proposals of the White Paper in her devastating January 1996 article "The Copyright Grab."[17] If the NII proposals are enacted, warned Samuelson, "your traditional user rights to browse, share or make private noncommercial copies of copyrighted works will be rescinded. Not only that, your online service provider will be forced to snoop through your files, ready to cut you off and turn you in if it finds any unlicensed material there. The White Paper regards digital technology as so threatening to the future of the publishing industry that the public must be stripped of all the rights copyright law has long recognized— including the rights of privacy. Vice President Al Gore has promised that the National Information Infrastructure will dramatically enhance public access to information; now we find out that it will be available only on a pay-per-use basis." [18]

The White Paper was not just an effort by Old Media to domesticate or eliminate the freedoms emerging on the Information Superhighway; it sought to set the stage for the internationalization of strict copyright norms, so that American-style copyright law would prevail around the world. To counter this effort, American University law professor Peter Jaszi convened a group of law professors, library organizations, and computer and consumer electronics makers, who promptly organized themselves as the Digital Future Coalition (DFC), the first broad-based coalition in support of the public's stake in copyright law.

The DFC attacked the White Paper as a copyright-maximalist nightmare and sought to rally civil liberties groups, Internet service providers, and electronics manufacturers. With modest industry support, the DFC was largely responsible for slowing progress on legislation that would have enacted Lehman's proposals. As domestic opposition grew, Lehman shrewdly decided to push for a new global copyright treaty that would embody similar principles. In the end, however, the World Intellectual Property Organization demurred.

By that time, however, the terms of debate had been set, and there was serious congressional momentum to adopt some variant of the White Paper agenda. The ultimate result, enacted in October 1998, was the Digital Millennium Copyright Act (DMCA), the crowning achievement of the copyright-maximalist decade. It contained dozens of highly specific provisos and qualifications to satisfy every special pleader. The law in effect authorized companies to eliminate the public's fair use rights in digital content by putting a "digital lock" around the content, however weak. Circumventing the lock, providing the software to do so, or even telling someone how to do so became a criminal offense.

The DMCA has been roundly denounced by software programmers, music fans, and Internet users for prohibiting them from making personal copies, fair use excerpts, and doing reverse engineering on software, even with legally purchased products. Using digital rights management systems sanctioned by the DMCA, for example, many CDs and DVDs are now coded with geographic codes that prevent consumers from operating them on devices on other continents. DVDs may contain code to prevent them from running on Linux-based computers. Digital journals may "expire" after a given period of time, wiping out library holdings unless another payment is made. Digital textbooks may go blank at the end of the school year, preventing their reuse or resale.

Critics also argue that the DMCA gives large corporations a powerful legal tool to thwart competition and interoperability. Some companies programmed garage door openers and printer cartridges so that the systems would not accept generic replacements (until a federal court found this behavior anticompetitive). Naturally, this sort of behavior, which the DMCA facilitates, lets companies avoid open competition on open platforms with smaller companies and entrepreneurs. It also gives companies a legal pretext for bullying Web site owners into taking down copyrighted materials that may in fact be legal to use.

In her excellent history of the political run-up to the DMCA, Litman notes, "There is no overarching vision of the public interest animating the Digital Millennium Copyright Act. None. Instead, what we have is what a variety of different private parties were able to extract from each other in the course of an incredibly complicated four-year multiparty negotiation."[19] The DMCA represents a new frontier of proprietarian control—the sanctioning of technological locks that can unilaterally override the copyright bargain. Companies asked themselves, Why rely on copyrights alone when technology can embed even stricter controls into the very design of products?

The year 1998 was an especially bad year for the public domain. Besides enacting the trademark dilution bill and DMCA, the Walt Disney Company and other large media corporations succeeded in their six-year campaign to enact the Sonny Bono Copyright Term Extension Act.[20] The legislation, named after the late House legislator and former husband of the singer Cher, retroactively extended the terms of existing copyrights by twenty years. As we will see in chapter 3, this law became the improbable catalyst for a new commons movement.

Confronting the Proprietarian Juggernaut

If there was ever a need for independent scholarship on copyright law and activism to challenge the new excesses, this was such a time. Fred von Lohmann, senior staff attorney for the Electronic Frontier Foundation in San Francisco, recalls, "Peggy Radin taught the first cyber-law class at Stanford Law School in 1995, and I was her research assistant. And at the end of that semester, I had read everything that had ever been written about the intersection of the Internet and the law—not just in the legal literature, but in almost all the literature. It filled about two boxes, and that was it. That was all there was."[21]

In about a dozen years, those two boxes of literature have grown into many shelves and countless filing cabinets of case law and commentary. Much of the legal scholarship was the fruit of a new generation of copyright professors who rose to the challenge of the time. An earlier generation of copyright scholars—Melville Nimmer, Alan Latman, Paul Goldstein—were highly respected titans, but they also enjoyed busy consulting practices with the various creative industries that they wrote about. Protecting the public domain was not their foremost concern.

By the 1980s, as law schools become more like graduate schools and less like professional schools, copyright commentary began to get more scholarly and independent of the industries it studied. People like Pamela Samuelson, Peter Jaszi, Jerome H. Reichman, Jessica Litman, L. Ray Patterson, and Wendy Gordon were among this cohort, who were soon joined in the 1990s by a new wave of thinkers such as James Boyle, Lawrence Lessig, Julie Cohen, Niva Elkin-Koren, and Yochai Benkler. Still others, such as Rose-mary Coombe and Keith Aoki, approached copyright issues from cross-cultural and globalization perspectives. These scholars were frankly hostile to the large copyright industries, and greatly concerned with how the law was harming democracy, science, culture, and consumers.

A number of activist voices were also coming forward at this time to challenge the proprietarian juggernaut. As the Internet became a popular medium, ordinary people began to realize that the new copyright laws were curtailing their creative freedoms and free speech rights. The obscure complexities of copyright law started to become a far more public and political issue. The pioneering activist organization was the Electronic Frontier Foundation. EFF was founded in 1990 by tech entrepreneur Mitch Kapor, the famed inventor of the Lotus 1-2-3 spreadsheet in the 1980s; John Perry Barlow, Grateful Dead lyricist and hacker; and John Gilmore, a leading privacy/cryptography activist and free software entrepreneur.

The organization was oriented to hackers and cyberlibertarians, who increasingly realized that they needed an organized presence to defend citizen freedoms in cyberspace. (Barlow adapted the term *cyberspace* from science-fiction writer William Gibson in 1990 and applied it to the then-unnamed cultural life on the Internet.) Initially, the EFF was concerned with hacker freedom, individual privacy, and Internet censorship. It later went through some growing pains as it moved offices, changed directors, and sought to develop a strategic focus for its advocacy and litigation. In more recent years, EFF, now based in San Francisco, has become the leading litigator of copyright, trademark, and Internet free expression issues. It also has more than ten thousand members and spirited outreach programs to the press and public.

John Perry Barlow was an important visionary and populizer of the time. His March 1994 article "The Economy of Ideas" is one of the most prophetic yet accessible accounts of how the Internet was changing the economics of information. He astutely realized that information is not a "product" like most physical property, but rather a social experience or form of life unto itself. "Information is a verb, not a noun," he wrote. "Freed of its containers, information obviously is not a thing. In fact, it is something that happens in the field of interaction between minds or objects or other pieces of information. . . . Sharks are said to die of suffocation if they stop swimming, and the same is nearly true of information." [22]

Instead of the sober polemics of law professors, Barlow—a retired Wyoming cattle rancher who improbably doubled as a tech intellectual and rock hipster—spiced his analysis of information with colorful metaphors and poetic aphorisms. Comparing information to DNA helices, Barlow wrote, "Information replicates into the cracks of possibility, always seeking new opportunities for *Lebensraum*." Digital information, he said, "is a continuing process more like the metaphorphosing tales of prehistory than anything that will fit in shrink-wrap."

Since hyperbole is an occupational reflex among cyberjournalists, Barlow's *Wired* piece bore the obligatory subtitle, "Everything you know about intellectual property is wrong." Yet reading Barlow more than a decade later confirms that, posturing aside, he *was* on to the big story of our time: "Notions of property, value, ownership and the nature of wealth itself are changing more fundamentally than at any time since the Sumerians first poked cuneiform into wet clay and called it stored grain. Only a very few people are aware of the enormity of this shift, and fewer of them are lawyers or public officials." [23]

With a nod to Professor Samuelson, Barlow was prescient enough to compare the vulnerability of indigenous peoples to the coming dispossession of Internet communities: "Western countries may legally appropriate the music, designs and biomedical lore of aboriginal people without compensation to their tribes of origins since those tribes are not an 'author' or 'investors.' But soon most information will be generated collaboratively by the cyber-tribal hunter-gatherers of cyberspace. Our arrogant legal dismissal of the rights of 'primitives' will soon return to haunt us."

No account of cyberactivism in the 1990s is complete without mention of James Love, a feisty advocate with a brilliant strategic mind and an extraordinary ability to open up broad new policy fronts. For example, Love, as director of the Ralph Nader–founded

Consumer Project on Technology, worked with tech activist Carl
Malamud to force the U.S. Securities and Exchange Commission to
put its EDGAR database of corporate filings online in 1994, at a
time when the SEC was planning to give the data to private vendors
to sell. By prevailing at the SEC, Love and Malamud set an important precedent that government agencies should post their information on the Internet for free. A few years later, in 1997, Love
convened a conference to assess Microsoft's troubling monopoly
power, an event that emboldened the Department of Justice to
launch its antitrust lawsuit against the company. Love later played a
key role in persuading an Indian drugmaker to sell generic
HIV/AIDS drugs to South Africa, putting Big Pharma on the defensive for its callous patent and trade policies and exorbitant drug
prices. Love's timely gambit in 1996 to organize broader advocacy
for the public domain failed, however. He co-founded the Union
for the Public Domain, with a board that included Richard Stallman, but the project never developed a political following or raised
much money.

The American Library Association was the largest and best-
funded advocate on copyright issues in the 1990s, but its collaborations with other Washington allies tended to be modest, and its
grassroots mobilization disappointing. Libraries are respected in
the public mind precisely because they are stable, apolitical civic institutions—that is, not activists. Despite its valuable presence on
copyright and Internet policy issues, the library lobby was tempera-
mentally disinclined to get too far ahead of the curve.

By the end of the decade, a muscular, dissenting discourse about
copyright law was starting to take shape. On one side was a complicated body of industry-crafted copyright law that claimed imperial
powers to regulate more and more aspects of daily life—your Web
site, your music CDs, your electronic devices, your computer practices. On the other side were ordinary people who loved how the
Internet and digital devices were empowering them to be creators
and publishers in their own right. They just wanted to indulge their
natural human urge to share, tinker, reuse, and transform culture.

The dissent of the progressive copyright scholars and activists, though pungent, was hardly insurrectionist. These critics were re-formers, not bomb throwers. Most objected to the overreaching scope and draconian enforcement of copyright law, not to its philo-sophical foundations. They generally argued that the problem wasn't copyright law per se, but the misapplication and overexten-sion of its core principles.

A New Story About the Public Domain

One of the most notable outgrowths of all this activity was the de-velopment of a new story about the public domain. Scholars took a range of legal doctrines that were scattered among the sprawling oeuvre of copyright law and consolidated them under one banner, *the public domain*. The new framing helped give the public's rights in cultural works a new moral standing and intellectual clarity.

Even though copyright law has existed for three centuries, the term "public domain" did not surface in a U.S. Supreme Court de-cision until 1896. The public domain was first mentioned in U.S. copyright law in 1909, and while it occasionally merited passing ref-erence or discussion in later decades, the concept was not the sub-ject of a significant law review article until 1981. That article was "Recognizing the Public Domain," by Professor David Lange.[24] "David's article was an absolutely lovely piece that sunk without a trace," recalls Jessica Litman. "When a bunch of us discovered [Lange's article] in the late 1980s, it had been neither cited nor ex-cerpted nor reprinted nor anything—because nobody was looking for a defense of the public domain. People were looking for argu-ments for extending copyright protection. David was ahead of his time."

The main reason that the public domain was ignored was that it was generally regarded as a nullity. "Public domain in the fields of literature, drama, music and art is the other side of the coin of copy-right," wrote M. William Krasilovsky in 1967.[25] "It is best defined in negative terms." Edward Samuels wrote that the public domain "is simply whatever remains after all methods of protection are taken into account."[26]

Lange himself acknowledged this conventional wisdom when he wrote that the public domain "amounts to a dark star in the constellation of intellectual property." He took issue with this history, however, and insisted upon the affirmative value of the public domain. Lange dredged up a number of "publicity rights" cases and commentary to shed light on the problem: Bela Lugosi's widow and son claimed that they, not Universal Pictures, should own the rights to the character Dracula. Representatives of the deceased Marx Brothers sought to stop a Broadway production spoofing 1930s musicals from using the Marx Brothers' characters. DC Comics, owner of a trademark in the Superman character, sued to prevent a group of Chicago college students from calling their newspaper *The Daily Planet*. And so on.

From such examples, Lange drove home a commonsense lesson about the derivative nature of creativity: we all depend on others to generate "new" works. Groucho, Chico, and Harpo Marx couldn't "invent" their stage personas until, in classic vaudevillian tradition, they had adapted jokes and shtick from their peers. "In time," Groucho wrote in his memoirs, "if [a comedian] was any good, he would emerge from the routine character he had started with and evolve into a distinct personality of his own. This has been my experience and also that of my brothers, and I believe this has been true of most of the other comedians."

To which Lange added, "Of course, what Groucho is saying in this passage is that although he and his brothers began as borrowers they ended as inventors. . . . It is a central failing in the contemporary intellectual property literature and case law that that lesson, so widely acknowledged, is so imperfectly understood."[27]

In example after example, Lange made the point that "as access to the public domain is choked, or even closed off altogether, the public loses too: loses the rich heritage of its culture, the rich presence of new works derived from that culture, and the rich promise of works to come." Lange warned that "courts must dispel" the "impression of insubstantiality" from which the public domain suffers. Nothing will be resolved, he warned, "until the courts have come to see the public domain not merely as an unexplored abstraction but as a field of individual rights as important as any of the new property rights."

What Is "Authorship"?

Besides honoring the public domain, copyright reformers sought to develop a second, more subversive narrative. They questioned the very idea of individual "authorship" and "originality," two central pillars of copyright law. The standard moral justification for granting authors exclusive rights in their works is the personal originality that they supposedly show in creating new works. But can "originality" and "authorship" be so neatly determined? What of the role of past generations and creative communities in enabling the creation of new works? Don't we all, in the words of Isaac Newton, stand on the shoulders of giants?

The idea that sharing, collaboration, and adaptation may actually be important to creativity, and not merely incidental, was a somewhat daring theme in the early 1990s, if only because it had little recognition in copyright scholarship. While this line of analysis preceded the Internet, the arrival of the World Wide Web changed the debate dramatically. Suddenly there was a powerful, real-life platform for *collective* authorship. Within fifteen years, sharing and collaboration has become a standard creative practice, as seen in Wikipedia, remix music, video mashups, machinima films, Google map mashups, social networking, and much else.

Of course, in the early 1990s, the promise of online networks was only dimly understood. But for Jessica Litman, the tightening noose of proprietary control had troubling implications for fair use and the ability of people to create and share culture: "Copyright law was no longer as open and porous as it had been, so I felt compelled to try to defend the open spaces that nobody was paying attention to." Litman published a major article on the public domain in 1990, instigating a fresh round of interest in it and establishing lines of analysis that continue to this day.[28]

She made the then-startling claim, for example, that "the very act of authorship in *any* medium is more akin to translation and re-combination than it is to creating Aphrodite from the foam of the sea. Composers recombine sounds they have heard before; play-wrights base their characters on bits and pieces drawn from real human beings and other playwrights' characters. . . . This is not parasitism; it is the essence of authorship. And, in the absence of a vigorous public domain, much of it would be illegal." Litman argued that the public domain is immensely important because all authors depend upon it for their raw material. Shrink the public domain and you impoverish the creative process.

The problem, said Litman, is that copyright law contains a struc-tural contradiction that no one wants to acknowledge. The law re-quires "originality" in order for a work to be protected—but it cannot truly determine what is "original." If authors could assert that their works were entirely original, and courts conscientiously enforced this notion, copyright law would soon collapse. Everyone would be claiming property rights in material that had origins else-where. Shakespeare's estate might claim that Leonard Bernstein's *West Side Story* violates its rights in *Romeo and Juliet*; Beethoven would prevent the Bee Gees from using the opening chords of his Fifth Symphony.

When one person's copyright claims appear to threaten another person's ability to create, the courts have historically invoked the public domain in order to set limits on the scope of copyright pro-tection. In this backhanded way, the public domain helps copyright law escape from its own contradictions and ensures that basic cre-ative elements remain available to all. As Litman explained:

> Because we have a public domain, we can permit authors to avoid the harsh light of a genuine search for provenance, and thus maintain the illusion that their works are indeed their own creations. We can tolerate the grant of overbroad and overlapping deeds through the expedient assumption that each author took her raw material from the commons, rather than from the property named in prior deeds.[29]

In effect, copyright law sets up a sleight of hand: it invites authors to plunder the commons with the assurance that their borrowings will be politely ignored—but then it declares the resulting work of authorship "original" and condemns any further follow-on uses as "piracy." This roughly describes the early creative strategy of the Walt Disney Company, which built an empire by rummaging through the public domain of fairy tales and folklore, adding its own creative flourishes, and then claiming sole ownership in the resulting characters and stories.

As Litman unpacked the realities of "authorship," she showed how the idea of "originality" serves as a useful fiction. Any author must draw upon aspects of culture and recombine them without ever being able to identify the specific antecedents, she pointed out. Judges, for their part, can never really make a rigorous factual determination about what is "original" and what is taken from the public domain. In reality, said Litman, authorship amounts to "a combination of absorption, astigmatism and amnesia." The public domain is vague and shifting precisely because it must constantly disguise the actual limits of individual "originality."

English professor Martha Woodmansee and law professor Peter Jaszi helped expose many of the half-truths about "authorship" and "originality." Their 1994 anthology of essays, *The Construction of Authorship*, showed how social context is an indispensable element of "authorship," one that copyright law essentially ignores.[30] Thus, even though indigenous cultures collectively create stories, music, and designs, and folk cultures generate works in a collaborative fashion, copyright law simply does not recognize such acts of collective authorship. And so they go unprotected. They are vulnerable to private appropriation and enclosure, much as Stallman's hacker community at MIT saw its commons of code destroyed by enclosure.

Before the Internet, the collaborative dimensions of creativity were hardly given much thought. An "author" was self-evidently an individual endowed with unusual creative skills. As the World Wide Web and digital technologies have proliferated, however, copyright's traditional notions of "authorship" and "originality" have come to seem terribly crude and limited. The individual creator still matters and deserves protection, of course. But when dozens of people contribute to a single entry of Wikipedia, or thousands contribute to an open-source software program, how then shall we determine who is the "author"?[31] By the lights of copyright law, how shall the value of the public domain, reconstituted as a commons, be assessed?[32]

The Bellagio Declaration, the outgrowth of a conference organized by Woodmansee and Jaszi in 1993, called attention to the sweeping deficiencies of copyright law as applied. One key point stated, "In general, systems built around the author paradigm tend to obscure or undervalue the importance of the 'public domain,' the intellectual and cultural commons from which future works will be constructed. Each intellectual property right, in effect, fences off some portion of the public domain, making it unavailable to future creators."[33]

Another fusillade of flaming arrows engulfed the fortress of "authorship" and "originality" in 1996, when James Boyle published *Shamans, Software, and Spleens.* With sly wit and deep analysis, this landmark book identified many of the philosophical paradoxes and absurdities of property rights in indigenous knowledge, software, genes, and human tissue. Boyle deftly exposed the discourse of IP law as a kind of Möbius strip, a smooth strip of logic that confusingly turns back on itself. "If a geography metaphor is appropriate at all," said Boyle, "the most likely cartographers would be Dali, Magritte and Escher."[34]

"You Have No Sovereignty Where We Gather"

The deconstruction of copyright law over the past twenty years has been a significant intellectual achievement. It has exposed the copyright law's philosophical deficiencies, showed how social practice deviates from it, and revealed the antisocial effects of expanding copyright protection. Critics knew that it would be impossible to defend the fledgling cyberculture without first documenting how copyright law was metastasizing at the expense of free expression, creative innovation, consumer rights, and market competition.

But as the millennium drew near, the tech-minded legal community—and law-minded techies—knew that critiques and carping could only achieve so much. A winnable confrontation with copyright maximalists was needed. A compelling counternarrative and a viable long-term political strategy had to be devised. And then somehow they had to be pushed out to the wider world and made real.

That task was made easier by the intensifying cultural squeeze. The proprietarian lockdown was starting to annoy and anger people in their everyday use of music, software, DVDs, and the Web. And the property claims were growing more extreme. The American Society of Composers, Authors and Publishers had demanded that Girl Scout camps pay a public performance license for singing around the campfire. Ralph Lauren challenged the U.S. Polo Association for ownership of the word *polo*. McDonald's succeeded in controlling the Scottish prefix *Mc* as applied to restaurants and motels, such as "McVegan" and "McSleep."[35]

The mounting sense of frustration fueled a series of conferences between 1999 and 2001 that helped crystallize the disparate energies of legal scholarship into something resembling an intellectual movement. "A number of us [legal scholars] were still doing our own thing, but we were beginning to get a sense of something," recalls Yochai Benkler. "It was no longer Becky Eisenberg working on DNA sequences and Pamela Samuelson on computer programs and Jamie Boyle on 'environmentalism for the 'Net' and me working on spectrum on First Amendment issues," said Benkler. "There was a sense of movement."[36] ("Environmentalism for the 'Net" was an influential piece that Boyle wrote in 1998, calling for the equivalent of an environmental movement to protect the openness and freedom of the Internet.)[37]

"The place where things started to get even crisper," said Benkler, "was a conference at Yale that Jamie Boyle organized in April 1999, which was already planned as a movement-building event." That conference, Private Censorship/Perfect Choice, looked at the threats to free speech on the Web and how the public might resist. It took inspiration from John Perry Barlow's 1996 manifesto "A Declaration of the Independence of Cyberspace." It is worth quoting at length from Barlow's lyrical cri de coeur—first published in *Wired* and widely cited—because it expresses the growing sense of thwarted idealism among Internet users, and a yearning for greater self-determination and self-governance among commoners. Barlow wrote:

> Governments of the Industrial World, you weary giants of flesh and steel, I come from Cyberspace, the new home of Mind. On behalf of the future, I ask you of the past to leave us alone. You are not welcome among us. You have no sovereignty where we gather.
>
> We have no elected government, nor are we likely to have one, so I address you with no greater authority than that with which liberty itself always speaks. I declare the global social space we are building to be naturally independent of the tyrannies you seek to impose on us. You have no moral right to rule us nor do you possess any methods of enforcement we have true reason to fear.
>
> Governments derive their just powers from the consent of the governed. You have neither solicited nor received ours. We did not invite you. You do not know us, nor do you know our world. Cyberspace does not lie within your borders. Do not think that you can build it, as though it were a public construction project. You cannot. It is an act of nature and it grows itself through our collective actions.
>
> You have not engaged in our great and gathering conversation, nor did you create the wealth of our marketplaces. You do not know our culture, our ethics, or the unwritten codes that already provide our society more order than could be obtained by any of your impositions.
>
> You claim there are problems among us that you need to solve. You use this claim as an excuse to invade our precincts. Many of these problems don't exist. Where there are real conflicts, where there are wrongs, we will identify them and

address them by our means. We are forming our own Social Contract. This governance will arise according to the conditions of our world, not yours. Our world is different.

As Barlow made clear, the Internet was posing profound new questions—not just about politics, but about the democratic polity itself. What would be the terms of moral legitimacy and democratic process in cyberspace? Would the new order be imposed by a Congress beholden to incumbent industries and their political action committees, or would it be a new social contract negotiated by the commoners themselves? In posing such questions, and doing it with such rhetorical panache, Barlow earned comparisons to Thomas Jefferson.

The stirrings of a movement were evident in May 2000, when Benkler convened a small conference of influential intellectual property scholars at New York University Law School on "A Free Information Ecology." This was followed in November 2001 by a large gathering at Duke Law School, the first major conference ever held on the public domain. It attracted several hundred people and permanently rescued the public domain from the netherworld of "nonproperty." People from diverse corners of legal scholarship, activism, journalism, and philanthropy found each other and began to reenvision their work in a larger, shared framework.

Over three decades, copyright scholarship had become more incisive, impassioned, and focused on the public good—but much of the talk remained within the rarefied circles of the academy. What to *do* about the disturbing enclosures of the cultural commons remained a vexing, open question. The 1990s saw an eclectic smattering of initiatives, from EFF lawsuits and visionary manifestos to underfunded advocacy efforts and sporadic acts of hacker mischief and civil disobedience. All were worthwhile forms of engagement and exploratory learning. None were terribly transformative. Free software was growing in popularity in the 1990s, but its relevance to broader copyright struggles and the Internet was not yet recognized. Congress and the courts remained captive to the copyright-maximalist worldview. The idea of organizing a counter-constituency to lay claim to the public domain and forge a new social contract for cyberspace was a fantasy. Copyright law was just too obscure to excite the general public and most creators and techies. The commoners were too scattered and diverse to see themselves as an insurgent force, let alone imagine they might create a movement.

3

WHEN LARRY LESSIG MET ERIC ELDRED

A constitutional test case becomes the seed for a movement.

Once the value of the public domain became evident, and a few visionaries realized that the commons needed to be protected somehow, an important strategic question arose: Which arena would offer the best hope for success—politics, culture, technology, or law?

The real answer, of course, was all of the above. Building a new digital republic would require a wholesale engagement with the politics of effecting democratic change and the challenges of building a cultural movement. It would require the invention of a shared technological infrastructure, and the development of legal tools to secure the commons. All were intertwined. But as a practical matter, anyone who aspired to stop the mass-media-driven expansions of copyright law had to choose where to invest his or her energy. In the mid-1990s, Lawrence Lessig decided that the greatest leverage would come through law.

Lessig, usually referred to as Larry, had the knowledge, talent, and good timing to conceptualize the politics of digital technologies at a ripe moment, the late 1990s, when the World Wide Web was exploding and people were struggling to understand its significance. However, Lessig was not content to play the sage law professor dispensing expertise at rarefied professional and scholarly gatherings; he aimed to become a public intellectual and highbrow activist. Through a punishing schedule of public speaking and a series of high-profile initiatives starting in 1998 and 1999, Lessig became a roving demigod-pundit on matters of the Internet, intellectual property, and cultural freedom.

In the course of his frequent travels, he had a particularly significant rendezvous at the Starbucks on Church Street in Cambridge, Massachusetts. It was November 1998. A month earlier, Congress had enacted the Sonny Bono Copyright Extension Act. Lessig was eager to meet with one Eric Eldred, a retired navy contractor, to see if he would agree to be a plaintiff in the first federal case to challenge the constitutionality of the copyright clause.

Eldred was a book enthusiast and computer programmer who had reached the end of his rope. Three years earlier, in 1995, he had launched a simple but brilliant project: a free online archive of classic American literature. Using his PC and a server in his home in New Hampshire, Eldred posted the books of Nathaniel Hawthorne, Henry James, Wallace Stevens, and dozens of other great authors whose works were in the public domain. Eldred figured it would be a great service to humanity to post the texts on the World Wide Web, which was just beginning to go mainstream.

Eldred had previously worked for Apollo Computer and Hewlett-Packard and was experienced in many aspects of computers and software. In the late 1980s, in fact, he had developed a system that enabled users to post electronic text files and then browse and print them on demand. When the World Wide Web arrived, Eldred was understandably excited. "It seemed to me that there was a possibility of having a system for electronic books that was similar to what I had done before. I was interested in experimenting with this to see if it was possible."[1]

So Eldred set out to build his own archive of public-domain books: "I got books from the library or wherever, and I learned how to do copyright research and how to scan books, do OCR [optical-character recognition] and mark them up as HTML [the programming language used on the Web]," he said. "I just wanted to make books more accessible to readers."[2]

Eldred didn't realize it at the time, but his brave little archive, Eldritch Press, embodied a dawning cultural archetype—the self-published digital work meant to be freely shared with anyone in the world, via the Internet. Thanks to the magic of "network effects"— the convenience and value that are generated as more people join a network—Eldred's Web site was soon receiving more than twenty thousand hits a day. A growing community of book lovers came together through the site. They offered annotations to the online books, comments, and links to foreign translations and other materials. In 1997, the National Endowment for the Humanities considered the site so educational and exemplary that it formally cited Eldritch Press as one of the top twenty humanities sites on the Web.

Although it was only a one-person project, Eldritch Press was not just an idiosyncratic innovation. The convergence of telecommunications, personal computers, and software in the 1990s, otherwise known as the Internet, was facilitating an explosion of new genres of public expression. We are still grappling with how this new type of media system is different from broadcasting and other mass media. But we do know this: it invites mass participation because the system doesn't require a lot of capital or professional talent to use. The system favors decentralized interactivity over centralized control and one-way communication. Ordinary people find it relatively inexpensive and versatile. Since everyone has roughly the same access and distribution capacities, the Internet is perhaps the most populist communication platform and egalitarian marketplace in human history.

This was not the goal of the computer scientists who invented the Internet, of course. Working under the auspices of the U.S. military, they were chiefly concerned with building a communications system that would allow academic researchers to share computerized information cheaply and easily. The idea was that intelligence and innovation would arise from the "edges" of a "dumb" network, and not be controlled by a centralized elite in the manner of broadcasting or book publishing. The Internet—a network of networks—would be a platform open to anyone who used a shared set of freely accessible "protocols," or standardized code, for computer hardware and software.*

What was radically new about the network architecture was its

---

* The Internet protocols that enable different computers and networks to connect despite their differences is TCP/IP, which stands for Transmission-Control Protocol/Internet Protocol. These protocols enabled the commons known as the Internet to emerge and function, and in turn to host countless other commons "on top" of it.

freedom: No special qualifications or permissions were needed to communicate or "publish." No one needed to pay special fees based on usage. Anyone could build her own innovative software on top of the open protocols. It is a measure of the system's power that it has spawned all sorts of innovations that were not foreseen at the outset: in the 1990s, the World Wide Web, instant messaging, peer-to-peer file sharing, and Web logs, and, in the 2000s, podcasts, wikis, social networking software, and countless other applications. The open, shared protocols of the Internet provided an indispensable communications platform for each of these innovations to arise.

In building his online archive, Eric Eldred was part of this new cultural cohort of innovators. He not only shared Richard Stallman's dream—to build an open, sharing community. He also came to share Stallman's contempt for the long arm of copyright law. The problem, in Eldred's case, was the corporate privatization of large portions of the public domain. In the 1990s, the Walt Disney Company was worried that its flagship cartoon character, Mickey Mouse, would enter the public domain and be freely available for anyone to use. Mickey, originally copyrighted in 1928, was nearing the end of his seventy-five-year term of copyright and was due to enter the public domain in 2003.

Disney led a concerted campaign to extend the term of copyrights by twenty years. Under the new law, all works copyrighted after January 1, 1923, would be privately controlled for another twenty years. Corporations would be able to copyright their works for ninety-five years instead of seventy-five years, and the works of individual authors would be a private monopoly for the author's lifetime plus seventy years. Thousands of works that were expected to enter the public domain in 1999 and following years would remain under copyright until 2019 and beyond.

Congress readily enacted this twenty-year giveaway of monopoly rights on a unanimous vote, and without any public hearings or debate. Disney was the most visible beneficiary of the law, prompting critics to dub it the Mickey Mouse Protection Act. But its more significant impact was to deprive Americans of access to an estimated four hundred thousand cultural works from the 1920s and 1930s. Books by Sherwood Anderson, music by George Gersh-win, poems by Robert Frost, and tens of thousands of other works would remain under private control for no good reason. The law was the eleventh time in the course of four decades that Congress had extended the term of copyright protection. American University law professor Peter Jaszi complained that copyright protection had become "perpetual on the installment plan."

The law was astonishingly inefficient and inequitable as well. To preserve the property rights of the 2 percent of works from this period that still had commercial value, the law also locked up the remaining 98 percent of works (whose owners are often unknown or unable to be located in order to grant permissions). Indeed, it was these "orphan works"—works still under copyright but not commercially available, and with owners who often could not be found—that represent an important "feedstock" for new creativity. The Sonny Bono Act showered a windfall worth billions of dollars to the largest entertainment businesses and authors' estates.

At a more basic level, the copyright term extension showed contempt for the very rationale of copyright law. Copyrights are intended as an inducement to authors to create works. It is a government grant of monopoly property rights meant to help authors earn money for producing books, music, film, and other works. But, as Lessig pointed out, "You can't incent a dead person. No matter what we do, Hawthorne will not produce any more works, no matter how much we pay him." Jack Valenti replied that longer copyright terms would give Hollywood the incentive to preserve old films from deteriorating and make them available.

The copyright term extension act privatized so many of the public domain books on the Eldritch Press Web site, and so offended Eldred's sense of justice, that in November 1998 he decided to close his site in protest. The new law meant that he would not be able to add any works published since 1923 to his Web site until 2019. "I can no longer accomplish what I set out to do," said Eldred.[3]

As luck had it, Larry Lessig was looking for an Everyman of the Internet. Lessig, then a thirty-seven-year-old professor at Harvard

Law School, was looking for a suitable plaintiff for his envisioned constitutional test case. He had initially approached Michael S. Hart, the founder of Project Gutenberg, the first producer of free electronic books. At the time, the project had nearly six thousand public-domain books available online. (It now has twenty thousand books; about 3 million books are downloaded every month.) Hart was receptive to the case but had his own ideas about how the case should be argued. He wanted the legal complaint to include a stirring populist manifesto railing against rapacious copyright holders. Lessig demurred and went in search of another plaintiff.[4]

After reading about Eldred's protests in the *Boston Globe,* and meeting with him over coffee, Lessig asked Eldred if he would be willing to be the plaintiff in his envisioned case. Eldred readily agreed. As a conscientious objector and draft resister during the Vietnam War, he was ready to go to great lengths to fight the Sonny Bono Act. "Initially, I volunteered to violate the law if necessary and get arrested and go to jail," Eldred said. "But Larry told me that was not necessary." A good thing, because under the No Electronic Theft Act, passed in 1997, Eldred could be charged with a felony. "I could face jail, fines, seizure of my computer, termination of my Internet service without notice—and so all the e-books on the Web site could be instantly lost," he said.

It was the beginning of a landmark challenge to the unchecked expansion of copyright law. The case would turbocharge Lessig's unusual career and educate the press and public about copyright law's impact on democratic culture. Most significantly, it would, in time, spur the growth of an international free culture movement.

Larry Lessig's Improbable Journey

Since Lessig looms so large in this story, it is worth pausing to understand his roots. Raised by culturally conservative, rock-ribbed Republican parents in central Pennsylvania, Lessig was a bright kid with a deep enthusiasm for politics. "I grew up a right-wing lunatic Republican," Lessig told journalist Steven Levy, noting that he once belonged to the National Teen Age Republicans, ran a candidate's unsuccessful campaign for the Pennsylvania state senate, and attended the 1980 Republican National Convention, which nominated Ronald Reagan for president. Larry's father, Jack, was an engineer who once built Minuteman missile silos in South Dakota (where Lessig was born in 1961), and who later bought a steel-fabrication company in Williamsport, Pennsylvania.[5]

Lessig initially thought he would follow in his father's footsteps, and so he went to the University of Pennsylvania to earn degrees in economics and management. Later, studying philosophy at Trinity College in Cambridge, England, he faced growing doubts about his deep-seated libertarian worldview. Hitchhiking through Eastern Bloc countries, Lessig gained a new appreciation for the role of law in guaranteeing freedom and making power accountable. "There were many times when people in Eastern Europe would tell me stories about the history of the United States that I had never been taught: things like the history of how we treated Native Americans; and the history of our intervention in South America; and the nature of our intervention in South East Asia," Lessig told Richard Poynder in 2006. "All of those were stories that we didn't tell ourselves in the most accurate and vivid forms." These experiences, said Lessig, "opened up a channel of skepticism in my head."[6]

Lessig's sister Leslie once told a reporter that Larry came back from Cambridge a very different person: "His views of politics, religion, and his career had totally flipped."[7] No longer aspiring to be a businessman or a philosopher, Lessig set his sights on law and entered the University of Chicago Law School in 1986. He transferred the next year to Yale Law School (to be near a girlfriend), groomed himself to be a constitutional law scholar, and graduated in 1989.

Although he now considered himself a liberal, Lessig spent the next two years in the service of two of the law's most formidable conservatives. He clerked for circuit court judge Richard Posner in 1988–89, followed by a year clerking for Supreme Court justice Antonin Scalia during the 1990–91 term. His educational odyssey complete, the thirty-year-old Lessig settled into the life of a tenured law professor at the University of Chicago Law School.

One of Lessig's early scholarly concerns—adjudication—was

not exactly a warm-up for tub-thumping activism. But it did curiously prefigure his later interest in using law as a tool to effect political change. In a 1993 law review article, Lessig wondered how courts should interpret the law when public sentiment and practice have changed. If a judge is going to be true to the original meaning of a law, Lessig argued, he must make a conscientious "translation" of the law by taking account of the contemporary context. A new translation of the law is entirely justified, and should supplant an old interpretation, Lessig argued, if prevailing social practices and understandings have changed. The important thing in interpreting law, therefore, is "fidelity in translation."[8]

Lessig elaborated on this theme in a 1997 article that spent twenty-seven dense pages pondering how two different Supreme Courts, separated by nearly a century, could look to identical words in the Constitution and reach precisely opposite conclusions.* It is not as if one Court or the other was unprincipled or wrong, Lessig wrote. Rather, any court must take account of contemporary social norms and circumstances in "translating" an old law for new times. Lessig called this dynamic the "*Erie*-effect," a reference to the U.S. Supreme Court's 1938 ruling in *Erie Railroad Co. v. Tompkins*. The *Erie*-effect is about the emergence of "a kind of contestability about a practice within a legal institution," which prompts "a restructuring of that practice to avoid the rhetorical costs of that contestability."[9]

Lessig described how an *Erie*-effect might be exploited to catalyze a political shift (paraphrased here): *identify* a socially contested law, aim to *force* the conflicting social practice into the foreground by *inflaming* conventional discourse, and then *argue* for a change in legal interpretation in order to relieve the contestability that has been alleged.[10] If the conflict between the law and actual social practice can be made vivid enough, a court will feel pressure to reinterpret the law. Or the court will defer to the legislature because the very contestability of the law makes the issue a political question that is inappropriate for a court to resolve. One notable instance of

---

* The *Erie* ruling held that federal common law, previously recognized by the U.S. Supreme Court in 1842, was unconstitutional.

the *Erie*-effect in our times, Lessig pointed out, was the successful campaign by feminist law scholar Catherine MacKinnon to define sexual harassment in the workplace as a form of illegal discrimination. The point was to transform popular understanding of the issue and then embody it in law.

Lessig was not especially focused on tech issues until he ran across Julian Dibbell's article "A Rape in Cyberspace," which appeared in the *Village Voice* in December 1993.[11] The piece described the social havoc that ensued in an online space, LambdaMOO, hosted at Xerox Palo Alto Research Center. One pseudonymous character "raped" another in the virtual space, using cruel words and graphic manipulations. The incident provoked an uproar among the thousand members of LambdaMOO, and had real emotional and social consequences. Yet, as Dibbell pointed out, "No bodies touched. Whatever physical interaction occurred consisted of a mingling of electronic signals sent from sites spread out between New York City and Sydney, Australia."

For Lessig, the LambdaMOO "rape" had an obvious resonance with Catherine MacKinnon's arguments in her 1993 book *Only Words*. Does a rape in cyberspace resemble the harms inflicted on real women through pornography? Lessig saw intriguing parallels: "I really saw cyberspace as a fantastic opportunity to get people to think about things without recognizing the political valences. That's all I was interested in; it was purely pedagogical."[12]

To explore the issues further, Lessig developed one of the first courses on the law of cyberspace. He taught it in the spring semester of 1995 at Yale Law School, where he was a visiting professor, and later at the University of Chicago and Harvard law schools. During the Yale class, an exchange with a student, Andrew Shapiro, jarred his thinking in a new direction: "I was constantly thinking about the way that changing suppositions of constitutional eras had to be accounted for in the interpretation of the Constitution across time. Andrew made this point about how there's an equivalent in the technical infrastructure [of the Internet] that you have to think about. And then I began to think about how there were norms and law and infrastructure—and then I eventually added markets into this—which combine to frame what policymaking is in any particular context."[13]

This line of analysis became a central theme of Lessig's startling first book, *Code and Other Laws of Cyberspace*, published in 1999.[14] *Code* took on widespread assumptions that the Internet would usher in a new libertarian, free-market utopia. Cyberlibertarian futurists such as Alvin Toffler, Esther Dyson, George Gilder, and John Gilmore had routinely invoked cyberspace as a revolutionary force that would render government, regulation, and social welfare programs obsolete and unleash the transformative power of free markets.[15] In the libertarian scenario, individual freedom can flourish only if government gets the hell out of the way and lets individuals create, consume, and interact as they see fit, without any paternalistic or tyrannical constraints. Prosperity can prevail and scarcity disappear only if meddling bureaucrats and politicians leave the citizens of the Internet to their own devices. As Louis Rossetto, the founder and publisher of *Wired,* bluntly put it: "The idea that we need to worry about anyone being 'left out' is entirely atavistic to me, a product of that old economics of scarcity and the 19th century social thinking that grew out of it."[16]

Lessig was more wary. In *Code,* he constructed a sweeping theoretical framework to show how freedom on the Internet must be actively, deliberately constructed; it won't simply happen on its own. Inspired by conversations with computer programmer Mitch Kapor, who declared that "architecture is politics" in 1991, Lessig's book showed how software code was supplanting the regulatory powers previously enjoyed by sovereign nation-states and governments. The design of the Internet and software applications was becoming more influential than conventional sources of policymaking—Congress, the courts, federal agencies. *Code is law,* as Lessig famously put it.

What was worrisome, Lessig warned, was how relatively small changes in software code could alter the "architecture of control" governing the Internet. The current architecture was not necessarily stable and secure, in other words. Moreover, any future changes were likely to be animated by private, commercial forces and not publicly accountable and democratic ones. Lessig illustrated this point with a disarmingly simple drawing of a dot representing an individual, whose range of behaviors is affected by four distinct forces: software architecture, the market, law, and social norms. Each of these factors conspires to regulate behaviors on the Internet, Lessig argued—and commercial forces would clearly have the upper hand.

Code was a powerful and sobering rebuttal to libertarian assumptions that "keeping government out" would safeguard individual freedom. Its analysis quickly became the default conceptual model for talking about governance on the Internet. It helped situate many existing policy debates—Internet censorship, digital privacy, copyright disputes—in a larger political and policy framework. Although many readers did not share Lessig's pessimism, *Code* helped expose an unsettling truth—that a great many legislators, federal agencies, and courts were largely oblivious to the regulatory power of software code. They didn't have a clue about the technical structures or social dynamics affecting life on the Internet, let alone how existing law would comport with this alien domain.

Code was widely praised and widely read. But it was only one project of that period that catapulted Lessig to international prominence. In the mid-1990s, Charles Nesson, a bold-thinking, high-flying evidence professor at Harvard Law School, was organizing the Berkman Center for Internet & Society. The new project aspired to study "the most difficult and fundamental problems of the digital age," and show public-interest leadership in addressing them. Nesson, who had become modestly famous for his role in the W. R. Grace litigation chronicled in Jonathan Harr's *A Civil Action*, recruited Lessig to be the Berkman Center's marquee star in 1997. It was an irresistibly prestigious and visible perch.

This was demonstrated within months, when Judge Penfield Jackson tapped Lessig to be a "special master" in one of the most important antitrust cases in a generation, *U.S. v. Microsoft*.[17] Lessig's assignment was to sift through the welter of technical claims and counterclaims in the case and produce a report with recommendations to the court. The government alleged that Microsoft had abused its monopoly power in its sales of its operating system and

Web browser, particularly in "bundling" the browser with the Windows operating system.

Microsoft soon raised questions about Lessig's neutrality as a special master. Among other objections, the company cited his book's claim that software code is political and a passage that said Microsoft was "absolutely closed" compared to an open-standards body. It also dredged up an e-mail in which Lessig facetiously equated using Microsoft's Internet Explorer with "selling one's soul." After nearly eight weeks on the job, the Court of Appeals, citing a technicality, took Lessig off the case, to his enduring disappointment. He has been deeply frustrated by the implication that he had been removed for bias (the court made no such finding) and by his abrupt banishment from a plum role in a landmark case.

Waging the *Eldred* Case

Back at the Berkman Center, however, there were plenty of opportunities to influence the digital future. The center was a hothouse of venturesome ideas and eccentric visionaries. It was a place where John Perry Barlow could drop by to talk with Lessig and Berkman co-founder Jonathan Zittrain, one of the early cyberlaw experts. The center drew upon the ideas of intellectual property guru William (Terry) Fisher; Charles Nesson, who specialized in launching Big Ideas; and a self-renewing batch of bright law students eager to make their mark on a hip and emerging field of law. Richard Stallman at nearby MIT was an occasional visitor, as was MIT computer scientist Hal Abelson, who combined deep technical expertise with an appreciation of the social and democratic implications of digital technologies. It was during this time, in 1998, that Lessig and Abelson jointly taught The Law of Cyberspace: Social Protocols at Harvard Law School. The class was an attempt to make sense of some novel legal quandaries exploding on the Internet, such as computer crime, identity authentication, digital privacy, and intellectual property.

While nourished by the work of his academic colleagues, Lessig was determined to come up with ingenious ways to *do something* about the distressing drift of copyright law. It was important to take the offensive. Notwithstanding the pessimism of *Code*, Lessig's decidedly optimistic answer was to gin up a constitutional challenge to copyright law. Many legal experts and even sympathetic colleagues were skeptical. Peter Jaszi, a leading intellectual law professor at American University, told a reporter at the time, "It's not so much that we thought it was a terrible idea but that it was just unprecedented. Congress has been extending copyright for 180 years, and this is the first time someone said it violated the Constitution." [18] Others worried that an adverse ruling could set back the larger cause of copyright reform.

In the spirit of the commons, Lessig and his Berkman Center colleagues decided that the very process for mounting the *Eldred* lawsuit would be different: "Rather than the secret battles of lawyers going to war, we will argue this case in the open. This is a case about the commons; we will litigate it in the commons. Our arguments and strategy will be developed online, in a space called 'openlaw.org.' Key briefs will be drafted online, with participants given the opportunity to criticize the briefs and suggest other arguments. . . . Building on the model of open source software, we are working from the hypothesis that an open development process best harnesses the distributed resources of the Internet community. By using the Internet, we hope to enable the public interest to speak as loudly as the interests of corporations." [19]

Emulating the open-source development model was a nice touch, and perhaps useful; dozens of people around the world registered at the Openlaw site and posted suggestions. Some of the examples and legal critiques were used in developing the case, and the model was later used by lawyers in the so-called DeCSS case, in which a hacker broke the encryption of a DVD. But it turns out that open, distributed creativity has its limits in the baroque dance of litigation; it can't work when secrecy and confidentiality are important, for example.

The case, *Eldred v. Reno*—later renamed *Eldred v. Ashcroft* when the Bush II administration took office—was filed in federal district court in Washington, D.C., on January 11, 1999. [20] The complaint argued that the Copyright Term Extension Act violated Article 1, section 8, clause 8, of the Constitution, which provides that copyright protection shall be of limited duration. It also argued that the Term Extension Act violated the free speech clause of the First Amendment. In some respects, the case could never have been waged without the foundation of legal scholarship produced in the 1990s, which rehearsed a great many of the arguments presented to the Court. In opposition were motion picture studios, the music industry, and book publishers. They argued that Congress had full authority under the Constitution to extend copyright terms, as it had done since the beginning of the republic.

In October 1999, the U.S. District Court brusquely dismissed the case without even holding a trial. Lessig and his Berkman colleagues were not entirely surprised, and quickly set about filing an appeal with the U.S. Court of Appeals for the District of Columbia Circuit. Going beyond the Openlaw experiment at Berkman, they enlisted the support of several lawyers at Jones, Day, Reavis & Pogue. On appeal, Lessig was allowed to argue the case personally to a panel of judges. But once again, in February 2001, the case was dismissed. Lessig considered it a significant victory that it was a 2-1 ruling, however, which meant that a further appeal was possible. Lessig was also encouraged that the dissenter had been the court's most conservative member, Judge David Sentelle. Lessig requested that the full circuit court hear the case—a petition that was also rejected, this time after picking up support from a liberal dissenter, Judge David Tatel.

Normally, this would have been the end of the road for a case. Very few appeals court cases are accepted for review by the U.S. Supreme Court, particularly when the case has not even been argued at trial and no other courts have passed judgment on the statute. So it was quite surprising when the Supreme Court, in February 2002, accepted *Eldred* for review and scheduled oral arguments for October 2002.

At this point, Lessig realized he needed the advice and support of some experienced Supreme Court litigators. He enlisted help from additional lawyers at Jones, Day; Alan Morrison of Public Citizen Litigation Group; Kathleen Sullivan, the dean of Stanford Law School; and Charles Fried, a former solicitor general under President Reagan. Professor Peter Jaszi and the students of his law clinic drafted an amicus brief.

A key concern was how to frame the arguments. Attorney Don Ayer of Jones, Day repeatedly urged Lessig to stress the dramatic harm that the Bono Act was inflicting on free speech and free culture. But as Lessig later confessed, "I hate this view of the law. . . . I was not persuaded that we had to sell our case like soap."[21] Lessig was convinced that the only way *Eldred* could prevail at the Supreme Court would be to win over the conservative justices with a matter of principle. To Lessig, the harm was obvious; what needed emphasis was how the Sonny Bono Act violated "originalist" principles of jurisprudence. (Originalist judges claim to interpret the Constitution based on its "original" meanings in 1791, which includes a belief that Congress has strictly enumerated powers, not broad legislative discretion.)

"We tried to make an argument that if you were an originalist—in the way these conservative judges said they were in many other cases—then you should look to the original values in the Copyright Clause," said Lessig. "And we argued that if you did that then you had to conclude that Congress had wildly overstepped its constitutional authority, and so the law should be struck down."[22] Flaunting the harm caused by the copyright term extension struck Lessig as showy and gratuitous; he considered the harm more or less self-evident. In the aftermath of a public debate that Lessig once had with Jack Valenti, a questioner on Slashdot, a hacker Web site, suggested that Lessig would be more persuasive if he asserted "a clear conception of direct harm . . . than the secondary harm of the copyright holders getting a really sweet deal." Lessig conceded that such a focus "has been a weakness of mine for a long time. In my way of looking at the world, the point is a matter of principle, not pragmatics. . . . There are many others who are better at this pragmatism stuff. To me, it just feels insulting."[23]

And so, despite warnings to the contrary, Lessig's legal strategy relied on a call to uphold originalist principles. Having clerked for

Justice Scalia and Judge Posner, Lessig felt that he understood the mind-set and sympathies of the conservative jurists. "If we get to the Supreme Court," Lessig told Slashdot readers in December 2001, "I am certain that we will win. This is not a left/right issue. The conservatives on the Court will look at the framers' Constitution— which requires that copyrights be granted for 'limited times'—and see that the current practice of Congress . . . makes a mockery of the framers' plan. And the liberals will look at the effect of these never-ending copyrights on free speech, and conclude that Congress is not justified in this regulation of speech. The Supreme Court doesn't give a hoot about Hollywood; they will follow the law." [24]

Lessig took pride in the fact that thirty-eight amicus briefs were filed on behalf of *Eldred*. They included a wide range of authors, computer and consumer electronics companies, and organizations devoted to arts, culture, education, and journalism. Besides the usual suspects like the Free Software Foundation, Electronic Frontier Foundation, and Public Knowledge, supporting briefs were filed by fifteen economists including Kenneth Arrow and Milton Friedman, Phyllis Schlafly of the Eagle Forum, and the Intel Corporation.

At oral arguments, Lessig immediately confronted a skeptical bench. Justice Sandra Day O'Connor worried about overturning years of previous copyright term extensions. Justice William Rehnquist proposed. "You want the right to copy verbatim other people's books, don't you?" And when Justice Anthony Kennedy invited Lessig to expound upon the great harm that the law was inflicting on free speech and culture, Lessig declined the opportunity. He instead restated his core constitutional argument, that copyright terms cannot be perpetual. "This was a correct answer, but it wasn't the right answer," Lessig later confessed in a candid postmortem of the case. "The right answer was to say that there was an obvious and profound harm. Any number of briefs had been written about it. Kennedy wanted to hear it. And here was where Don Ayer's advice should have mattered. This was a softball; my answer was a swing and a miss." [25] No justices spoke in defense of the Sonny Bono Act.

Yet they had clear reservations about the Supreme Court's authority to dictate the length of copyright terms.

A few months later, on January 15, 2003, the Supreme Court announced its ruling: a 7-2 defeat for Eldred. The majority opinion, written by Justice Ruth Bader Ginsburg, did not even raise the "enumerated powers" argument or engage with originalist philosophy. "We are not at liberty to second-guess Congressional determinations and policy judgments of this order, however debatable or arguably unwise they may be," Ginsburg wrote.[26] She likewise ignored the idea that there is a "copyright bargain" between the American people and copyright holders, which entitles the public to certain rights of access to the public domain. As for copyright's impact on free speech, Ginsburg invoked the fair use doctrine and the "idea/expression dichotomy" (the notion that ideas are freely available but expression can be copyrighted) as sufficient protections for the public. She ignored the fact that both doctrines were (and are) under fierce assault.

Justices Stephen Breyer and John Paul Stevens accepted Lessig's arguments, and wrote separate dissents. Breyer—a respected scholar of copyright law since his famous 1970 essay "The Uneasy Case for Copyright"[27]—agreed that copyright terms had effectively become perpetual, and that the law was therefore unconstitutional. Stevens complained that the majority decision reneged on the copyright bargain and made copyright law "for all intents and purposes judicially unreviewable."

In assessing the broad impact of the *Eldred* ruling, copyright scholar Siva Vaidhyanathan cited law professor Shubha Ghosh's observation that the *Eldred* ruling had effectively "deconstitutionalized" copyright law. *Eldred* pushed copyright law

farther into the realm of policy and power battles and away from principles that have anchored the system for two centuries. That means public interest advocates and activists must take their battles to the public sphere and the halls of Congress. We can't appeal to the Founders' wishes or repub-

lican ideals. We will have to make pragmatic arguments in
clear language about the effects of excessive copyright on research, teaching, art and journalism. And we will have to
make naked mass power arguments with echoes of "we want
our MP3" and "it takes an industry of billions to hold us
back." [28]

A Movement Is Born

The *Eldred* case had a paradoxical effect. Early on, Lessig had said,
"We didn't want to make it a big political cause. We just wanted to
make it an extension of the existing Supreme Court jurisprudence,
because we realized that the only way to win the case was to win the
conservatives' view, and the conservatives were not likely to be motivated by great attacks on media concentration." [29] The upshot of
the Court's ruling was to intensify the political battles over copyright law. While such resistance was already growing, the *Eldred* ruling and the publicity surrounding it spawned a new generation of
"copyfighters." Lessig had wanted to protect the commons through
law, only to find that the courts were unwilling to offer any help.
Any answers would now have to be pursued through politics, culture, and technology—and ingenious uses of law where feasible.
How to proceed in this uncharted territory became the next challenge, as we see in chapter 4.

After four years of relentless work, Lessig was frustrated and de-
jected. "I had failed to convince [the Supreme Court] that the issue
was important," he wrote in a frank confessional, "and I had failed to
recognize that however much I might hate a system in which the
court gets to pick the constitutional values that it will respect, that is
the system we have." [30] For a constitutional law scholar, it was a rude
awakening: constitutional originalists could not be taken at their
word! Scalia and fellow justice Clarence Thomas had declined to
stand behind their jurisprudential principles.

Yet Lessig had certainly been correct that *Eldred* would not succeed unless it convinced the Court's conservative majority. The fact
that the originalist gambit failed was perhaps the strongest message

of all: *nothing* would convince this Court to rein in the excesses of copyright law.

Even before the Supreme Court had delivered its ruling, Lessig admitted his misgivings about the power of law to solve copyright's failings: "The more I'm in this battle, the less I believe that constitutional law on its own can solve the problem. If Americans can't see the value of freedom without the help of lawyers, then we don't deserve freedom."[31] Yet mobilizing freedom-loving Americans to seek redress from Congress was also likely to be doomed. Hollywood film studios and record companies had showered some $16.6 million and $1.8 million, respectively, on federal candidates and parties in 1998. Legislators know who butters their bread, and the public was not an organized influence on this issue. No wonder a progressive copyright reform agenda was going nowhere.

Four years after the *Eldred* ruling, Lessig had some second thoughts about the "Mickey Mouse" messaging strategy. Opponents of the copyright term extension, including Lessig, had often flaunted Mickey motifs in their dealings with the press and railed at the "Mickey Mouse Protection Act." Yet in 2006, Lessig lamented to one interviewer that "the case got framed as one about Mickey Mouse. Whereas the reality is, who gives a damn about Mickey Mouse? The really destructive feature of the Sonny Bono law is the way it locks up culture that has no continuing commercial value at all. It orphaned culture. So by focusing on Mickey Mouse, the Court thought this was an issue of whether you believed in property or not. If, however, we had focused people on all the culture that is being lost because it is locked up by copyright, we might have succeeded."[32]

The lasting impact of the *Eldred* case, ironically, may have less to do with the law than with the cultural movement it engendered. The lawsuit provided a powerful platform for educating the American people about copyright law. A subject long regarded as arcane and complicated was now the subject of prominent articles in the *New York Times, Salon*, computer magazines, wire services, and countless other publications and Web sites. A cover story for the *Los Angeles*

Times's Sunday magazine explained how the case could "change the way Hollywood makes money—and the way we experience art." *Wired* magazine headlined its profile of Lessig "The Great Liberator." Lessig himself barnstormed the country giving dozens of presentations to librarians, technologists, computer programmers, filmmakers, college students, and many others. Even Lessig's adversary at the district court level, Arthur R. Miller, a Harvard Law School professor, agreed, "The case has sparked a public discussion that wasn't happening before."

Lessig's orations often provoked the fervor of a revival meeting—and led to more than a few conversions. This may appear surprising because Lessig, with his receding hairline and wireframe glasses, strikes an unprepossessing pose. In the professorial tradition, he can sometimes be didactic and patronizing. But on the stage, Lessig is stylish, poised, and mesmerizing. His carefully crafted talks are intellectual but entertaining, sophisticated but plainspoken—and always simmering with moral passion. He typically uses a customized version of Keynote, a Macintosh-based program similar to PowerPoint, to punctuate his dramatic delivery with witty visuals and quick flashes of words. (Experts in professional presentations have dubbed this style the "Lessig Method," and likened it to the Takahashi Method in Japan because slides often use a single word, short quote, or photo.)[33]

More than a sidebar, Lessig's public speaking has been an important aspect of his leadership in building a commons movement. His talks have helped some fairly sequestered constituencies in technical fields—computer programming, library science, Internet policy, copyright law—understand the larger political and cultural significance of their work. The results have sometimes been galvanizing. As one veteran hacker told me in 2006, "There's a whole connoisseurship of Lessig talks. He's a little past his peak right now—but there was a period where, like when he gave the lecture at OSCON [a conference of open-source programmers], when he was done, they wanted to start a riot. People were literally milling around, looking for things to smash. He was saying to these people who worked on open source, 'There's a larger world context to your work. The government is doing things—and you can stop them!' "[34]

Following oral arguments before the Supreme Court, the movement—such as it was—had a rare gathering of its leaders. Public Knowledge co-hosted a luncheon for those who had aided the lawsuit. The diners spanned the worlds of libraries, computers, Internet publishing, public-interest advocacy, and many other fields. The event was held at Washington's Sewall-Belmont House, where the National Woman's Party once led the fight for women's suffrage. This prompted Gigi Sohn, president of Public Knowledge, to declare, "We, too, are building a movement."[35]

So after arguing—and losing—before the U.S. Supreme Court, what does a copyright superstar do for an encore?

A seed had already been planted at the Starbucks meeting four years earlier. Eldred recalls telling Lessig, "I think this case is very important, and I think you're the right guy for this. But at the same time, I'd like to talk to you about something else. I really think that we need to start up some sort of a copyright conservancy, which would be sort of like a nature conservancy. It would allow people to donate books to the public domain; we could then take ownership of them. They could maybe have a tax deduction for them, and we could—instead of having the book privately owned—they would be in the public domain, maybe before the copyright term expired. We could sort of have an independent group maintain this conservancy, and allow the books to be put on the Internet for free."

Eldred remembers that Lessig "was sort of stunned. He didn't have anything to say for a little while. We sort of looked at each other, and I think he was very shocked and surprised that I said that. And he said, 'I don't think we can do it until we've done the work on the copyright term extension act suit, but I promise to do it.' "[36]

PART II

The Rise of Free Culture

To the commoners seeking to build a new cultural universe, the failure of the *Eldred* case in the U.S. Supreme Court was both depressing and liberating. It confirmed what the legal scholars of the 1990s had long suspected—that both Congress and the courts were captives to a backward-looking vision of copyright law. Government was tacitly committed to a world of centralized and commercial mass media managed by elite gatekeepers. That was not likely to change soon.

As for helping build a new digital republic with a more open, democratic character, the Clinton administration made its intentions clear in its infamous White Paper. It wanted to convert the gift economy of the Internet into a wall-to-wall marketplace. It wanted to give sellers absolute control over content and limit the disruptions of innovative newcomers. The government, acting on behalf of the film, record, and book industries, had no desire to legitimize or fortify the sharing culture that was fast gaining a hold on the Internet. Quite the contrary: strengthening the public's fair use rights, access to the public domain, and online free speech rights might interfere with the perceived imperatives of electronic commerce. *Freedom* would therefore have to be defined as the freedom of consumers to buy what incumbents were selling, not as a robust civic freedom exercised by a sovereign citizenry.

By the conclusion of *Eldred*, in 2003, it was clear that the copyright dissidents were not just confronting one policy battle or another; they were confronting an antiquated and entrenched worldview. While Lessig, Eldred, and the growing band of commoners realized that it was important to pay close attention to pending legislation and lawsuits, many of them also realized that the real challenge was to develop a new vision—and then try to actualize it.

A more affirmative, comprehensive vision was needed to supersede the limited intellectual parameters of copyright law. Copyright law was a mode of property discourse, after all, and that discourse simply could not adequately express the aspirations of hackers, citizen-journalists, librarians, academics, artists, democrats, and others trying to secure open online spaces for themselves. The online insurgents acknowledged the great importance of fair use and the public domain, but they also considered such doctrines to be vestiges of an archaic, fraying legal order. It was time to salvage what was valuable from that order, but otherwise instigate a new language, a new aesthetic, a new legal regime, a new worldview.

This meant venturing into risky, unknown territory. Law professors accustomed to working within the comfort of the academy would have to clamber onto public stages and set forth idealistic, politically inflected scenarios for Internet culture. Activists accustomed to rhetorical critiques would have to initiate pragmatic, results-driven projects. Free software hackers would have to invent new software and digital protocols. Volunteers would need to be enlisted and organized and funding secured to sustain bare-boned organizational structures. Wholly new constituencies would have to be imagined and mobilized and brought together into something resembling a new movement. Part II, The Rise of Free Culture, describes the building of this foundation from 2000 to 2005.

4

INVENTING THE CREATIVE COMMONS

A public-spirited cabal schemes for a way to legalize sharing.

Larry Lessig remembers his Starbucks conversation with Eric Eldred as a "crystallizing moment," a revelation that the stakes in copyright reform were much higher than he had originally imagined. Both Lessig and Eldred obviously wanted to win the lawsuit and recognized its importance. But Eldred had made clear that he didn't just want to roll back regressive laws; he wanted to develop an affirmative and sustainable alternative.

This got Lessig thinking: "So, okay—you get the Supreme Court to strike the laws down, but you still live in a world where people think that everything is property and has to be owned. If nobody has a political awareness about why the judicial response makes sense, then it's a pretty empty result."[1] Throughout the *Eldred* case, paradoxically enough, Lessig says he was "skeptical" of the traditional liberal strategy of seeking redress through the courts.

The turning point for him, Lessig recalled, was in recognizing that Eldred was not just a plaintiff in a test case but "someone trying to build a movement around a practice of making things available in a way that took advantage of the infrastructure of the Net."[2] True, Eldritch Press resembled an old-style archive of canonical works. Yet Eldred's goal all along had been to host an active social community of book lovers, not just provide a repository for old texts. The Web site's real importance was in the social activity it represented—the fact that thousands of participant-readers could come together around a self-selected amateur eager to build a new type of social community and information genre.

Lessig told me that when he recognized Eldred's Web site as a new type of social practice, it helped define the challenge: "The question became a very technical, legal one: How could we instantiate that movement?" Lessig said he needed to find a way to "disambiguate the social practice." By that bit of tech-legalese, he meant, How could the practices and values animating Eldred's Web site be articulated in law, denoted on the Web, and thereby be seen for what they were: a new mode of social practice and cultural freedom?

It helps to remember that in 1998 and the following years, the legality of sharing online works and downloading them was highly ambiguous. Prevailing legal discourse set forth a rather stark, dualistic world: either a work is copyrighted with "all rights reserved," or a work is in the public domain, available to anyone without restriction. The mental categories of the time offered no room for a "constituency of the reasonable," in Lessig's words.

Copyright law made nominal provisions for a middle ground in the form of the fair use doctrine and the public domain. But Lessig realized that fair use was "just a terrible structure on which to build freedom. There are basically no bright lines; everything is a constant debate. Of course, we don't want to erase or compromise or weaken [these doctrines] in any sense. But it's very important to build an infrastructure that doesn't depend upon four years of litigation." Or as Lessig was wont to put it in his impassioned performances on the stump: "Fuck fair use." [3]

This was a theatrical flourish, of course. Back in Palo Alto, Lessig in 2001 had launched the Center for Internet & Society at Stanford Law School, which actively takes on lawsuits seeking to vindicate the public's fair use rights, among other things. One notable case was against Stephen Joyce, the grandson of novelist James Joyce. As executor of the Joyce literary estate, Stephen Joyce steadfastly prevented dozens of scholars from quoting from the great writer's archive of unpublished letters. [4] (After losing a key court ruling in February 2007, the Joyce estate settled the case on terms favorable to a scholar who had been denied access to the Joyce papers.)

But Lessig's intemperance toward fair use has more to do with the almost subliminal void in legal discourse and political culture. There was no way to talk about the social behaviors exemplified by

Eldred's Web site except through crabbed, legalistic rules. The only available language, the default vocabulary, is copyright law and its sanctioned zones of freedom, such as fair use. Lessig wanted to open up a new, more bracing line of discourse. "We wanted to rename the social practice," he said. It sounds embarrassingly grandiose to state it so bluntly, but in later years it became clear to Lessig and his loose confederation of colleagues that the real goal was to *imagine and build a legal and technical infrastructure of freedom.*

Initially, the goal was more exploratory and improvisational—an earnest attempt to find leverage points for dealing with the intolerable constraints of copyright law. Fortunately, there were instructive precedents, most notably free software, which by 2000, in its opensource guise, was beginning to find champions among corporate IT managers and the business press. Mainstream programmers and corporations started to recognize the virtues of GNU/Linux and opensource software more generally. Moreover, a growing number of people were internalizing the lessons of *Code*, that the architecture of software and the Internet really does matter.

Even as he sought to prevail in *Eldred*, Lessig understood that enduring solutions could not be conferred by the U.S. Supreme Court; they had to be made real through people's everyday habits. The commoners needed to build a new set of tools to actualize freedom on the Internet, and to develop a new language, a new epistemology, a new vision, for describing the value proposition of sharing and collaboration. The big surprise, as we will see in chapter 6, was the latent social energies poised to support this vision.

What If . . . ?

Shortly after the *Eldred* case was filed in January 1999, a number of Harvard Law students working with Lessig announced the formation of a new group, "Copyright's Commons."[5] Led by Jennifer Love and Ashley Morgan, Copyright's Commons published a monthly Web newsletter that provided updates on the progress of the *Eldred* case and miscellaneous news about the public domain.

Copyright's Commons described itself as "a coalition devoted to promoting the public availability of literature, art, music, and film." It was actually a named plaintiff in the *Eldred* case.

That spring, Copyright's Commons announced a new project that it called the "counter-copyright [cc] campaign." Billed as "an alternative to the exclusivity of copyright," the campaign invited the general public to "show your support for the public domain by marking your work with a [cc] and a link to the Copyright's Commons website. . . . If you place the [cc] icon at the end of your work, you signal to others that you are allowing them to use, modify, edit, adapt and redistribute the work that you created."

The project may have been an imaginative call to arms, but there was no infrastructure behind it except one Web page, and no background material except a Web link to the Open Source Initiative. Wendy Seltzer, a Harvard Law student at the time, recalled that the [cc] symbol produced by Copyright's Commons "was supposed to be a public domain dedication, but nobody had yet gone through all of the thinking about what was actually required to put something into the public domain, and did this satisfy the 'affirmative act' requirements [of the law]? Part of the germ of the Creative Commons was thinking about what would it take to make this—the [cc] symbol—an actual, meaningful, legally binding statement." [6]

Lessig, in the meantime, was keeping a frenetic schedule. He was overseeing the progress of the *Eldred* lawsuit; traveling to give speeches to dozens of conferences and forums every year; promoting his book *Code*; and writing a monthly column in the *Industry Standard* until it went under with the tech bubble collapse in 2001. The year before, Kathleen Sullivan of Stanford Law School persuaded Lessig to join its faculty and supervise a new law clinic, the Center for Internet and Society. [7] Along the way Lessig also got married to Bettina Neuefeind, a human rights lawyer.

Work on *Eldred* intensified after the district court dismissed the case in October 1999. Lessig embarked on a new round of legal strategizing with colleagues to prepare the appeals court brief, which was submitted in May 2000. Throughout this period, intellectual property (IP) thinkers and tech activists—especially those in the Lessig/Cambridge/Stanford axis—were highly attuned to the gathering storm in copyright and software policy.

One of the most tumultuous developments was Napster, a homemade file-sharing software program that had become an international sensation. Released in June 1999, Napster was the creation of hacker Shawn Fanning, then a student at Northeastern University in Boston. Within a year, the free program had been downloaded by an estimated 70 million users, drawing fierce denunciations by the recording industry and Washington officials. Napster used centralized file directories on the Internet to connect users to music files on thousands of individual computers. By enabling people to download virtually any recorded music in existence, for free, it was as if the fabled "cosmic jukebox" had arrived. Of course, much of the copying was blatantly illegal. Yet consumers welcomed Napster as one of the few vehicles they had for thumbing their nose at a reactionary music industry that refused to offer digital downloads. The Recording Industry Association of America (RIAA) sued Napster in December 1999, and succeeded in shutting it down in July 2001.[8]

The Napster craze intensified the polarized property discourse that Lessig and his colleagues were trying to transcend. Napster encouraged an either/or debate by suggesting that a song is either private property or contraband; there was no middle ground for fair use or the public domain. While the RIAA and acts like Metallica and Madonna railed against massive copyright infringements, defenders of Napster were quick to point out its promotional power. An album produced by the English rock band Radiohead, for example, was downloaded for free by millions of people before its release—a fact that many credit with pushing the album, *Kid A*, to the top of the Billboard CD sales chart. But such claims carried little weight against those defending what they considered their property rights.

The controversy over Napster was clearly influential in shaping the debate over how to protect the public domain. Berkman Center co-director Jonathan Zittrain recalls, "If we're trying to hang the hopes of the community on the right just to copy stuff, we're going to lose—and maybe we should. [The issue] is actually about the right to manipulate the symbols and talismans of our culture"— what Professor Terry Fisher likes to call "semiotic democracy." [9]

The problem was that copyright discourse, at least in the hands of the record and film industries, refused to acknowledge that the sharing and reuse of works might be necessary, desirable, or legal. The concept did not compute. There was a conspicuous void in the prevailing terms of debate. So the challenge facing the Cambridge copyright cabal was really a riddle about epistemology, law, and culture rolled into one. How could a new type of free culture, independent of the market, be brought into existence? And how could the creative works of this imagined culture be made legally "shareable" instead of being automatically treated as private property?

This was an unprecedented challenge. When culture was chiefly a set of analog media—books, records, film—there had been affirmative legal limits on the scope of copyright. Before 1978, the law regulated only commercial uses of a work and only works that had been formally registered, which meant that most works automatically remained in the public domain. Moreover, there was a natural, physical "friction" preventing copyright holders from overcontrolling how a work could circulate and be used. When words were fixed in books and sounds embedded in vinyl, people could circulate those objects freely, without having to ask permission from copyright holders. In the digital world, however, the physical constraints of analog media disappeared. Copyright holders now claimed that every digital blip, however transient, constituted a "copyright event" subject to their unilateral control. In practice, this greatly weakened the rights a person could enjoy under the fair use doctrine.

In a sense, the entire legal and cultural framework for free culture needed to be reimagined so it could function in the digital environment. The terms of fair use essentially had to be renegotiated—an undertaking that copyright law had never had to tackle in the past. But how might that be achieved when both Congress and the courts were beholden to the copyright maximalists' worldview?

Such were the kinds of conversations that swirled around the Berkman Center, Harvard Law School, MIT, and a handful of progressive intellectual property circles. Such discussions had been going on for years, especially in the context of free software and public-domain scholarship, but now they were reaching the lay public. The Napster and *Eldred* cases were vehicles for educating the press and the public, and Lessig's book *Code* was becoming must reading for anyone who cared about Internet governance and digital culture.

Amid this swirl of copyright controversy, MIT professor Hal Abelson had lunch with Lessig at the Harvard Faculty Club in July 2000. The two had co-taught a class on cyberlaw two years earlier and shared many interests in the confluence of copyright and technology. One topic that day was Eric Eldred's idea of a copyright conservancy—a "land trust" for public-domain works. On August 1, 2000, Abelson sent Zittrain an e-mail:

> *Here's an idea that we might be able to get going, and where the Berkman Center could help.*
>
> *Let's set up a tax-free, charitable foundation to which artists and record label companies could donate the copyright for recorded music. I'm thinking of all the old music for which there isn't currently an active market.*
>
> *The foundation would arrange for this stuff to be loaded for free onto the internet and give the public permission to use it. The artists and record labels get a tax writeoff. The RIAA and Napster hug and kiss, and everyone goes home happy.*
>
> *What do you think?*
>
> *Hal*

Zittrain loved the idea, and suggested that it might make a great clinical project for Harvard Law students that fall. But he wondered if the Copyright Clearinghouse Center—a licensing and permissions organization for music—already offered such a service (it didn't). Lessig proposed that Stanford and Harvard law schools jointly develop the program. He immediately identified one glaring problem: it would be difficult to "establish a process for valuing gifts of copyrighted stuff that would be clearly understood and would be accepted by the IRS."

What ensued was a lengthy and irregular series of e-mail conversations and social encounters through which the idea was chewed over and refined. Lessig acted as the "supernode" among a small group of participants that initially included Zittrain, Eldred, Nesson, and Diane Cabell, a lawyer and administrator at the Berkman Center. Within a month, others were invited into the conversation: Richard Stallman; Duke Law professors James Boyle and Jerome H. Reichman; and documentary film producer Eric Saltzman, who had just become director of the Berkman Center.

A digital archive for donated and public-domain works had great appeal. Just as land trusts acted as trustees of donated plots of land, so the Copyright's Commons (as Lessig proposed that it be named) would be a "conservancy" for film, books, music, and other works that were either in the public domain or donated. Six weeks after Abelson's original suggestion, Lessig produced a "Proposal for an Intellectual Property Conservancy" for discussion purposes.[10] He now called the concept "an IP commons"—"the establishment of an intellectual property conservancy to facilitate the collection and distribution under a GPL-like license of all forms of intellectual property." As elaborated by two Harvard Law School students, Chris Babbitt and Claire Prestel, "The conservancy will attempt to bridge the gap between authors, corporate copyright holders and public domain advocates by providing a repository of donated works which we believe will create a more perfect 'market' for intellectual property."[11]

Friendly critiques started arriving immediately. Stallman considered the proposal a "good idea overall," but as usual he objected to the words, such as "intellectual property" and "copyright protection," which he considered "propaganda for the other side."[12] Abelson, a friend and colleague of Stallman's at MIT, was not finicky about word choices, but he did believe that software donations should be directed to the Free Software Foundation, not to the envisioned project. FSF already existed, for one thing, but in addition, said Abelson, "It may be detrimental to have people initially associate this [new project] too closely with the FSF. . . . We need to craft a public position that will unify people. An FSF-style 'let's undo the effects of all those evil people licensing software' is not what we want here."[13] Some people suggested attracting people to the conservancy by having "jewels" such as material from the estates of deceased artists. Another suggested hosting special licenses, such as the Open Audio License, a license issued by the Electronic Frontier Foundation in 2001 that lets musicians authorize the copying and reuse of their songs so long as credit is given and derivative songs can be shared.

The most difficult issue, said Abelson, was the economics of the project. The care and maintenance of donations, such as the master version of films, could be potentially huge expenses. Digitizing donated works could also be expensive. Finally, there were questions about the economic incentives to potential donors. Would people really wish to donate works that have significant cash value?

Answers to such questions were hardly self-evident, but there were encouraging signs. After Lessig gave a speech at the University of Michigan in September 2000, a man came up to him and announced, "I'm one of the people who benefited by the Mickey Mouse Protection Act." It was Robert Frost, Jr., son of the great poet. Frost said, "I obviously need to check with my family, but we may be interested in becoming a contributor to your conservancy."[14] If Robert Frost's estate could come forward with his literary legacy, perhaps there were others willing to do the same.

When Berkman Center director Eric Saltzman joined the conversation, he raised a series of difficult questions about the whole idea:

> Why would a person or corp. donate copyrighted materials? Larry's draft implies a benefit to the IP owner—does this mean broader Internet facilitated use, and not merely a tax deduction? Under what circumstances, if any, does the Conservancy charge for use of its IP? If a user modifies a story,

say, producing a screenplay, to whom does that screenplay
belong? Would a motion picture based upon that screenplay
owe $$ to the Conservancy? If so, how much (this is the
damages phase of the *Rear Window* case)? [15] Wouldn't a new,
hopeful band prefer to allow free use of its song(s) on a com-
mercially promoted site like MP3.com rather than the Con-
servancy site? All asking: How to make the Conservancy
into a useful garden, not a well-meaning weed patch of un-
wanted, neglected IP? [16]

By early October 2001, some of these questions had been provi-
sionally answered. For example: Only digital works would be ac-
cepted initially. No limitations or restrictions would be set on the
use of donated works. Prospective academic partners would include
the University of California at Berkeley, Duke, Harvard, MIT, and
Stanford. Lessig suggested both Richard Stallman and Jack Valenti as
possible board members. The central goal was to develop a new sort
of noncommercial space in cyberspace for the sharing and reuse of
music, visual art, film, literature, nonfiction, academic work, soft-
ware, and science. [17]

But many questions still hung in the air. Could the free software
ethic really translate to other creative genres? Would tax incentives
elicit donations of works? Would independent appraisals of donated
works be needed? How would the conservancy search the titles of
works and get permissions clearances?

For all of its brainpower and commitment, Lessig's rump caucus
might not have gotten far if it had not found a venturesome source
of money, the Center for the Public Domain. The center—origi-
nally the Red Hat Center—was a foundation created by entrepre-
neur Robert Young in 2000 following a highly successful initial
public offering of Red Hat stock. As the founder of Red Hat, a
commercial vendor of GNU/Linux, Young was eager to repay his
debt to the fledgling public-domain subculture. He also realized,
with the foresight of an Internet entrepreneur, that strengthening
the public domain would only enhance his business prospects over
the long term. (It has; Young later founded a print-on-demand pub-

lishing house, Lulu.com, that benefits from the free circulation of electronic texts, while making money from printing hard copies.)

The director of the center, Lauric Racine, a former geneticist and business professor, was skilled at making shrewd strategic grants and "character bets" in public-domain activism. Because the center was not hobbled by the bureaucracy or timidity that afflicts many large foundations, it was able to make swift decisions and bold bets on innovative projects. (I came to work closely with Racine on a number of projects, including the co-founding of Public Knowledge, in 2001.)

Lessig met with Racine in October 2000. On a napkin, he sketched his idea for expanding copyright for authors. He came away with funding for a meeting at the Berkman Center and, later, a $100,000 commitment to launch the IP conservancy; the Center for the Public Domain eventually put up $1 million to get the project going, well before other funders saw the promise of the idea. Racine wanted her new center to be associated with "a project that has broad vision, credibility, range and staying power." She saw Lessig's project as having all of those things.[18] The grant was based more on the concept than a specific plan, however. At the time it was not entirely clear if the project would own and manage digital works, host Web services that made things freely available, or provide legal and software tools—or something else.[19] There was, nonetheless, a great sense of mission and urgency to get under way.

Interestingly, two similar initiatives were also in the early stages of development. The Knowledge Conservancy, led by David Bearman at Carnegie Mellon University in Pittsburgh, had a similar model of accepting donations of materials and making them available online. It focused more on sponsorship donations and memberships, while Lessig's group was more oriented toward legal research and Web hosting of works. Another project, OpenCulture.org, planned to compensate artists for contributions to the public domain, but apparently it never took off.[20] Lessig and his group were not averse to joining forces with others, but they were intent on vetting their own business model, such as it was, before joining anyone else's venture.

One turning point came in January 2001 after Saltzman had met with several lawyers at Wilmer, Cutler & Pickering, a prominent law firm in Washington, D.C.[21] After conversations with attorneys David Johnson and Michael W. Carroll, it became clear that a non-profit trust managing donated material could face considerable liability if it turned out that the donors did not actually own the works. To explore this issue, Carroll produced a much-praised legal memo that raised a red flag: "What if we were fools, and the person who gave us the rights [to a work] actually never had the rights and suddenly we get sued for infringement?" asked Carroll.[22] One successful lawsuit could sink the whole enterprise.

The project was caught in a conundrum. It wanted to legalize a whole set of social practices for sharing and reusing creative works—but establishing a content intermediary for that purpose appeared to be financially prohibitive under the law. It could be hugely expensive to clear titles and indemnify the organization and future users against copyright infringement risks.

For a few months, various people in Lessig's orbit suggested complicated schemes to try to finesse the legal problems. For example, one way that the conservancy could reduce its liability would be to simply point to the Web locations of public-domain materials, in the style of Napster's centralized index of songs. This would also avoid the nuisance and expense of clearing titles on thousands of works. Another idea was to create a "three zone system" of content—Zone A for content that the conservancy owned and licensed; Zone B for content that was merely hosted at the conservancy site with no copyright representations; and Zone C, a simple search engine with links to public-domain content. Each of these zones, in turn, raised a flurry of complicated, speculative legal issues.[23]

None of the proposed alternatives got much traction, especially when Saltzman took a closer look at the realities of tax deductions for donors. Saltzman came to see that tax breaks would have very little incentive value for most potential donors, and establishing the cash value of donations would be difficult in any case. Moreover, if donors were getting little in return for their donations, they would be wary of signing a form indemnifying the conservancy against legal liability. On top of all this, Saltzman, like others, had misgiving about "the idea of the federal treasury contributing public money [in the form of tax expenditures]." In short, the conservancy approach seemed plagued with many complicated and perhaps insoluble problems.

As if to keep the pot boiling, newcomers kept adding new thoughts. Two leading thinkers about the public domain in science, Paul Uhlir and Jerome H. Reichman, urged that the group expand its mission to include scientific research and take an international perspective.[24] (Uhlir directs the international scientific and technical information programs at the National Academy of Sciences/National Research Council; Reichman is an intellectual property professor at Duke Law School.) Both were keenly aware of the dangers to scientific progress if copyright and patent protection continued to expand.

In January 2001, the caucus reached one point of consensus—that the primary function of this commons should be "to facilitate free/low-cost public use of original works." It also agreed upon a name. Asked to vote on a name from a list that included IP Commons, Dot-commons, Sui Generous, IP Conservancy, and Public Works, Saltzman piped up, "May I suggest another name? CREATIVE COMMONS." When the final poll results were counted, Creative Commons was the clear winner with five votes, with one vote apiece for the remaining names. A later poll pitted "The Constitution's Commons" against "Creative Commons" (CC) in a final runoff. The vote tally is lost to history, but we do know which name prevailed.[25]

Viewpoints quickly diverged on how a commons ought to be structured and what metrics of success should be used. Should it seek to maximize the number of donations or the number of downloads? Should it develop quality holdings in a given field or provide the widest possible breadth of content? Should it focus on social interaction and creative reuses of works? Should the focus be on producers or consumers of intellectual property? Should the organization focus on individuals or institutions? And how would it be different from other rights clearance organizations and content archives? The group seemed mired in a great cloud of uncertainty.

For the next nine months, the group intensified its debate about how to build the envisioned conservancy. After law student Dotan Oliar sketched out possible "business models," Saltzman persuaded a friend at McKinsey & Company, the consulting firm, to provide a pro bono assessment.[26] "The McKinsey folks were very skeptical and, I think, had a hard time fitting this into their [business] framework," recalled one student at the meeting, Chris Babbitt. After the meeting, he was convinced that Creative Commons could not possibly host a content commons: "It would just be huge amounts of material, huge costs, and we didn't have the money for that."[27]

Feeling the need to force some concrete decisions, Saltzman and Lessig convened twenty-eight people for an all-day meeting in Hauser Hall at Harvard Law School, on May 11, 2001, to hash out plans. "What we're trying to do here is *brand the public domain*," Lessig said. A briefing book prepared by Chris Babbitt posed a pivotal question to the group: Should Creative Commons be structured as a centralized Web site or as an distributed, open-source licensing protocol that would allow content to be spread across cyberspace? The centralized model could be "an eBay for open-source IP" or a more niche-based commons for out-of-print books, film, or poetry. A mock Web site was actually prepared to illustrate the scenario. The home page read: "The member sites listed on the CommonExchange have been certified by Creative Commons to offer high-quality, non-infringing content on an unrestricted basis. Please feel free to use and pass these works along to others. We invite you to donate works of your own to help maintain the digital Commons."[28]

The distributed commons model would resemble the Chicago Mercantile Exchange or the New York Stock Exchange—"a trusted matchmaker to facilitate the transaction of securing rights," according to the briefing book. "Just as corporations or commodities producers must meet certain criteria before they are listed on the Exchange, we could condition 'listing' in the Commons on similar criteria, albeit reflecting open source rather than financial values." [29] The virtue of the distributed model was that it would shift costs, quality control, and digitization to users. Creative Commons would serve mostly as a credentialing service and facilitator. On the other hand, giving up control would be fraught with peril—and what if Creative Commons' intentions were ignored?

Several participants remember Lessig, Nesson, and Zittrain pushing for the distributed model, which seemed a bolder and riskier option. "Larry was the lead advocate for a distributed commons, where it would be focused on a license mechanism that we then would release to the world, and we let the world do with it what it will," one attendee recalled. "At the time, I think, XML-type capabilities were just coming around, and Larry was very confident that that was the direction to go." [30] XML, or Extensible Markup Language, is a programming language that uses self-created "tags" that help Internet users aggregate and share digital content residing on different computer systems. Lessig envisioned XML tags embedded in any Creative Commons–licensed work, which could then be used to identify shareable content on the Internet.

This perspective carried the day, and the "conservancy" model of the commons was formally abandoned. CC would serve as a licensing agent. The licenses would enable authors' works to be made available online in an easy, low-cost way without the full restrictions of copyright law. A standardized set of licenses would overcome the ambiguities of the fair use doctrine without overriding it. Creators could voluntarily forfeit certain copyright rights in advance—and signal that choice—so that others could freely reuse, share, and distribute CC-licensed works.

Jonathan Zittrain remembers being skeptical at first: "So this whole thing is just about some tags? It's about *licensing*? How boring." Upon reflection, however, he saw the value of CC licensing as a way to create a new default. "As soon as you realize—'Well, wait a minute! It's just about authors being able to express their desires!' " [31]

More than a menu of individual choices, the licenses would constitute an embryonic cultural order—a "constitutional system" to direct how text, images, and music could circulate in the online world, based on authors' individual choices. But the new focus on licenses raised its own set of novel quandaries. What options should an author be able to choose? What suite of licenses made sense? While licensing terms may be boring and legalistic, the architecture could have potentially profound implications for cultural freedom—which is why the legal minds involved in the licenses spent so much time arguing seemingly obscure points.

However these debates were resolved, everyone agreed that it was time to incorporate Creative Commons as a nonprofit group, assemble a board, recruit a chief executive officer, and of course raise more money. The stated goal: "to expand the shrinking public domain, to strengthen the social values of sharing, of openness and of advancing knowledge and individual creativity." [32]

There was a certain audacity if not unreality to the whole venture. Law professors don't go around inventing ambitious public projects to revamp the social applications of copyright law. They don't generally muck around with software, contract law, and artists to build an imagined "sharing economy." "There was always this lingering suspicion in the back of my mind," recalled Babbitt in 2006, "that it [Creative Commons] would be kind of a rich man's folly, and this would just be some little thing—a niche experiment—that really wouldn't turn out to have merited the sort of sustained interest of this high-caliber group of people." [33]

Crafting the Licenses

If Creative Commons licenses were going to enable artists to determine future uses of their works—on less restrictive terms than copyright law—what did actual artists think of the whole idea? To get a crude baseline of opinion, Laura Bjorkland, a friend of Lessig's and manager of a used-book store in Salem, Massachusetts, conducted an unscientific survey. She asked about a dozen writers, photographers, painters, filmmakers, and a sculptor if they would be interested in donating their works to a commons, or using material from one? Most of them replied, "I've never even *thought* of this before. . . ." [34]

A classical composer said he "loved the idea of a Nigerian high school chamber group playing one of my string quartets without paying royalties . . . but I would not want a film studio or pop song writer using one of my themes on a commercial project, even if my name's attached, without royalties." Some artists worried about others making money off derivatives of their work. Many complained that artists earn so little anyway, why should they start giving away their work? Others were reluctant to see their work altered or used for violence or pornography. Photographers and visual artists found it "a little scary" to let their signature style be used by anyone.

In short, there was no stampede for starting a public-domain conservancy or a set of licenses. Some worried that the CC licenses would be a "case of innovation where's there's no current demand." Another person pointed out, more hopefully, that it could be a case of "changing the market demand with a new model." [35]

The Lessig caucus was clearly struggling with how best to engage with the networked environment. Napster had demonstrated that, in the dawning Internet age, creativity would increasingly be born, distributed, and viewed on the Web; print and mass media would be secondary venues. For a society still deeply rooted in print and mass media, this was a difficult concept to grasp. But Michael Carroll, the Washington lawyer who had earlier vetted the conservancy's liability issues, shrewdly saw network dynamics as a potentially powerful tool for building new types of digital commons. In 2001, he had noticed how a bit of Internet folk art had become an overnight sensation. Mike Collins, an amateur cartoonist from Elmira, New York, had posted the cartoon below on Taterbrains, a Web site. [36] The image suddenly rocketed throughout the cyberlandscape. Everyone was copying it and sharing it with friends.

Carroll observed:

[Collins] distributed his design initially without a motive to profit from it. But the scale of distribution surpassed what he imagined, and in a subsequent interview he expressed some resentment over those who had made money from T-shirts and other paraphernalia using his design. But he appears to have taken no actions to enforce his copyright, the notice

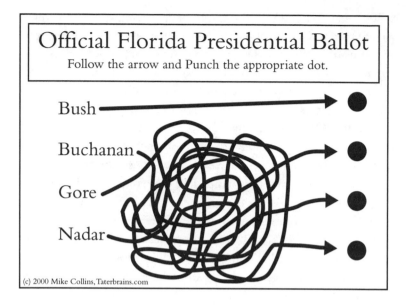

Official Florida Presidential Ballot
Follow the arrow and Punch the appropriate dot.

Bush

Buchanan

Gore

Nadar

(c) 2000 Mike Collins, Taterbrains.com

notwithstanding. Copyright lawyers would consider the un-licensed distribution of this work "leakage"—that is, a viola-tion of law but not worth pursuing.

But if we could take steps to make it cheap, easy and de-sirable for the Mike Collinses of the world to stick a CC tag on something like this before sending it out, "leakage" be-comes legal, changing the terms of the debate.[37]

CC tags could make nonproprietary culture the default, revers-ing the presumption of copyright law. Everyone agreed with this general approach, but implementing it was rife with difficult ques-tions. As Saltzman recalled: "What kind of relationship did we want to encourage between the creator/licensor and the user? Should it be totally automated? Should it invite some back-and-forth? Should there be a requirement that licensors provide contact infor-mation?"[38] The General Public License for software had shown the feasibility of a license for safeguarding a commons of shared code. Could it work in other creative sectors? It would be critical to strike the right balance. As law student Chris Babbitt put it, "Too little protection for the donor's interests and no one will donate; too little room for the users to use the work, and the service is useless." [39]

If there were going to be several licenses, the next question was how many, and of what sort? There are many different types of creativity, after all. Should each one have its own set of special licenses? The Berkman conclave agreed that there should be a public-domain license enabling creators to grant a nonexclusive, royalty-free license on their works, without the viral conditions of the GPL. As for other licenses, five ideas were put on the table for consideration: a license authorizing free reuses of a work so long as proper attribution is given to the author; a license authorizing noncommercial uses; and a license authorizing free reuses but prohibiting derivative uses. Other suggestions included a license authorizing academic uses only and a "timed donations" license, which would allow an artist to revoke a work from the commons after a stipulated number of years. [40] Neither of these two licenses gained support from the group.

There were also lots of open questions about how to structure the specific terms of the licenses. Should they be perpetual? Will the licensor be liable for "downstream" uses of a work that are deemed an infringement? Will licensors be required to identify themselves? Should licensors be able to add their own separate warranties and representations? Crafting the licenses meant going beyond the abstract rhetoric of the commons. These licenses had to be serious, operational legal instruments that courts would recognize as valid.

Another concern was making the new CC licenses compatible with existing licenses seeking similar goals. MIT had produced the first such license for its OpenCourseWare initiative, which allows Internet users to use the university's curricula and syllabi (see chapter 12). To ensure that CC- and MIT-licensed content would be compatible, the CC lawyers deliberately wrote a license that would meet MIT's needs. Another license, the GNU Free Documentation License (FDL), was being used on Wikipedia, among other online sites. But the FDL, originally intended for software documentation materials, was incompatible with the CC licenses. Stallman refused to alter the FDL, and Wikpedia was already under way and committed to the FDL. This quirk of history meant that Wikipedia content and CC-licensed content could not legally be combined. As we will see in chapter 9, this was the beginning of a rancorous schism in the free culture world, and the beginning of a heated philosophical/political debate over which licenses truly promote "freedom."

As this overview suggests, licensing complexities can quickly soar out of control and become overwhelming. Yet the very point of the Creative Commons licenses was to simplify the sharing and reuse of digital material. CC planners wanted to help ordinary people bypass the layers of mind-numbing legalese that make copyright law so impenetrable and inaccessible. The Creative Commons was all about empowering individuals and avoiding lawyers. A proliferation of licensing choices would only lead to license incompatibilities, a Balkanization of content on the Internet, and more lawyers. Sharing and interoperability go together, as Stallman's early experiences with his Emacs Commune showed.

Somehow, therefore, the licenses had to thread three needles at once. They needed to align (1) the technical dynamics of the Internet with (2) the legal realities of copyright law and (3) the everyday needs of people. The ingenious solution was to create licenses on three layers: a "lawyer-readable" license that could stand up in court, a "human-readable" license that could be understood by ordinary people, and a "machine-readable" license that could be recognized by search engines and other software on the Internet. Each "layer" expressed the same license terms in a different way—an unexpected twist on Lessig's concern for "fidelity in translation." The formal license was called the "Legal Code" (or "legal source code"); the machine-readable translation of the license was called "Digital Code"; and the plain-language summary of the license, with corresponding icons, was the "Commons Deed" (or the "happy deed").

Branding the Public Domain in Code

As the lawyers brooded and debated the licensing terms, another complicated debate was unfolding on the tech side of CC: how to brand the public domain in software code. If code is law, then it was imperative for Creative Commons to find some way to represent CC licenses in digital code. Abelson, Lessig, and others understood that the future of the Internet was likely to include all sorts of automated, computer-to-computer functions. One of the best ways to promote a new body of "free content" on the Web, therefore, would be to develop machine-readable code that could be inserted into any digital artifact using a Creative Commons license. That way, search engines could more easily identify CC-licensed works by their terms of use, and help assemble a functionally accessible oeuvre of digital content that was free to use.

At this time, in 2001, the founder of the World Wide Web, Tim Berners-Lee, and others at the World Wide Web Consortium, based at MIT, were trying to conceptualize the protocols for a new "logical layer" of code on top of the World Wide Web. They called it the Semantic Web. The idea is to enable people to identify and retrieve information that is strewn across the Internet but not readily located through conventional computer searches. Through a software format known as RDF/XML,* digital content could be tagged with machine-readable statements that would in effect say, "This database contains information about x and y." Through Semantic Web protocols and metatags on content, it would be possible to conduct searches across many types of digital content—Web pages, databases, software programs, even digital sensors—that could yield highly specific and useful results.

Unfortunately, progress in developing the Semantic Web has been bogged down in years of technical disagreement and indifference among the larger Web community. Some critics argue that the project has stalled because it was being driven by a small corps of elite software theorists focused on databases, and not by a wider pool of decentralized Web practitioners. In any case, the Creative Commons became one of the first test cases of trying to implement

---

* RDF, or Resource Description Framework, is a way to make a statement about content in a digital artifact. XML, or Extensible Markup Language, is a way to write a specialized document format to send across the Web, in which certain content can be marked up, or emphasized, so that other computers can "read" it.

RDF/XML for the Semantic Web.[41] The project was led initially by Lisa Rein, a thirty-three-year-old data modeler who met Lessig at an O'Reilly open-source software conference. Lessig hired her as CC's first technical director in late 2001 to embed the CC legal licenses in machine-readable formats.

Writing the XML code was not so difficult, said Rein; the real challenge was "deciding what needed to be included and how you represent the licenses as simply as possible."[42] This required the lawyers and the techies to have intense dialogues about how the law should be faithfully translated into software code, and vice versa. Once again, there were complicated problems to sort through: Should there be a central database of CC–licensed content? How could machine-readable code be adapted if the legal licenses were later modified?

Rein got an unexpected assist in the project from programming whiz Aaron Swartz, who had heard about Creative Commons and volunteered to help write the RDF/XML code. Swartz was an esteemed member of the RDF core working group at the World Wide Web Consortium (W3C), and so was intimately involved in Semantic Web deliberations. He was also a fifteen-year-old junior high school student living with his parents in Chicago. "I remember these moments when I was sitting in the locker room, typing on my laptop, in these [W3C] debates, and having to close it because the bell rang and I had to get back to class," Swartz recalled. At CC, he was given the title of "Volunteer Metadata Coordinator." His job was "to design the RDF schema and what the XML documents would look like, and work that out with my friends at the W3C and get their approval on things."[43] For his troubles, Swartz received an in-kind donation of a laptop computer and travel expenses, rather than a salary. "At the time, I felt bad," said Swartz. "They were a nonprofit doing work I believe in. I didn't feel I should be taking their money when I didn't need it." With later help from Ben Adida, the CC team managed to develop an RDF that could attach CC licenses to Web pages. But since the Semantic Web protocols were still in flux, and not widely used, the effort amounted to a speculative gamble on future and widespread adoption of those protocols.

Although inspired by the Semantic Web and by Lessig's analysis in *Code*, the RDF/XML coding was also provoked by the growing specter of digital rights management (DRM), the reviled systems used by film and music companies to lock up their content. The Creative Commons dreamed of developing an "anti-DRM" code to express the idea, "This content is and shall remain free." Professor Hal Abelson remembered that "we even used the phrase, 'DRM of the public domain.' "[44] The coinage that Lessig later popularized is "digital rights expression"—metadata that indicate that a digital object can be shared and reused. There was a passing fear that CC's digital rights expression code might infringe on DRM patents; one company known for its aggressive patent defense raised concerns. But once it was made clear that the CC's RDF code amounted to a label, and did not execute online rights on a person's computer, the problem disappeared.

The machine-readable CC licenses were one of the first major buildouts of RDF protocols. Swartz ruefully recalled the reaction of his friends at W3C: "I got the sense that they thought it was sort of a silly project, that they were thinking about bigger and longer-term things." Adida, who later replaced Swartz as the CC representative at the W3C, played a major role in helping develop the metatags and protocols.

The RDF/XML coding was part of a larger CC strategy to brand the public domain via software code. Since RDF code alone is like a nail without a hammer, Creative Commons decided to develop a specialized search engine so that Internet users could locate CC-licensed content. Without such a search engine, Lessig said in April 2002, "there will be no way to demonstrate that we've produced anything useful."[45] Swartz, who was not involved in the project, said, "I was impressed that they did it, because it was probably the biggest programming job I'd seen them do at the time." In the meantime, the CC began a series of overtures to Google and Yahoo in an attempt to get their search engines to search for CC-licensed content. After years of lukewarm interest, both Google and Yahoo added CC-search capabilities in 2005. Creative Commons also nurtured the hope that once enough content contained CC metadata, software developers would develop new applications to let people browse, use, and distribute CC-tagged content.

The Action Shifts to Palo Alto

By the fall of 2001, Creative Commons was still an idea without definition. The project gained new momentum in September 2001 when Lessig hired a former student, Molly Shaffer Van Houweling, to be the first director of the organization. Van Houweling, a sophisticated yet plainspoken law scholar with strong executive skills, had just finished clerking for Supreme Court justice David Souter. She set about incorporating the Creative Commons, organizing the board, building a Web site, and hammering out final versions of the licenses.

Once a key foundation grant was secured—$1 million from the Center for the Public Domain—the Creative Commons was incorporated in Massachusetts (home to many key backers of the project) on December 21, 2001. The first board members included several legal scholars (Boyle, Carroll, Lessig), a computer scientist (Abelson), two filmmakers (Saltzman and Davis Guggenheim, a friend of Lessig's), and a Web publisher (Eldred). Charged with breathing life into a fragile idea, Van Houweling settled into a small office on the third floor of Stanford Law School (before the project was reassigned to basement offices).

In January 2002, Glenn Otis Brown, a lawyer and former student of Lessig's, was hired as assistant director. Brown had been a law student at Harvard Law School, where he had known Van Houweling and taken a constitutional law course from Lessig. An affable Texan who had flirted with a journalism career, Brown had just finished a year of clerking for a circuit court judge. He was due to start a job in New York City the following week when he got a call from Van Houweling. "She and Larry were starting something to do with copyright at Stanford," recalled Brown. "I knew pretty much nothing else about it except it was a nonprofit and it was going to be a full-time job. . . . The next thing I knew, I was moving to California."[46]

Lessig, Van Houweling, and Brown took the menu of licenses proposed by two graduate students, Dotan Oliar and Oren Bracha, and sought to refine them and make them as legally bulletproof as possible.[47] They were torn about the process to adopt. "We didn't want to do a collective drafting process with the entire Internet community," said Van Houweling. "That didn't seem practical. And yet we were a little nervous, I think, about not knowing what our potential user base would want to use." Lessig was unfazed. Release of the licenses "isn't going to be like a movie premiere," he told Van Houweling, but more of an evolutionary process. The idea was to get the licenses in circulation, monitor their progress, and make changes as necessary.[48]

Two of the most prestigious law firms in Silicon Valley, Cooley Godward Kronish and Wilson, Sonsini, offered pro bono legal assistance to the effort. Attorney John Brockland, an expert in open-source software licenses at Cooley Godward and a former student of Lessig's, was the architect of the final licenses, assisted by Catherine Kirkman, a licensing attorney at Wilson, Sonsini. Brockland recalled, "One of the drafting challenges was to write something that could be broadly useful across a wide range of copyrighted works and would not be tied to particular nuances of the way the copyright statute works."[49] Most copyright licenses are drafted for specific clients and particular circumstances, not for the general public and all types of copyrighted works.

Much of the discussion, said Van Houweling, "revolved around the values that we wanted to embed in the licenses, and what were the outer limits of those values?" Ultimately, she said, "we opted for a menu of licenses that was weighted toward the nonproprietary [content]. . . . We wanted to subsidize a certain set of choices that are otherwise underserved."[50] The point was to facilitate the rise of a sharing culture, after all, not to replicate the baroque dysfunctions of copyright law.

Since the CC licenses were trying to articulate a new "middle ground" of voluntary choices for sharing, it had to grapple with all sorts of fine legal complexities. How exactly should they define a derivative work? What should be considered a noncommercial reuse of a work? Can you dedicate a work to the public domain?

Some artists felt that they ought to be able to prohibit derivative uses of their works in pornography or hate speech. Hal Abelson adamantly disagreed. If the licenses had an "offensive uses" clause, as either a standard or optional term, it would open up a can of worms and put Creative Commons on the side of censors. That view readily prevailed.

A primary concern was anticipating how the licenses might be interpreted by the courts. Wendy Seltzer was worried that the CC licenses might become entangled with court cases involving the fair use doctrine. She wanted to make sure that the CC licenses were not seen as limiting or waiving a person's fair use rights in any way. Her concern, shared by many others, resulted in an explicit disclaimer stating that intention. "I'm really glad that we did that," recalled Glenn Brown, then the assistant director of CC, "because we ended up pointing to that over and over and over again—to make clear that this was something that went above and beyond fair use."[51]

To ensure that the licenses would be enforceable, the CC lawyers built on the same legal base as the GPL; the licenses were crafted not as contracts, but as conditional permissions based on copyright law. A contract requires that the licensee have the opportunity to accept or reject the terms of an agreement, which would not be the case here. A conditional permission, by contrast, is the legal prerogative of a copyright holder. She is simply offering advance permission to use a CC-licensed work (to share, modify, distribute, etc.) so long as the specified terms are respected.

Countless lawyerly refinements of a very technical nature were made to the licenses to ensure that they would be specific as needed, vague enough to be versatile, and rigorous enough to survive a court's scrutiny.[52]

The first set of licenses, version 1.0, was completed in the spring of 2002 and included eleven choices. The six basic licenses, listed here in order of least restrictive to most restrictive, included:

Attribution (BY). Authorizes free reuses (download, distribution, modifications, commercial uses, etc.) so long as the author is credited for the original creation.

ShareAlike (SA). Authorizes free reuses so long as credit is given and the new work is licensed under the same terms.

No Derivatives (ND). Authorizes free reuses so long as the new work is unchanged and in whole.

NonCommercial (NC). Authorizes free reuses so long as they are not commercial in nature.

NonCommercial ShareAlike (NC-SA). Requires free reuses so long as the new work is passed along on the identical terms as the original work (so, for example, works that use a NonCommercial ShareAlike work will also have to be distributed as NonCommercial Share-Alike works).

NonCommercial No Derivatives (NC-ND). Authorizes free reuses so long as credit is given, no changes are made, the work is kept intact, and it is not used commercially. This is the most restrictive CC license.

Because each of these six basic choices can be combined with other CC licenses, copyright holders had five additional choices:

Attribution-ShareAlike (BY-SA). Authorizes free reuses so long as the author is credited and the new work is licensed under the same terms.

Attribution-NonCommercial (BY-NC). Authorizes free reuses so long as the author is credited and the new work is used for noncommercial purposes.

Attribution NonCommercial-ShareAlike (BY-NC-SA). Authorizes free reuses so long as the author is credited, the new work is used for noncommercial purposes, and the new work is passed along using this same license.

Attribution-No Derivatives (BY-ND). Authorizes free

reuses so long as the author is credited and the new work is unchanged and in whole.

Attribution No Derivatives-ShareAlike (BY-ND-SA). Authorizes free reuses so long as the author is credited, the new work is unchanged and in whole, and the new work is passed along using this same license.

It soon became clear that very few people were choosing any of the five licenses that did not require attribution of the author (the SA, ND, NC, NC-SA, and NC-ND licenses). So in May 2004 Creative Commons decided to "retire" those licenses, leaving the six most commonly used ones today (BY, BY-SA, BY-NC, BY-NC-SA, BY-ND, and BY-ND-SA).

Still another choice was offered to copyright holders, a "public domain dedication," which is not a license so much as "an overt act of relinquishment in perpetuity" of any rights in the work. The public domain dedication places no restrictions whatsoever on subsequent reuses of the work.

To the first-time user, the licenses may seem a little daunting.[53] The full implications of using one or another license are not immediately obvious. The tagline for the licenses, "Some Rights Reserved," while catchy, was not really self-explanatory. This became the next big challenge to Creative Commons, as we see in chapter 6: how to educate creators about a solution when they may not have realized they even had a problem.

By December 2002, the three levels of code—legal, digital, and human—had been coordinated and finalized as version 1.0. The organization was set to go public, which it did at a splashy coming-out party in San Francisco. The gala featured appearances by the likes of rapper DJ Spooky (an ardent advocate for remix culture) and a London multimedia jam group, People Like Us. Lessig proudly introduced the licenses as "delivering on our vision of promoting the innovative reuse of all types of intellectual works, unlocking the potential of sharing and transforming others' work."[54]

Perhaps the biggest surprise was a set of video testimonials from both ends of the copyright spectrum—John Perry Barlow of Electronic Frontier Foundation and Jack Valenti of the Motion Picture Association of America. With uncharacteristic solemnity, Barlow said: "I personally think there is something deeply oxymoronic about the term 'intellectual property.' But as long as we have set up a huge matrix of laws and social understandings that traffic in that assumption, we have to meet the conditions as we have found them and use what exists to preserve the human patrimony." The silvermaned Valenti saluted the "Lessig compact" that is both "respectful of, and supports, copyright" while allowing people "to give up some of their copyrighted material, or all of it, and put it on the creative commons for others to view it or hear it." "Larry, I hope that my supporting you in this doesn't ruin your reputation," Valenti joked.[55]

Many copyfighters were not thrilled to have an arch-adversary like Valenti praise their efforts at their moment of triumph. Yet that was a deliberate part of Lessig's strategy: to assert a politically neutral middle ground from which to remake the social landscape of creativity. The question raised in some people's mind was whether something so politically unassailable could have significant impact. Still others saw it as a welcome base upon which to build a new sharing economy.

The CC launch party can be seen as a watershed moment in the struggle to protect the public domain. It announced a novel gambit to transcend the political impasse over copyright reform, a way to address copyright abuses without getting embroiled in a pitched and unwinnable confrontation. It legitimized all sorts of activities that had historically been seen as morally problematic, if not illegal. While building on the idea of the public domain developed over the preceding twenty years, Creative Commons inaugurated a new story about the commons, creativity, and the value of sharing. Watching the rocking party and savoring the hard work completed, Glenn Brown remembers a friend musing to him, "I wonder if we'll see another legal hack like this in our careers."

5

NAVIGATING THE GREAT VALUE SHIFT

Amateurs discover new tools for creating value:
open networks and self-organized commons.

"It was never really clear to me what was going to happen after we launched the licenses," recalled Glenn Otis Brown. "Would our work be done?" The intense push to craft the licenses and release them now over, Brown and his colleagues were only too happy to ease up in their work. (Van Houweling had left in 2002 to teach law; she is now at the University of California at Berkeley.) Despite his enthusiasm for the licenses, Brown had his private doubts about their future success. "To be honest, I was pretty scared," he said. "I was worried they were going to go nowhere, and that I was going to be blamed for that." [1]

In January 2003, a month after the CC licenses were announced, however, the project took on a new urgency. The Supreme Court handed down its *Eldred* ruling, sending a clear signal that the courts were not much interested in reforming copyright law. Soon after this crushing disappointment, Lessig began to intensify his focus on the Creative Commons. "The pressure really increased," said Brown, "but that's also when things started to get a lot more fun. That's when the staff started working on things *all the time* and we got a stable, permanent staff, instead of contractors."

What began as a modest licensing experiment began to take on the character of a permanent campaign. Working from the themes in *The Future of Ideas*, Lessig came to see the Creative Commons as more than a nonprofit custodian of some free public licenses; it was a champion for a bracing new vision of culture. This broader orientation meant reaching out to various creative sectors and the general public with messages that were both practical ("here's how to use the licenses") and idealistic ("you, too, can build a better world").

The band of enterprising law scholars and techies who once saw their challenge as one of bolstering the public domain began to widen their gaze to the vast world of creativity and democratic culture. Social practice, not theory, became the animating force in their work.

This meant reaching out to writers, musicians, filmmakers, photographers, librarians, academics, and other creators. All faced worrisome threats to their freedoms in the digital environment, as we saw in chapter 2. Lessig and the small Creative Commons staff made it their job to speak to these threats, promote the licenses, and set forth an alternative to the corporate media's vision of culture.

"Our single, overarching aim," said Lessig in December 2002, "is to build the public domain, by building projects that expand the range of creative work available for others to build upon."[2] In an attempt to credential the licenses, the Creative Commons touted endorsements by a number of educational institutions (MIT, Rice University, Stanford Law School), public-spirited tech enterprises (iBiblio, the Internet Archive, O'Reilly & Associates), and venturesome musicians (DJ Spooky, Roger McGuinn of the Byrds).

As if by spontaneous replication, people from far-flung corners of the Internet began to use the licenses on their blogs, their MP3 music files, their photographs, their books. Week after week, the Creative Commons's blog trumpeted the new recruits—the blog for book designers (Foreword), the database of metadata about music (MusicBrainz), the online storytelling Web site (Fray), the 2004 presidential campaign of Dennis Kucinich.

But the larger challenge for Creative Commons was finding ways to reach new constituencies who knew little about technology or copyright law. Why should they bother to use a CC license? This was a major public education challenge. Besides appearing at many conferences and cultivating press coverage, Glenn Brown spent a lot of time developing a Web site that could explain the licenses clearly. Great pains were taken to develop a precise, intuitive user interface to help people learn about the licenses and choose the right one for them. Copyright law was complicated enough; the CC licenses had to be seen as a simple alternative.

Advertisers have plenty of trouble communicating the virtues of mouthwash in a crowded public sphere. Could something as dry and forbidding as copyright law ever be made lucid and even hip? Although not a trained marketer, Glenn Brown had a knack for communicating things simply. Working with graphic designer Ryan Junell and Web designer Matt Haughey, Brown developed a site that combined a certain institutional authority with contemporary pizzazz. This style was on abundant display in a series of jaunty and entertaining Flash animations that explained the rationale for Creative Commons.

Junell designed the now-familiar CC logo as a deliberate counterpoint to the copyright logo, ©. "I thought that Creative Commons should have something like the copyright logo since it deals with the same stuff," said Junell. "It should be something really simple and pure."[3] Junell set his sights on making the CC logo a standard, ubiquitous symbol. He hoped that it would eventually be incorporated into the Unicode, an international registry for every character in any language used in software, from % to Δ to ≠.

In promoting its licenses, Creative Commons fashioned itself as a neutral, respectable defender of individual choice. "Our tools are just that—tools," said Haughey, who was then developing the CC Web site. "Our model intentionally depends on copyright holders to take responsibility for how they use those tools. Or how they don't use them: If you're unsure and want to keep your full copyright, fine. If you choose to allow others to re-use your work, great."[4] While many CC users were enthusiastically bashing copyright law, Lessig and the CC staff made it a point to defend the basic principles of copyright law—while extolling the value of collaborative creativity and sharing under CC licenses.

Despite praise by the heads of the Motion Picture Association of America and the Recording Industry Association of America, the licenses nonetheless did attract critics. Some in the music industry regarded the licenses as a Trojan horse that would dupe unsuspecting artists. David Israelite, president and CEO of the National Music Publishers' Association, told *Billboard*, "My concern is that many who support Creative Commons also support a point of view that would take away people's choices about what to do with their own property."[5] *Billboard* went on to cite the cautionary tale of a song writer who was being kept alive by his AIDS medications, thanks to the royalties from a highly successful song. "No one should let artists give up their rights," said Andy Fraser of the rock group Free. Other critics, such as John Dvorak of *PC Magazine*, called the CC licenses "humbug" and accused them of adding "some artificial paperwork and complexity to the mechanism [of copyright]," while weakening the rights that an author would otherwise enjoy.[6] Still others had cultural scores to settle and criticized "anything advocated by clever, sleek young lawyers."[7]

Putting aside such quibbles and prejudices, the CC licenses seemed a benign enough idea. Given its reliance on copyright law, how could any entertainment lawyer object? Yet the real significance of the licenses was only appreciated by those who realized that a Great Value Shift was kicking in. For them, the licenses were a useful legal tool and cultural flag for building a new sharing economy.

The Great Value Shift

In retrospect, the CC licenses could not have been launched at a more propitious moment. Networked culture was exploding in 2003. Broadband was rapidly supplanting dial-up Internet access, enabling users to navigate the Web and share information at much faster speeds. Prices for personal computers were dropping even as computing speeds and memory capacity were soaring. Sophisticated new software applications were enabling users to collaborate in more powerful, user-friendly ways. The infrastructure for sharing was reaching a flashpoint.

Put another way, the original promise of the Internet as a gift economy was coming into its own. Originally built as a platform for efficient sharing among academic researchers, the Internet by 2003 was being used by some 600 million people worldwide.[8] The open framework for sharing was no longer just a plaything of technophiles and academics; it was now insinuated into most significant corners of the economy and social life. As it scaled and grew new muscles and limbs, the Internet began to radically change the ways in which wealth is generated and allocated.

I call this the Great Value Shift—a deep structural change in how valuable things are created for commerce and culture. The shift is not only a fundamental shift in business strategy and organizational behavior, but in the very definition of wealth. On the Internet, wealth is not just financial wealth, nor is it necessarily privately held. Wealth generated through open platforms is often *socially created value* that is shared, evolving, and nonmonetized. It hovers in the air, so to speak, accessible to everyone.

Creative Commons had the good fortune to introduce its licenses just as the Great Value Shift was picking up momentum. The types of distributed innovation first seen in free software were now popping up in every imaginable corner of cyberspace. The social content was not just about listservs and newsgroups, but instant messaging networks, Web logs, podcasts, wikis, social networking sites, collaborative archives, online gaming communities, and much else.

"What we are seeing now," wrote Yochai Benkler in his book, *The Wealth of Networks,* "is the emergence of more effective collective action practices that are decentralized but do not rely on either the price system or a managerial structure for coordination." Benkler's preferred term is "commons-based peer production." By that, he means systems that are collaborative and nonproprietary, and based on "sharing resources and outputs among widely distributed, loosely connected individuals who cooperate with each other."[9]

Informal social relationships, working in the unregimented, free space of open platforms, were beginning to change economic production and culture. "Behaviors that were once on the periphery— social motivations, cooperation, friendship, decency—move to the very core of economic life," Benkler argued.[10] Money and markets do not necessarily control the circulation of creativity; increasingly, online communities—large numbers of people interacting with one another on open platforms—are the engines that create value.

The CC licenses were launched at a moment when the new modes of value creation were just gaining a foothold.

We do not yet have well-accepted theoretical models for understanding this new "socioeconomic space"; the online environments are still so new, and much is still in flux.[11] But it has not escaped the notice of major corporations that online social dynamics can result in some radically more effective models for organizing employees and engaging with customers. A *BusinessWeek* cover story touted "The Power of Us" in June 2005, profiling the ways in which companies like Procter & Gamble use mass collaboration for R&D; Hewlett-Packard had created a virtual stock market among its staff to gather collective estimates that have improved sales forecasts.[12] The *Economist* has written about the "fortune of the commons" that can result when there are open technical standards, and business professors such as Henry Chesbrough have examined new "open business models."[13]

Before looking at the many creative sectors that have adopted the CC licenses—the focus of chapter 6—it helps to understand the Great Value Shift that open networks have catalyzed. In one market after another, open networks have helped new competitors slash all sorts of business costs while enhancing their capacity to innovate and respond to changing consumer demand. Open networks have also given rise to new types of social platforms on the Web, often known as Web 2.0, which are making it economically attractive to serve niche markets. This is the so-called Long Tail. Yet even these sweeping changes in market structure are facing a qualitatively different kind of competition—from the commons sector. It turns out that informal online communities based on trust, reciprocity, and shared social norms can perform a great many tasks more efficiently than markets, and with some measure of social pleasure and fun.

The Endangered Economics of Centralized Media

The dominant systems of communications in the twentieth century—radio, broadcast and cable television, recorded music, theatrical film—required large amounts of centralized capital, corporate management, and professional control. These media have very different business models and practices, but they all rely upon centralized control of capital and distribution to large, fairly undifferentiated audiences. Each depends upon efficiencies derived from high-volume sales and a limited spectrum of commercial choices.

Centralized Media also dictate certain economic and social identities for people. There are "sellers," who are the prime source of expertise, innovation, and production, and there are "consumers," who passively buy, or don't buy, what is offered. Sellers mostly determine what choices are offered to buyers, and they tend to have greater market power and information than consumers. Interactions between sellers and consumers are mostly brief and transactional; there is little ongoing conversation or relationship between seller and buyer.

Much of the strength of the Centralized Media derives from its control of critical "choke points" of product development and distribution. By controlling the technical standards for a product, its retail distribution or its brand identity, a company can maximize its competitive advantages and limit competition. The high concentration of capital needed to communicate through a Centralized Media outlet is itself a useful way to limit competition. No surprise that only large, publicly traded corporations and rich individuals own and control Centralized Media—and that their messages tend to be overtly commercial or commercial-friendly.

While this paradigm is obviously quite attractive for those investors with a piece of the action, it also entails some very large costs that are not readily evident. Companies have to spend a lot on advertising to build a brand identity that can enhance sales. Their "blockbuster" business model entails large upfront costs in order to reap large financial returns. Centralized Media require expensive systems for finding, recruiting, and developing stars; an elaborate marketing apparatus to find and retain customers; and legal and technological means to identify and prosecute "piracy" of creative works.

In a more static environment, this model worked fairly well. But as the Internet revolution proceeded in the 2000s, distributed media started to undercut the economic logic of Centralized Media. Your personal computer, connected to other computers via inexpensive telecommunications and software, can do things more cheaply. Distributed online media not only avoid the costly overhead needed by Centralized Media, they can generate dynamic, interactive, and sociable types of communication: *user-generated content!* While this amateur content is wildly variable in quality, it does have this virtue: it is more culturally diverse and authentic than the homogenous, overproduced programming of Centralized Media. And because distributed media are not economically driven to amass large, undifferentiated audiences, the content can be more idiosyncratic, passionate, and, in its own ways, creative. There is no "fifty-seven channels and nothing on" problem. The problem is how to locate what you want from among millions of choices.

For all these reasons—but mostly because of the economics— conventional media are becoming more vulnerable to the most advanced Internet-based competitors (Amazon, eBay, Google, Yahoo) as well as to new types of nonmarket social production (e.g., Craigslist, Wikipedia, special-interest affinity groups). We may even be approaching a point at which the historic cost structures and risk management strategies of major media companies are no longer sustainable. Some analysts fret about the long-term viability of American newspapers, whose stock value fell by 42 percent, or $23 billion, between 2005 and 2008. Broadcast and cable television have similar fears. They worry, correctly, that Internet venues are siphoning away "eyeballs" by providing more timely and convenient alternatives. While the amateur videos of YouTube may not have the production quality of NBC, broadcast and cable television cannot ignore an upstart platform that in 2006 was attracting more than 100 million video downloads *per day* and had a market valuation of $1.65 billion when bought by Google that year. No wonder Cable News Network co-hosted a presidential debate with YouTube in 2007; it needed to reassert its cultural relevance.

Large media companies are struggling to support some huge financial, administrative, and marketing burdens simply to "tread

water" and retain some measure of their customary market dominance. This helps explain why Centralized Media are so keenly focused on influencing Congress and the Federal Communications
Commission. They want to lock in competitive advantages through
regulation. (Consider the fierce battles over media ownership rules,
spectrum allocation policies, anticopying technology mandates such
as the "broadcast flag," new copyright and trademark protections,
must-carry rules for cable operators, and on and on.) Centralized
Media's great interest in securing legal and regulatory privileges for
themselves suggests their relative weakness and decline. For them, it
is easier to chase market advantages through political interventions
than through innovation, superior performance, and price.

The Economic Advantages of Open Media

By contrast, a profusion of new ventures are finding that a company
can thrive on the open networks of the Internet. Even a startup
without brand recognition or regulatory preferences can compete
on the merits—price, quality, responsiveness—against entrenched
giants. They can leverage user-generated content and the vast reser-
voir of value previously known as the public domain. The success of
thousands of new Internet businesses reflects an epochal shift in the
terms of competition—a Great Shift in how value is created.

The most significant shifts in the history of capitalism have
come when new mechanisms lower the costs of managing risk
and serving latent market demand. We are apparently in such a
stage of economic transformation today. The genius of the Renaissance banks and the Dutch insurance and shipping companies, for
example, was to reinvent the structure of markets through new financial and legal instruments that enabled commercial trust and
transparency to work on a larger scale. The limited liability corporation was also a powerful innovation for diversifying risk, coordi-
nating people, and deploying capital on a scale that was previously
impossible.[14]

In like fashion, the Internet is now facilitating some deep shifts
in the cost structures and scale of markets. Innovative online busi-

ness models are significantly undercutting the (expensive) cost structures of traditional Centralized Media, and in the process sometimes creating entirely new sorts of markets (search engine advertising, discounted travel, specialty niches) and more open, competitive markets.

One of the most intriguing developments is a set of "open business models" that shun closed, proprietary technical standards and content restrictions. Unlike the classic industrial business models of the twentieth century, the new open business models make money by aggressively insinuating themselves into open networks. They are able to identify new trends, mobilize talent, interact with customers, and develop customized products more rapidly than competitors. They are also building ingenious new business models "on top of" social behaviors of online users. (See chapter 10.)

MySpace, for example, hosts a social network of more than 100 million "friends" (a claim that, even if inflated by inactive user accounts, is indisputably huge). eBay consolidated the world's garage sales and flea markets into a more efficient market by developing Web-based software that "manages" social trust and reputation and evolves with user interests. Amazon has become a premier online retail Web site by hosting a platform open to all sorts of online vendors and spurred by the recommendations and collective purchase records of buyers. Google devised its famous PageRank search algorithms to aggregate the Web-surfing "wisdom of the crowd," making online searches vastly more useful.

The basic point is that open media platforms are significantly reducing business coordination and communication costs by leveraging people's natural social behaviors in ways that conventional businesses simply cannot. Open Web platforms allow large and diverse groups to organize themselves and their projects more easily. Individuals have greater self-defined choice and the capacity to express their own market demand; they need not be constrained by the choices presented to them in the market. The Internet has opened up gushing channels of virtual word of mouth, which is a more trusted form of consumer information than advertising. Those companies with excellent products use favorable word of mouth to reduce their marketing and distribution costs. "Smart mobs" can elevate obscure bloggers and Web sites because they regard them as more trustworthy, expert, and authentic (or entertaining) than those of Centralized Media. Many conservatives now trust the Drudge Report and Free Republic more than CBS News, just as many liberals trust DailyKos and Huffington Post more than CBS News. Indeed, the very genre of "objective journalism"—an artifact of the economic necessity of appealing to broad, lowest-common-denominator audiences—is now in jeopardy.

As people migrate to the Web, advertising revenues for Centralized Media are eroding further, setting off a scramble to devise new advertising vehicles to reach fugitive Internet users. It is a chase that cannot be avoided because that's where the eyeballs are. Moreover, the value proposition of open networks is too attractive to ignore. But because that value proposition is so radically different from conventional media—a company must revamp its organizational structures, strategies, marketing, etc.—it raises some wrenching choices for Centralized Media: Should they "go native" and let their products loose on open networks? Or would that destroy their entrenched business models for television shows, theatrical films, music CDs, and other content? The vast infrastructure and business practices of Centralized Media cannot be summarily abandoned, but neither can they remain economically tenable over the long haul without significant changes. For now, Centralized Media are attempting an ungainly straddle of both worlds.

Web 2.0: A New Breed of Participatory Media

At the time, Eric Eldred's Web repository of public-domain books could be seen as a modest little experiment. In retrospect, it can be seen as a dawning cultural archetype. It betokened the power of the amateur.[15] While Centralized Media continue to have greater resources, talent, and political clout, amateurs are finding their voices and new online venues. A significant cultural emancipation is under way. Creative expression need no longer cater to corporate gatekeepers and the imperatives of the mass market. A no-name amateur can produce useful and influential work without having to go through New York, Los Angeles, London, or Tokyo. The do-it-yourself culture is flourishing and expanding. With little money or marketing, anyone can launch a viral spiral that, with enough luck and panache, can sweep across global culture.

It is only now dawning on some media chieftains that the biggest threat to Centralized Media is not piracy or online competitors, but *nonmarket alternatives*: you, me, and the online friends that we can attract. Hollywood and record labels might rail against "pirates" and demand stronger copyright protection, but the real long-term threat to their business models is the migration of consumer attention to amateur creativity and social communication. Social production on open networks has become a powerful creative and economic force in its own right. Ordinary people can now find their own voices and develop folk cultures of their own that may or may not use the market.

After the tech bubble of 2000–2001 burst, the surviving techies and entrepreneurs developed a remarkable range of cheap, versatile software that took to heart the lessons of free software and open networks. Blogs, wikis, social networking software, peer-to-peer file-sharing and metadata tools began to migrate from the tech fringe to the mainstream. There have been many conceptual frames and buzzwords associated with this new order—"smart mobs" (Howard Rheingold), "the wisdom of crowds" (James Surowiecki), "wikinomics" (Don Tapscott and Anthony D. Williams)—but the catchphrase that has gained the most currency is "Web 2.0," a term launched by Tim O'Reilly in a canonical 2003 essay.[16]

O'Reilly, a prominent publisher of books on open-source software, coined Web 2.0 to describe the fluid social dynamics that occur on open Web platforms—wikis, blogs, social networking Web sites, and other open, collaborative platforms—where people have the freedom to share and reuse work. Web 2.0 amounts to a worldview that celebrates open participation as a way to create valuable collective resources. It regards open technical protocols and content as the basis for this process (whether managed as a commons or a business), and dismisses closed, proprietary regimes as both socially and economically questionable. In essence, Web 2.0 honors socially created value as the basis for value creation, which market players may or may not be able to exploit.

Blogging is more of a social medium than is generally supposed, for example. It is not just the outburst of some ranter in his pajamas, as the stereotype has it, but a social medium that connects people in new ways. Most blogs have a blogroll—a list of admired blogs—which enables the readers of one blog to identify other bloggers engaged in similar conversations. Permalinks—stable Web addresses for blog content—enable people to make reliable Web citations of content, which means that people can coalesce around a shared body of work. And RSS feeds—"Really Simple Syndication"—allow people to "subscribe" to individual blogs and Web sites, enabling them to keep abreast of a sprawling set of communities.

The rise of blog-tracking companies like Technorati and Alexa has also helped blogging become a durable social genre. These companies inventory and rank blogs, and help people discover blogs for virtually any subject of interest—cocktail mixing, high-energy physics, needlework design. By 2007, there were an estimated 100 million blogs in existence (although many were inactive or abandoned), making the blogosphere a powerful cultural force in its own right. There was also a flood of online "news aggregators"—Web sites that cherry-pick their own mix of pieces from the wire services, newspapers, Web sites, blogs, and other online sources. With huge audiences, news aggregators like the Drudge Report (1.6 million unique monthly visitors) and the Huffington Post (773,000 visitors) have begun to rival major daily newspapers in reach and influence.

Another seminal social innovation has been Wikipedia, a strange and wondrous cultural eruption. Founded by Jimmy Wales and Larry Sanger in January 2001, the English-language Wikipedia began to gain serious momentum in the months after the CC licenses were released, and by early 2003 hosted 100,000 articles. (A "wiki" is a special type of Web site that allows anyone who accesses it to add or modify its contents.) After two years, Wikipedia had amassed a collection of 400,000 articles and inspired the launch of affiliated Wikipedias in more than 100 languages. In May 2008,

Wikipedia featured 10.2 million articles in 255 languages; 2.3 million of the articles were in English. By harnessing the energies of tens of thousands of volunteers to write an infinitely expandable "encyclopedia," Wikipedia has become the leading symbol for a radically new way of compiling and editing knowledge.[17] Remarkably, the Wikimedia Foundation, the umbrella organization that funds Wikipedia and many sister projects, had fewer than twenty paid employees in 2008 and a budget of less than $2 million.

Wikipedia has also spun off affiliated multilingual, free-content wikis on various subjects. Wikispecies is compiling an inventory of the world's species, Wikiquote is collecting thousands of memorable quotations, the Wikimedia Commons is providing freely usable media files, and Wikibooks is assembling open-content textbooks. Wiki software has been adopted by dozens of different online communities, giving rise to scores of collaborative Web sites such as Conservapedia (for American political conservatives), Intellipedia (for U.S. intelligence agencies), Wookieepedia (for *Star Wars* fans), Wikitravel (for travelers), and OpenWetWare (for biological researchers).

In the months following the launch of the CC licenses, peer-to-peer (P2P) file sharing was also expanding rapidly. Long associated with illicit sharing of copyrighted music, P2P software in fact has many entirely legitimate uses in science, education, and diverse creative sectors. One of the key attractions of P2P software is its efficiency. It does not need to route information through centralized servers; information can be rapidly shared by routing digital files directly to participants, computer to computer, or by passing it through key nodes in an on-the-fly manner. Even after the courts shut down Napster in 2002, a variety of other P2P software applications—Grokster, Lime Wire, KaZaA, Gnutella, BitTorrent—continued to facilitate online sharing and collaboration. Some thirty-five companies, including Hollywood studios, are sufficiently impressed with the efficiencies of P2P that they have licensed BitTorrent technology to distribute their video content.

Peer-to-peer file sharing has also unleashed radically new types of knowledge creation: volunteers who join the NASA Clickworkers project to count and classify craters on Mars, "citizen scientists" who help compile an interactive database of butterfly and bird sightings, or geneticists from around the world who submit data to the Human Genome Project and share access to the database.

Although the tech world and some Internet users had known about various networking tools for years, the general public was largely in the dark until the presidential campaign of Vermont governor Howard Dean in 2002 and 2003. At the time, Dean was considered a long-shot antiwar candidate with little base and little money. Within a few short months, however, thanks to Dean's outspoken style and his campaign's skillful use of the Internet, he became the front-runner in a field of twelve candidates. Dean did not use the Internet as a simple publishing tool, but as a way to stimulate decentralized collaboration and thereby organize a diverse community of supporters. The campaign was not just about Dean, but about the participation of 640,000 volunteers who virtually organized themselves through various online tools. The campaign became a dynamic conversation between the candidate and voters—and generated a gusher of more than $50 million, most of it donations of a hundred dollars or less. So much was raised that Dean famously asked his supporters whether he should forgo federal matching funds, and instead raise more money from them. They agreed. The campaign ultimately imploded, of course, after his famous "Dean's Scream" speech—itself a complex story—but what is notable is how the Dean campaign vividly demonstrated the speed and power of viral networks.

By 2003 many ordinary people knew about the Napster controversy, the record industry's scorched-earth litigation tactics against consumers, and the Supreme Court's ruling in the *Eldred* case. So people welcomed blogs, wikis, and other Web 2.0 applications as tools to emancipate themselves culturally. In the mass media era, people had few tools or sufficient money to speak to the general public or organize their own communities of interest. But now, using a lightweight infrastructure of software code and telecommunications, people could build stable online communities that reflected their own values and social practices. No permission or payment necessary. No expensive capital investments

In many instances, amazingly, virtual communities are performing tasks that existing markets are not performing as efficiently or with as much social trust and goodwill. Craigslist, the free want-ad service that has significantly undercut classified advertising in newspapers, is one of the more stellar examples. In South Korea, OhmyNews.org uses thirty-six thousand citizen-journalists to write up to two hundred online stories a day. The publication is considered the sixth-most influential media outlet in Korea, based on a national magazine poll. Countless specialty blogs are considered more expert and timely sources of information and analysis than mainstream newspapers and magazines.

Taken together, the new participatory media platforms constitute something new under the sun—a globally accessible space that is both personal and public, individual and social. The riot of unfiltered expression that has materialized on the Internet is often dismissed as stupid, unreliable, and silly; or praised as brilliant, stylish, and specialized; or simply accepted as idiosyncratic, irregular, and local. It is all of these things, of course, and that is precisely the point.

If print culture honors the ethic of "edit, then publish," the Internet inverts it: *anything* can be made public . . . and then it is up to users to become their own editors. On the Internet, people do not "consume" content, they become active writers, editors, and critics in their own right. They use search engines, news aggregators, and favorite bloggers to identify what they want—or they create their own content, as desired. They are *participants*, not merely informed consumers who choose what some professional editor offers to them.

The Web 2.0 environment was quite hospitable for the spread of the CC licenses. It enabled people to signal their willingness to share and their enthusiasm for cool niche fare as opposed to mass-audience kitsch. Members of online communities could confidently share their work on wikis and collaborative Web sites, knowing that no one could appropriate their content and take it private. Socially, the licenses let people announce their social identity to others and build a countercultural ethos of sharing. The ethos became hipper and more attractive with every new antipiracy measure that Centralized Media instigated.

Open Networks and the Long Tail

While technology and economics have been driving forces in shaping the new participatory platforms, much of their appeal has been frankly cultural. Amateur content on the Net may be raw and irregular, but it also tends to be more interesting and authentic than the highly produced, homogenized fare of commercial media. Some of it vastly outshines the lowest common denominator of mass media. Again, the cheap connectivity of the Internet has been key. It has made it possible for people with incredibly specialized interests to find one another and organize themselves into niche communities. For closeted homosexuals in repressive countries or isolated fans of the actor Wallace Beery, the Internet has enabled them to find one another and mutually feed their narrow interests. You name it, there are sites for it: the fans of obscure musicians, the collectors of beer cans, Iranian exiles, kite flyers. Freed of the economic imperative of attracting huge audiences with broad fare, niche-driven Internet content is able to connect with people's personal passions and interests: a powerful foundation not just for social communities, but for durable markets.

This, truly, is one of the more profound effects of networking technologies: the subversion of the "blockbuster" economics of the mass media. It is becoming harder and more expensive for film studios and broadcast networks to amass the huge, cross-demographic audiences that they once could. In the networked environment, it turns out that a diversified set of niche markets can be eminently profitable with lower-volume sales. While Centralized Media require a supply-side "push" of content, the Internet enables a demand-side "pull" of content by users. This radically reduces transaction costs and enhances the economic appeal of niche production. It is easier and cheaper for a company (or single creator) to "pull" niche audiences through word of mouth than it is to pay for expensive "push" advertising campaigns. Specialty interests and products that once were dismissed as too marginal or idiosyncratic to be profitable can now flourish in small but robust "pull markets." [18]

The term associated with this phenomenon is the "Long Tail"—the title of a much-cited article by Chris Anderson in the October 2004 issue of *Wired* magazine, later expanded into a book. Anderson explained the "grand transition" now under way:

> For too long we've been suffering the tyranny of lowest-common-denominator fare, subjected to brain-dead summer blockbusters and manufactured pop. Why? Economics. Many of our assumptions about popular taste are actually artifacts of poor supply-and-demand matching—a market response to inefficient distribution. . . . Hit-driven economics is a creation of an age without enough room to carry everything for everybody. Not enough shelf space for all the CDs, DVDs, and games produced. Not enough screens to show all the available movies. . . . [19]

The "Long Tail" refers to the huge potential markets that can be created for low-volume niche books, CD, DVDs, and other products. More than half of Amazon's book sales, for example, come from books that rank below its top 130,000 titles. The implication is that "the market for books that are not even sold in the average bookstore is larger than the market for those that are," writes Anderson. "In other words, the potential book market may be twice as big as it appears to be, if only we can get over the economics of scarcity."

Unconstrained by the size and tastes of a local customer base or by limited shelf space, online retailers such as Amazon, Netflix (DVDs), Rhapsody (music), and iTunes (music) are showing that the Long Tail can be a very attractive business model. These companies have developed new tools, such as collaborative filtering software and user recommendations, to drive demand for lesser-known titles at the far end of the Long Tail. This is just another instance of using new technologies that leverage people's natural social dynamics, and in so doing inventing new types of markets.

Another Vehicle for Niche Communities: The Commons

If the Long Tail is a market vehicle for amassing niche communities, the commons is the social analogue. A commons does not revolve around money and market exchange, but around collective participation and shared values. It does not use property rights and contracts in order to generate value; it uses gift exchange and moral commitments to build a community of trust and common purpose. Such communities, it turns out, can generate significant "wealth"— as Richard Stallman demonstrated with free software.

Generically speaking, a commons is a governance regime for managing collective resources sustainably and equitably. The commons is generally associated with open fields, forests, and other natural resources that were collectively used by villagers for their subsistence needs. During the "enclosure movement" in medieval times and extending through the eighteenth century, British gentry and entrepreneurs began to privatize the commons and convert its resources into marketable commodities. Enclosures essentially dispossessed the commoners and installed a new market regime to manage resources that were previously shared. The commoners, unable to feed themselves or participate in markets, migrated to the industrial cities of England to become the wage slaves and beggars who populate Charles Dickens's novels.

Although markets tend to be more efficient than commons, they also tend to focus on that which can be sold and converted into cash. Markets presume that deserts and the public domain have no value because they have no marketable output. Markets also presume that a commons cannot be sustained because inevitably someone will overuse a shared resource—a practice known as "free riding"—and ruin it. This is the famous "tragedy of the commons" notion popularized by biologist Garret Hardin in a 1968 essay, which described how a few farmers will let their sheep overgraze a common pasture and so destroy it

The "tragedy of the commons" metaphor has ossified into a truism of neoclassical economics. It takes for granted that shared resources cannot be managed sustainably, and that private property regimes are much better stewards of resources. This prejudice was powerfully rebutted by political scientist Elinor Ostrom in her noted 1990 book *Governing the Commons*, which marshaled many empirical examples of natural resource commons that have been managed responsibly for decades or even hundreds of years. Ostrom's scholarship has since given rise to a great deal of academic study of commons, particularly through the International Association for the Study of the Commons and the Workshop in Political Theory and Policy Analysis at Indiana University. It also inspired thinking about the commons by law scholars like Yochai Benkler, Lawrence Lessig, and James Boyle, who saw close parallels with the commons as they watched corporations use copyright law to enclose culture and information.

Cultural commons differ significantly from natural resource commons in this key respect: they are not finite, depletable resources like pastures or forests. Online commons tend to *grow* in value as more people participate, provided there is sufficient governance and common technical standards to enable sharing. Online commons, in short, are less susceptible to the dreaded "tragedy of the commons" and, indeed, tend to be highly generative of value. Their output does not get "used up" the way natural resources do.

The burden of Lessig's 2001 book *The Future of Ideas* was to argue that the Internet constitutes a great, underappreciated commons. It can serve as the infrastructure for tremendous wealth and innovation if its "layers"—the hardware, software, and content—remain sufficiently open and usable by all. The problem, he warned with great prescience, is that policymakers are generally blind to the value of the commons and markets are too eager to reap short-term individual gains. They fail to appreciate that too much private control at any "layer" of the Internet—through proprietary hardware or software, or excessive copyright or patent protection—can stifle personal freedom, market competition, and innovation. Lessig wanted to name the book *Dot.commons*, but his publisher rejected it as too obscure.

One of the key advantages of treating key infrastructure (such as Internet transmission protocols and computer operating systems) as a commons is that people have the freedom to modify and improve them, with resulting benefits for all. Innovation and competition can flourish more readily. At the content layer, much of the appeal of the commons is the creative freedom, above and beyond what the market may enable. Precisely because it is a commons, and not a market, people's freedoms are not constrained by marketability. A commons is a noncommercial, nongovernmental space that is free from corporate manipulations and government meddling. It offers a qualitatively different type of experience than the marketplace or government power. A commons tends to be more informal, a place where people know you by name, and where your contributions are known and welcomed. A commons based on relationships of trust and reciprocity can undertake actions that a business organization requiring extreme control and predictable performance cannot.

Precisely because a commons is open and not organized to maximize profit, its members are often willing to experiment and innovate; new ideas can emerge from the periphery. Value is created through a process that honors individual self-selection for tasks, passionate engagement, serendipitous discovery, experimental creativity, and peer-based recognition of achievement. The Open Prosthetics Project, for example, invites anyone to contribute to the design of a prosthetic limb and/or the specification of limbs that ought to be designed, even if they don't know how to do it.[20] This has generated such unexpected innovations as limbs specifically adapted for rock climbers and an arm designed for fishing. Athletes who engage in "extreme sports"—skiing, biking, surfing—have been a rich source of ideas for new products, just as software hackers are among the first to come up with innovative programming ideas.

Part of the value proposition of the commons at the content layer is that it can host a more diverse range of expression—personal, social, and creative—than the market, in part because it does not have the burden of having to sustain costly overhead and sell a product. It has other goals—the personal interests and whims of the commoners—and it can often meet those needs inexpensively. Yet the commons does in fact generate many marketable innovations, thanks to its open accessibility, the social relationships it enables and the free sharing and circulation of work.

Seeing the success of online commons, Centralized Media have tried to fight back by embracing elements of user participation. They invite audiences to vote in polls (*American Idol*), publish lists of "most e-mailed" articles (major newspapers), and direct radio listeners to their Web sites for more information (National Public Radio). *Time* magazine's choice for the "Person of the Year" in 2006—"You," the primary driver of Web sites like MySpace and YouTube—was a landmark moment in media history: with a pinched smile and backhanded assertion of its cultural authority, Centralized Media formally acknowledged its most powerful competitor, Decentralized Media!

Yet for all the celebration of "you" as the master of your own fate in cyberspace, the question that is skirted is whether "you" can indeed retain control of your stuff in a Centralized Media environment. The point of conventional business models, after all, is to engineer a proprietary lock-in of customers through technological dependence, binding contract terms, frequent-buyer credits, brand loyalty, etc. That's how companies have traditionally secured a more durable customer base and preempted competition.

But the commons is about securing user freedoms, and not necessarily about prevailing in a market. Web 2.0 may or may not protect both concerns. Like the commons, Web 2.0 relies upon user-generated content, network effects, and bottom-up innovation. But Web 2.0 entrepreneurs, at the end of the day, need to make money. Their sites need to adopt business practices that protect revenue streams. Facebook is catering to advertisers, not users, when they sift through masses of users' personal data in order to sell targeted advertising. MySpace at one point refused to let its users connect to rival Web sites and outside software "widgets."[21] In this sense, Web 2.0 media may be "open," but they are not necessarily "free," as in freedom. Web 2.0 entrepreneurs are more likely to focus on protecting their market advantages than advancing user freedoms. The two issues may overlap substantially, but they are not identical.

Science-fiction writer William Gibson once wrote, "The future is already here; it's just not well-distributed yet." That sums up the Great Value Shift circa 2003. The efficiencies and affordances made possible by the Internet were there. They were enabling all sorts of pioneers to build new business models, new creative genres, and new online communities—but these innovations were unevenly distributed. More to the point, their potential was unevenly *perceived*, especially in many precincts of Washington officialdom and the corporate world. The challenge for amateurs venturing onto open platforms was to validate the new sorts of socially created value enabled by the Internet.

6

CREATORS TAKE CHARGE

Rip, remix, burn, mashup—legally. The CC licenses facilitate new Internet genres and business models.

The first users of CC licenses understood that something different was going on; a different order was taking shape. More than just a legal tool, the CC licenses gave the tech vanguard a way to express their inchoate sense that a new and better world was possible, at least on the Internet. They yearned for a noncommercial sharing economy with a different moral calculus than mass media markets, and for markets that are more open, accountable, and respectful of customers.

The early adopters were unusually informed about the politics of technology, skeptical of Big Media, and passionate about the artistic freedoms and social responsibility. They were a locally engaged but globally aware network of tech sophisticates, avant-garde artists, clued-in bloggers, small-*d* democratic activists, and the rebellious of spirit: the perfect core group for branding the Creative Commons and instigating a movement.

It only made sense that Cory Doctorow—copyfighter, science-fiction writer, tech analyst, co-editor of the popular Boing Boing blog—became the first book author to use a CC license. Doctorow—then a thirty-two-year-old native of Canada, the son of Trotskyite schoolteachers, the European representative for the Electronic Frontier Foundation from 2002 to 2006—is a singular character on the tech/intellectual property/free culture circuit. He can hold forth with intelligence, wry wit, and bravado on digital rights management, Internet economics, or the goofy gadgets and pop culture artifacts that he regularly showcases on Boing Boing.

In January 2003, a month after the CC licenses were released, Doctorow published his first novel, *Down and Out in the Magic King-*

dom, under an Attribution, NonCommercial, No Derivative Works license (BY-NC-ND). Simultaneously, his progressive-minded publisher, Tor Books of New York City, sold hard copies of the book. "Why am I doing this thing?" Doctorow asked rhetorically:

> Well, it's a long story, but to shorten it up: first-time novelists have a tough row to hoe. Our publishers don't have a lot of promotional budget to throw at unknown factors like us. Mostly, we rise and fall based on word-of-mouth. I'm not bad at word-of-mouth. I have a blog, Boing Boing (http://boingboingnet), where I do a *lot* of word-of-mouthing. I compulsively tell friends and strangers about things I like. And telling people about stuff is *way, way* easier if I can just send it to 'em. Way easier.[1]

A year later, Doctorow announced that his "grand experiment" was a success; in fact, he said, "my career is turning over like a goddamned locomotive engine." More than thirty thousand people had downloaded the book within a day of its posting. He proceeded to release a collection of short stories and a second novel under a CC license. He also rereleased *Down and Out in the Magic Kingdom* under a less restrictive CC license—an Attribution, NonCommercial, ShareAlike license (BY-NC-SA), which allows readers to make their own translations, radio and film adaptations, sequels, and other remixes of the novel, so long as they are made available on the same terms.[2]

With some sheepish candor, Doctorow conceded: "I wanted to see if the sky would fall: you see writers are routinely schooled by their peers that maximal copyright is the only thing that stands between us and penury, and so ingrained was this lesson in me that even though I had the intellectual intuition that a 'some rights reserved' regime would serve me well, I still couldn't shake the atavistic fear that I was about to do something very foolish indeed."

By June 2006, *Down and Out in the Magic Kingdom* had been downloaded more than seven hundred thousand times. It had gone through six printings, many foreign translations, and two competing online audio adaptations made by fans. "Most people who download the book don't end up buying it," Doctorow conceded, "but they wouldn't have bought it in any event, so I haven't lost any sales. I've just won an audience. A tiny minority of downloaders treats the free e-book as a substitute for the printed book—those are the lost sales. But a much larger minority treats the e-book as an enticement to buy the printed book. They're gained sales. As long as gained sales outnumber lost sales, I'm ahead of the game. After all, distributing nearly a million copies of my book has cost me nothing."[3] In 2008, Doctorow's marketing strategy of giving away online books to stimulate sales of physical books paid off in an even bigger way. His novel for teenagers, *Little Brother*, about a youthful hacker who takes on the U.S. government after it becomes a police state, spent weeks on the *New York Times* bestseller list for children's books.

It is perhaps easier for a sci-fi futurist like Doctorow than a publishing business to take such a wild leap into the unknown. But that, too, is an important insight: artists are more likely to lead the way into the sharing economy than entrenched industries. "I'd rather stake my future on a literature that people care about enough to steal," said Doctorow, "than devote my life to a form that has no home in the dominant medium of the century." Book lovers and authors will pioneer the future; corporate publishing will grudgingly follow, or be left behind.

Over the past few years, a small but growing number of pioneering authors have followed Doctorow's lead and published books under Creative Commons licenses. While the hard evidence is scarce, many authors who use CC licenses believe that releasing free electronic versions of their books does not hurt, and probably helps, the sales of physical copies of their books. Lessig released his 2004 book, *Free Culture*, under an Attribution, NonCommercial license (BY-NC), and scores of authors and established publishers have since released books under CC licenses. Among the more notable titles: Yochai Benkler's *The Wealth of Networks* (Yale University Press, 2006), Kembrew McLeod's *Freedom of Expression* (Doubleday, 2005), Peter Barnes's *Capitalism 3.0* (Berrett-Koehler, 2006), and Dan Gillmor's *We the Media* (O'Reilly Media, 2004).

In 2006, Paulo Coelho, author of a bestselling book, *The Alchemist*, created a "pirate" blog site that invited readers to use BitTorrent and other file-sharing networks to download free copies of his books. After he put the Russian translation of *The Alchemist* online, sales of hardcover copies in Russia went from around 1,000 a year to 100,000, and then to more than 1 million. Coelho attributes the success of foreign translations of his book to their free availability online.[4] Experiments such as these were likely influential in the launch of LegalTorrents, a site for the legal peer-to-peer distribution of CC-licensed text, audio, video games, and other content.

The CC licenses have been useful, not just for helping individual authors promote their books, but in fueling open-access scholarly publishing. As we will see in chapter 11, the CC licenses help scientists put their "royalty-free literature" on the Internet—a move that enlarges their readership, enhances their reputations, and still enables them to retain copyrights in their works.

Free culture publishing models are popping up in many unusual quarters these days. LibriVox, to take one instance, is a nonprofit digital library of public-domain audio books that are read and recorded by volunteers.[5] Since it started in 2005, the group has recorded more than 150 books by classic authors from Dostoyevsky and Descartes to Jane Austen and Abraham Lincoln. All of them are free. Most are in English but many are in German, Spanish, Chinese, and other languages.

Founder Hugh McGuire said the inspiration for LibriVox was a distributed recording of Lessig's book *Free Culture* read by bloggers and podcasters, chapter by chapter. "After listening to that, it took me a while to figure out how to record things on my computer (which I finally did, thanks to free software Audacity). Brewster Kahle's call for 'Universal Access to all human knowledge' was another inspiration, and the free hosting provided by archive.org and ibiblio.org meant that LibriVox was possible: there was no worry about bandwidth and storage. So the project was started with an investment of $0, which continues to be our global budget." LibriVox's mission, said McGuire, is the "acoustical liberation of books in the public domain."

Several publishing businesses now revolve around CC licenses. Wikitravel is a collaborative Web site that amasses content about cities and regions around the world; content is licensed under the CC Attribution, ShareAlike license (BY-SA).[6] In 2007, its founder joined with a travel writer to start Wikitravel Press, which now publishes travel books in a number of languages. Like the Wikitravel Web pages, the text in the books can be freely copied and reused.

Another new business using CC licenses is Lulu, a technology company started by Robert Young, the founder of the Linux vendor Red Hat and benefactor for the Center for the Public Domain. Lulu lets individuals publish and distribute their own books, which can be printed on demand or downloaded. Lulu handles all the details of the publishing process but lets people control their content and rights. Hundreds of people have licensed their works under the CC ShareAlike license and Public Domain Dedication, and under the GNU Project's Free Documentation License.[7]

As more of culture and commerce move to the Internet, the question facing the book industry now is whether the text of a book is more valuable as a physical object (a codex) or as a digital file (intangible bits that can circulate freely), or some combination of the two. Kevin Kelly, the former editor of *Wired* magazine, once explained: "In a regime of superabundant free copies, copies lose value. They are no longer the basis of wealth. Now relationships, links, connection and sharing are. Value has shifted away from a copy toward the many ways to recall, annotate, personalize, edit, authenticate, display, mark, transfer and engage a work."[8]

What this means in practice, Kelly has pointed out, is that books become more valuable as they become more broadly known and socially circulated—the very functionalities that the Internet facilitates. If people can discover a book online and read portions of it, share it with friends, and add annotations and links to related materials, it makes a book more desirable than a hard-copy version that is an inert text on a shelf. As Kelly writes: "When books are digitized, reading becomes a community activity. Bookmarks can be shared with fellow readers. Marginalia can be broadcast. Bibliographies swapped. You might get an alert that your friend Carl has annotated a favorite book of yours. A moment later, his links are yours."[9]

Needless to say, most book publishers and authors' organizations are not yet prepared to embrace this newfangled value proposition. It seems way too iffy. A "sharing" business model would seemingly cannibalize their current revenues and copyright control with little guarantee of doing better in an open, online milieu. The bigger problem may be the cultural prejudice that an absolute right of control over any possible uses of a book is the best way to make money.

In general, the publishing trade remains skeptical of the Internet, clueless about how to harness its marketing power, and strangers to CC licenses. And it could be years before mainstream publishing accepts some of the counterintuitive notions that special-interest Internet communities will drive publishing in the future. In a presentation that caused a stir in the book industry, futurist Mike Shatzkin said in May 2007 that this is already happening in general trade publishing: "We're close to a tipping point, or maybe we're past it . . . where Web-based branding will have more credibility than print, because print, needing more horizontal reach to be viable, won't deliver the attention of the real experts and megaphones in each field."[10]

DIY Videos and Film

One of the biggest cultural explosions of the past decade has been amateur video on the Web. The volume of online video has been so great that there are actually many distinct genres of amateur video: short videos on YouTube, video mashups, "machinima" (a combination of video and online gaming images), amateur pornography, and hybrid forms that combine user videos with conventional broadcast and cable television shows. Just as the Great Value Shift has empowered musicians, so it is giving video- and filmmakers new powers to express themselves as they wish, and reach huge audiences via the Internet. This power represents a potentially major threat to the cultural dominance of the television and film industries, as reflected in various schemes by the networks and studios to establish their own online presences. The threat of do-it-yourself (DIY) video and film is big enough that Viacom alleged that YouTube's copyright infringements of Viacom-owned video should entitle Viacom to $1 billion in damages. The entertainment industry and the Writers Guild of America endured a long, bitter strike in 2007–2008 precisely because the projected revenues from Internet video are so large.

It is too early to know which new video styles will be flash-in-the-pan novelties and which will ripen into popular, and perhaps lucrative, genres. But rarely has a culture seen so many diverse experiments in amateur and indie video expression. One site, Justin.tv, is a free platform for broadcasting and viewing live video. Some people make round-the-clock "life casts" of their daily activities; others have used it to broadcast live from Baghdad, showing war-related events. Yahoo and Reuters have entered into a partnership to host amateur photojournalism by people using their digital cameras and camera phones. Machinima video, the product of the underground gaming community, blends filmmaking with online games to produce computer-generated imagery. As John Seely Brown describes it, "Basically, you can take Second Life or Worlds of Warcraft and have a set of avatars run all over the world, that come together and create their own movie, and then you can 'YouTube' the movie."[11]

As amateur video and film proliferate, thanks to inexpensive technologies and Internet access, the CC licenses have obvious value in letting the creator retain a copyright in the video while inviting its duplication and reuse by millions of people online. To industry traditionalists locked into binary options, the free circulation of a work precludes any moneymaking opportunities. But of course, that is precisely what is now being negotiated: how to devise ingenious new schemes to make money from freely circulating video. One option is to own the platform, as YouTube does. But there are also competitors such as Revver and blip.tv, which have established their own approaches based on advertising and commercial licensing of works. There are also schemes that use Internet exposure to drive paying customers into theaters and advertisers to buy commercial licenses. For some amateurs, DIY video is simply a way to get noticed and hired by a conventional media company.

That's what the Los Angeles–based comedy collective The Lonely Island did to promote themselves to national attention. They posted their comedy shorts and songs to their Web site using Creative Commons licenses. Soon other artists began making remixes of their songs. The remixes in effect served as free marketing, which caught the attention of the Fox Broadcasting Company, which in turn hired them to create a comedy pilot TV episode. In the end, Fox did not pick up the show, but as *Wired News* recounted, "Instead of letting the show wither on a shelf somewhere, the group posted the full video both cut and uncut. The edgy, quirky short— *Awesometown*—spread like wildfire online and eventually landed all three performers an audition spot for *Saturday Night Live.*"[12]

Perhaps the most successful example of leveraging free Internet exposure to reap commercial benefits is the sci-fi parody *Star Wreck*. Finnish producer Samuli Torssonen took seven years to shoot a full-length movie using a Sony DVCAM, computer-generated graphics, and a makeshift studio. Some three hundred people were involved in the project, including some professional actors and many amateurs. When *Star Wreck* was deliberately posted to the Internet in 2005, tagged with a CC-BY-NC-ND license (Attribution, Non-Commercial, No Derivatives), it was eventually downloaded 5 million times and became the most-watched Finnish film in history. Fans in Russia, China, and Japan soon copied the film, which stimulated broader viewer demand and led to commercial deals to distribute the film. *Star Wreck* became so popular that Universal Pictures, the American studio, signed a deal in 2006 to distribute DVD versions of the film. Torssonen says that the film has earned a 20-to-1 return on investment. "I wouldn't call free distribution stupid, as some people say, but a success," he told an audience in 2007.[13]

The lesson for Stephen Lee, CEO of Star Wreck Studios, is that "you don't need millions to make a quality movie. You need an active, passionate community." Lee says the plan for a peer-produced model of "wrecking a movie" is to develop an Internet collaboration, make the film popular through viral marketing, and then license it commercially. Star Wreck Studios is now developing a new movie, *Iron Sky*, about a Nazi base on the far side of the moon.

One of the more daring experiments in film production is being pioneered by the Blender Institute, a studio for open-content animation and game projects located in the Amsterdam docklands. Started in August 2007, the Institute employs fourteen full-time people who are obsessed with improving its three-dimensional open-source software, the so-called Blender 3D suite. The software is widely used by a large international user community for modeling, animation, rendering, editing, and other tasks associated with 3D computer-generated animation.

Ton Roosendaal, who directs the Blender Institute, is trying to demonstrate that a small studio can develop a virtuous cycle of economically sustainable creativity using open-source software, Creative Commons licenses, and talented programmers and artists from around the world. "We give programmers the freedom to do their best, and what they want to do is improve the technology," he said. "The market is too hyper-rational and nailed down and filled with limits," he argues, referring to his peers at major animation studios. "Open source is free of most of these constraints." [14]

In April 2008, the Blender Institute released a ten-minute animated short, *Big Buck Bunny*, which features a kind-hearted, fat white bunny who endures the abuse of three stone-throwing rodents until they smash a beautiful butterfly with a rock—at which point the bunny rallies to teach the bullies a lesson. [15] The film uses cutting-edge computer-generated animation techniques that rival anything produced by Pixar, the Hollywood studio responsible for *Toy Story, Cars*, and *Ratatouille. Big Buck Bunny* is licensed under a CC Attribution license, which means the digital content can be used by anyone for any purpose so long as credit is given to the Blender Institute.

Big Buck Bunny was initially distributed to upfront investors as a DVD set that includes extras such as interviews, outtakes, deleted scenes, and the entire database used in making the film. Then, to pique wider interest in sales of the DVD set, priced at thirty-four euros, a trailer was released on the Internet. This resulted in extensive international press coverage and blog exposure. Early signs are promising that Blender will be able to continue to make high-quality animation on a fairly modest budget without worries about illegal downloads or a digital rights management system. The Blender production model also has the virtue of enabling access to top creative talent and cutting-edge animation technologies as well as efficient distribution to paying audiences on a global scale.

While CC-licensed films are not common, neither are they rare. Davis Guggenheim, the filmmaker who directed *An Inconvenient Truth*, made a short film, *Teach*, to encourage talented people to become teachers. The film was released in 2006 under a CC BY-NC-ND license because Guggenheim wanted the film widely available to the public yet also wanted to preserve the integrity of the stories told, hence the NoDerivatives provision. A Spanish short film, *Lo que tú Quieras Oír*, became YouTube's fifth most-viewed video— more than 38 million views. The film's viral diffusion may have been helped by the CC BY-NC-SA (Attribution, NonCommercial, ShareAlike) license, which allows viewers not only to share the film, but to remix for noncommercial purposes so long as they use the same license.

In Brazil, director Bruno Vianna released his first full-length film, *Cafuné*, under a CC BY-NC-SA license (Attribution, Non-Commercial, ShareAlike) and put it on file-sharing networks at the same time that it was exhibited in a handful of theaters.[16] Each release had different endings; downloaders were invited to remix the ending as they wished. The film was financed by the government's culture ministry as part of a competition for low-budget films, but only about fifty Brazilian films are released to commercial theaters each year. Vianna saw the Internet release as a great way to build an audience for his debut film . . . which is exactly what happened. For some weeks, it made it into the list of twenty most-watched films in the country.

Letting the Music Flow

Media reform activist Harold Feld offers a succinct overview of why creativity in music—and therefore the business of selling recorded music—has suffered over the past two decades:

> The 1990s saw a number of factors that allowed the major labels to push out independents and dominate the market with their own outrageously priced and poorly produced products: consolidation in the music industry, the whole "studio system" of pumping a few big stars to the exclusion of others, the consolidation in music outlets from mom-and-pop record stores to chains like Tower Records and retail giants like Wal-Mart that exclude indies and push the recordings promoted by major labels, and the consolidation of radio—which further killed indie exposure and allowed the labels to artificially pump their selected "hits" through payola. All this created a cozy cartel that enjoyed monopoly profits.
>
> As a result, the major labels, the mainstream retailers, and the radio broadcasters grew increasingly out of touch with what listeners actually wanted. But as long as the music cartel controlled what the vast majority of people got to hear, it didn't matter . . . The music cartel remained the de facto only game in town.[17]

Changing the music industry is obviously a major challenge that is not going to be solved overnight. Still, there is a growing effort led by indie musicians, small record labels, Internet music entrepreneurs, and advocacy groups such as the Future of Music Coalition to address these problems. Creative Commons is clearly sympathetic, but has largely focused on a more modest agenda—enabling a new universe of shareable music to arise. Its chief tools for this mission, beyond the CC licenses, are new software platforms for legal music remixes, online commons that legally share music, and new business models that respect the interests of both fans and artists. Ultimately, it is hoped that a global oeuvre of shareable music will emerge. Once this body of music matures, attracting more artists and fans in a self-sustaining viral spiral, the record industry may be forced to give up its dreams of perfect control of how music may circulate and adopt fan-friendly business practices.

This, at least, is the theory, as Lessig explains it. He calls it the "BMI strategy," a reference to the strategy that broadcasters and musicians used to fight ASCAP's monopoly control over radio music in the early 1940s. ASCAP, the American Society of Composers, Authors and Publishers, is a nonprofit organization that collects royalties for musical performances. At the time, ASCAP required artists to have five hits before it would serve as a collection agency for them, a rule that privileged the playing of pop music on the radio at the expense of rhythm and blues, jazz, hillbilly, and ethnic music. Then, over the course of eight years, ASCAP raised its rates by 450 percent between 1931 and 1939—at which point, ASCAP then proposed *doubling* its rates for 1940. In protest, many radio stations refused to play ASCAP-licensed music. They formed a new performance-rights body, BMI, or Broadcast Music, Inc., which sought to break the ASCAP monopoly by offering free arrangements of public-domain music to radio stations. They also charged lower rates than ASCAP for licensing music and offered better contracts for artists.[18]

"The Internet is today's broadcasters," said Lessig in a 2006 speech. "They are facing the same struggle."[19] Just as ASCAP used its monopoly power to control what music could be heard and at what prices, he said, so today's media corporations want to leverage their control over content to gain control of the business models and technologies of digital environments. When Google bought YouTube, one-third of the purchase price of $1.65 billion was allegedly a financial reserve to deal with any copyright litigation, said Lessig. This is how the incumbent media world is trying to stifle the emergence of free culture.

The same questions that once confronted broadcasters are now facing Internet innovators, Lessig argues: "How do we free the future from the dead hand of the past? What do we do to make it so they can't control how technology evolves?" With copyright terms lasting so long, it is not really feasible to try to use public-domain materials to compete with a commercial cartel. Lessig's answer is a BMI-inspired solution that uses the CC licenses to create a new body of "free" works that, over time, can begin to compete with popular works. The legendary record producer Jerry Wexler recalled how ASCAP marginalized R & B, country, folk, and ethnic music, but "once the lid was lifted—which happened when BMI entered the picture—the vacuum was filled by all these archetypal musics. BMI turned out to be the mechanism that released all those primal American forms of music that fused and became rock-and-roll."[20] Lessig clearly has similar ambitions for Creative Commons.

For now, the subculture of CC-licensed music remains something of a fringe movement. It is easy to patronize it as small, amateurish, and quirky. Yet its very existence stands as a challenge to the music industry by showing the feasibility of a more artist- and fan-friendly way of distributing music. Is it visionary to believe that free culture artists will force the major labels to change—just as BMI forced ASCAP to lower prices—and make them more competitive and inclusive?

Creative Commons's primary task is practical—to help musicians reach audiences directly and reap more of the financial rewards of their music. So far, a wide range of indie bands, hip-hop artists, and bohemian experimentalists of all stripes have used the licenses. One of the most popular is the Attribution, NonCommercial license, which lets artists share their works while getting credit and retaining commercial rights. A number of marquee songwriters and performers—David Byrne, Gilberto Gil, the Beastie Boys, Chuck D—have also used CC licenses as a gesture of solidarity with free culture artists and as an enlightened marketing strategy. Inviting people to remix your songs is a great way to engage your fan base and sell more records. And tagging your music with a CC license, at least for now, wraps an artist in a mantle of tech sophistication and artistic integrity.

Guitarist Jake Shapiro was one of the first musicians to show the marketing potential of unleashing free music on the Internet. In 1995, Shapiro put MP3 files of music by his band, Two Ton Shoe, on the group's Web site. Within a few years, Two Ton Shoe was one of the most-downloaded bands on the Internet, developing fan bases in Italy, Brazil, Russia, and South Korea. One day Shapiro received a phone call out of the blue from a South Korean concert promoter. He wanted to know if the band would fly over to Seoul to perform four concerts. It turned out that fans in South Korea, where fast broadband connections are the norm, had discovered Two Ton Shoe through file sharing. A local CD retailer kept getting requests for the band's music, which led him to contact a concert promoter. In August 2005, Shapiro and his buddies arrived in Seoul as conquering rock stars, selling out all four of their concerts. "The kids who showed up knew all the words to the songs," Shapiro recalled. A year later, the band signed a deal to distribute a double CD to East Asia.[21]

While such stories of viral marketing success are not common, neither are they rare. Lots of bands now promote themselves, and find admiring (paying) fans, by posting their music, for free, on Web sites and file-sharing sites. Perhaps the most scrutinized example was Radiohead's decision to release its album *In Rainbows* for free online, while inviting fans to pay whatever they wanted. (The band did not release any numbers, but considered the move a success. They later released the album through conventional distribution channels as well.)[22]

Just as previous generations of fans came together around FM radio or live performance venues, the Internet is the new gathering place for discovering interesting, fresh, and authentic talent. The lesson that the record industry hasn't quite learned is that music is not just a commodity but a *social experience*—and social experiences lose their appeal if overly controlled and commercialized. If the music marketplace does not provide a place for fans to congregate and share in a somewhat open, unregimented way—if the commodity ethic overwhelms everything else—the music dies. Or more accurately, it migrates underground, outside the marketplace, to sustain itself. This is why so much of the best new music is happening on the fringes of the stagnant commercial mainstream.

It is also why the Creative Commons licenses have acquired such cachet. They have come to be associated with musicians who honor the integrity of music making. They symbolize the collective nature of creativity and the importance of communing freely with one's fans. Nimrod Lev, a prominent Israeli musician and supporter of the CC licenses, received considerable press coverage in his country for a speech that lamented the "cunning arrangement" (in Israeli slang, *combina*) by which the music industry has betrayed people's love of music, making it "only a matter of business and commerce." Said Lev:

> The music industry treats its consumer as a consumer of sex, not of love, the love of music. Just like everything else: a vacuum without values or meaning. But it is still love that everyone wants and seeks. . . . The music vendors knew then [a generation ago] what they have forgotten today, namely that we must have cultural heroes: artists that are not cloned in a manner out to get our money. There was an added value with a meaning: someone who spoke to our hearts in difficult moments, and with that someone, we would walk hand in hand for a while. We had loyalty and love, and it all meant something.[23]

At the risk of sounding naïve, Lev said he wanted to stand up for the importance of "authenticity and empathy and my own truth" in making music. It is a complaint that echoes throughout the artistic community globally. A few years ago, Patti Smith, the punk rocker renowned for her artistic integrity, decried the "loss of our cultural voice" as the radio industry consolidated and as music television became a dominant force. She grieved for the scarcity of places for her to "feel connected" to a larger musical community of artists and fans.[24]

The classic example of music as social experience—music as a vehicle for a community of shared values—is the Grateful Dead. The band famously invited its fans to record all of its concerts and even provided them with an authorized "tapers' section" in which to place their microphones and equipment. Fans were also allowed to circulate their homemade tapes so long as the music was shared, and not sold. This had the effect of building a large and committed fan base, which avidly archived, edited, and traded Grateful Dead cassettes. One reason that the Dead's "customer base" has been so lucrative and durable over several decades is that the fans were not treated as mere customers or potential pirates, but as a community of shared values. The music belonged to the fans as much as to the band, even though Deadheads were only too happy to pay to attend concerts and buy the officially released CDs and t-shirts.[25]

While the Grateful Dead may be an outlier case, it exemplifies the sharing ethic that the Internet is facilitating: the formation of communities of amateurs that flourish by sharing and celebrating music. Artists can make some money through CD sales, but much more through performances, merchandising, endorsements, and sales to films, television, and advertisers. If established singers and bands are reluctant to make a transition to this new business model, hungry newcomers are not.

The Mountain Goats, an indie rock group, authorized the Internet Archive to host their live shows on the Web because they realized the videos seed market demand for their music. The group's front man, John Darnielle, said, "I am totally in favor of tape trading, and file sharing never did anything wrong by me. People got into The Mountain Goats after downloading my stuff."[26] In 2001, two newcomers working out of a basement produced a cover version of Tears for Fears' "Mad World," which two years later went to the top of the British pop charts.[27] In a world where amateur creativity can easily migrate to the commercial mainstream, tagging works with a NonCommercial CC license is a valuable option. By requiring uses that fall outside the scope of the license to pay as usual, it can help artists get visibility while retaining their potential to earn money. A larger restructuring of the music industry, alas, will take longer to achieve.

Music as Remix

If any segment of the music world really understands the social dynamics of musical creativity, it is hip-hop artists. As Joanna Demers documents in her book about "transformative appropriation" in music, *Steal This Music*, hip-hop was born as a remix genre in the 1970s and 1980s.[28] In defiance of copyright law, which considers unauthorized borrowing as presumptively illegal, hip-hop artists used turntable scratching and digital sampling to transform existing songs into something new, which in time grew into a lucrative market segment. Hip-hop illustrates how the commons and the market need to freely interact, without undue restrictions, in order for both to flourish. It works because sampling is not a simple matter of "theft" but a mode of creativity, a way of carrying on a cultural conversation. Sampling is a way of paying tribute to musical heroes, mocking rivals, alluding to an historical moment, or simply experimenting with an arresting sound. When the rap group Run-DMC used Aerosmith's "Walk This Way" as the basis for a remix, it was not only a salute to the group's musical influence and a new turn of the creative wheel, it revived Aerosmith's sagging career (or, in economist's terms, it "created new value").

The problem, of course, is that most remix culture (and the value it creates) is illegal. By the late 1980s, in fact, the freedom of the commons that gave birth to hip-hop was coming under siege. Musicians and record labels were routinely invoking copyright law to demand permission and payments for the tiniest samples of music. Only wealthy artists could afford to clear the rights of familiar songs, and basement amateurs (who had given rise to the genre in the first place) were being marginalized. When George Clinton's group Funkadelic succeeded in its lawsuit against the rap group N.W.A. for using a nearly inaudible sample of a three-note, two-second clip from "Get Off Your Ass and Jam"—the infamous *Bridgeport v. Dimension Films* decision, in 2004—it became clear that the commons of hip-hop music was being enclosed.[29] Critics like Siva Vaidhyanathan and Kembrew McLeod believe that the legal crusade against sampling has significantly harmed the creative vitality of

hip-hop. Something is clearly amiss when the one of the most critically acclaimed albums of 2005—*The Grey Album*, a remix collection by DJ Danger Mouse—cannot be legally released. *The Grey
Album* artfully combined music from the Beatles's *White Album* with
lyrics from Jay-Z's *Black Album*, resulting in "the most popular
album in rock history that virtually no one paid for," according to
Entertainment Weekly.[30]

The impetus for a solution to the sampling problem started with
Negativland, an irreverent "sound collage" band known as much for
its zany culture jamming as for its anticopyright manifestos. (One of
its CDs includes a polemical booklet about fair use along with a
whoopee cushion with a © symbol printed on it.) Negativland
gained notoriety in the 1990s for its protracted legal battle with the
band U2 and Island Records over Negativland's release of a parody
song called "U2." Island Records claimed it was an infringement of
copyright and trademark law, among other things. Negativland
claimed that no one should be able to own the letter *U* and the numeral *2,* and cited the fair use doctrine as protecting its song and
title. The case was eventually settled.[31]

As an experienced sampler of music, Negativland and collagist
People Like Us (aka Vicki Bennett) asked Creative Commons if it
would develop and offer a music sampling license. Don Joyce of
Negativland explained:

> This would be legally acknowledging the now obvious
> state of modern audio/visual creativity in which quoting,
> sampling, direct referencing, copying and collaging have be-
> come a major part of modern inspiration. [A sampling op-
> tion would] stop legally suppressing it and start culturally
> encouraging it—because it's here to stay. That's our idea for
> encouraging a more democratic media for all of us, from
> corporations to the individual.[32]

With legal help from Cooley Godward Kronish and Wilson,
Sonsini, Goodrich & Rosati, Creative Commons did just that. During its consultations with the remix community, Creative Com-

mons learned that Gilberto Gil, the renowned *tropicalismo* musician and at the time the Brazilian minister of culture, had been thinking along similar lines, and so it received valuable suggestions and support from him.

In 2005, Creative Commons issued the Sampling license as a way to let people take pieces of a work for any purpose except advertising.[33] It also prohibited copying and distribution of the entire work.* For example, an artist could take a snippet of music, a clip of film, or a piece of a photograph, and use the sample in a new creation. Since its release, the Sampling license has been criticized on philosophical grounds by some commoners who say it does not truly enhance people's freedom because it prohibits copying and distribution of the entire work. This concern reached serious enough proportions that in 2007 Creative Commons "retired" the license; I'll revisit this controversy in chapter 9.

The CC Sampling license only whetted the imagination of people who wanted to find new ways to sample, share, and transform music. Neeru Paharia, then the assistant director of the Creative Commons, came up with the idea of developing ccMixter, a software platform for remixing music on the Web.[34] Paharia realized one day that "this whole remixing and sharing ecology is about getting feedback on who's using your work and how it's evolving. That's almost half the pleasure."[35] So the organization developed a Web site that would allow people to upload music that could be sampled and remixed. The site has about five thousand registered users, which is not terribly large, but it is an enthusiastic and active community of remix artists that acts as a great proof of concept while promoting the CC licenses. There are other, much larger remix sites on the Internet, such as Sony's ACIDplanet, but such sites are faux commons. They retain ownership in the sounds and

---

* A "Sampling Plus" license was also issued to allow noncommercial copying and distribution of an entire work, which means it could be distributed via file-sharing networks. Finally, a "NonCommercial Sampling Plus" license was devised to let people sample and transform pieces of a work, and copy and distribute the entire work, so long as it was for noncommercial purposes.

remixes that users make, and no derivative or commercial versions are allowed.

One feature of viral spirals is their propensity to call forth a jumble of new projects and unexpected partners. The CC licenses have done just that for music. ccMixter has joined with Opsound to offer a joint "sound pool" of clips licensed under an Attribution Share-Alike license. It also supports Freesound, a repository of more than twenty thousand CC-licensed samples ranging from waterfalls to crickets to music.[36]

Runoff Records, Inc., a record label, discovered a remix artist who teaches physics and calculus and goes by the name of Minus Kelvin. Runoff heard a podcast of Kelvin's CC-licensed music, and signed him up, along with another ccMixter contributor, to do music for three seasons of the television show *America's Next Top Model*.[37] A few months later, two ccMixter fans based in Poland and Holland started an online record label, DiSfish, that gives 5 percent of all sale proceeds to CC, another 5 percent to charity, with the remainder split between the label and the artist. All music on the label is licensed under CC.[38]

The CC licenses are not just the province of daring remix artists and other experimentalists. Disappointed by its CD sales through traditional channels, the Philharmonia Baroque Orchestra released its performance of Handel's 1736 opera, *Atalanta,* exclusively through the online record label Magnatune, using a CC license. Conductor Nicholas McGegan said the Internet "has potentially given the industry a tremendous shot in the arm," letting orchestras reach "new audiences, including ones that are unlikely to hear you in person."[39] A company that specializes in Catalan music collaborated with the Catalonian government to release two CDs full of CC-licensed music.[40] A group of Gamelan musicians from central Java who perform in North Carolina decided to release their recordings under a CC license.[41]

Big-name artists have gotten into the licenses as well. DJ Vadim created a splash when he released all the original solo, individual instrumental, and a cappella studio tracks of his album *The Sound Catcher* under an Attribution, NonCommercial license, so that remixers could have at it.[42] In 2004, *Wired* magazine released a CD with sixteen tracks by the likes of David Byrne, Gilberto Gil, and the Beastie Boys. "By contributing a track to *The Wired CD*, these musicians acknowledge that for an art form to thrive, it needs to be open, fluid and alive," wrote *Wired*. "These artists—and soon, perhaps, many more like them—would rather have people share their work than steal it."[43]

Soon thereafter, Byrne and Gil went so far as to host a gala benefit concert for Creative Commons in New York City. In a fitting fusion of styles, Gil sang a Brazilian arrangement of Cole Porter's cowboy song, "Don't Fence Me In." The crowd of 1,500 was high on the transcultural symbolism, said Glenn Brown: "Musical superstars from North and South, jamming together, building earlier works into new creations, in real time. Lawyers on the sidelines and in the audience, where they belong. The big Creative Commons logo smiling overhead."[44] The description captures the CC enterprise to a fault: the fusion of some clap-your-hands populism and hardheaded legal tools, inflected with an idealistic call to action to build a better world.

By 2008 the power of open networks had persuaded the major record labels to abandon digital rights management of music CDs, and more major artists were beginning to venture forth with their own direct distribution plans, bypassing the standard record label deals. Prince, Madonna, and others found it more lucrative to run their own business affairs and deal with concert venues and merchandisers. In a major experiment that suggests a new business model for major music acts, Nine Inch Nails released its album *Ghosts I-IV* under a Creative Commons NonCommercial Share-Alike license, and posted audio files of the album on its official Web site, inviting free downloads. It did not do advertising or promotion. Despite the free distribution—or because of it—the group made money by selling 2,500 copies of an "Ultra-Deluxe Limited Edition" of the album for $300; the edition sold out in less than three days. There were also nonlimited sales of a "deluxe edition" for $75 and a $10 CD. The scheme showed how free access to the music can be used to drive sales for something that remains scarce, such as a "special edition" CD or a live performance. One week after the album's release, the Nine Inch Nails' Web site reported that the group had made over $1.6 million from over 750,000 purchase and download transactions. Considering that an artist generally makes only $1.60 on the sale of a $15.99 CD, Nine Inch Nails made a great deal more money from a "free" album distribution than it otherwise would have made through a standard record deal.[45]

It is too early to know if Lessig's "BMI strategy" will in fact catalyze a structural transformation in the entertainment industries. But Lessig apparently feels that it is the only feasible strategy. As he said in a 2006 speech, intensified hacking to break systems of proprietary control will not work; new campaigns to win progressive legislation won't succeed within the next twenty years; and litigation is "a long-term losing strategy," as the *Eldred* case demonstrated. For Lessig and much of the free culture community, the long-term project of building one's own open, commons-friendly infrastructure is the only enduring solution.

In the music industry, the early signs seem to support this approach. When digital guru Don Tapscott surveyed the events of 2006, he concluded that "the losers built digital music stores and the winners built vibrant communities based on music. The losers built walled gardens while the winners built public squares. The losers were busy guarding their intellectual property while the winners were busy getting everyone's attention." In a penetrating analysis in 2007, music industry blogger Gerd Leonhard wrote: "In music, it's always been about interaction, about sharing, about engaging—not Sell-Sell-Sell right from the start. Stop the sharing and you kill the music business—it's that simple. When the fan/user/listener stops engaging with the music, it's all over."[46]

Serious change is in the air when the producer/consumer dichotomy is no longer the only paradigm, and a vast network of ordinary people and talented creators are becoming active participants in making their own culture. They are sharing and co-creating. Markets are no longer so separate from social communities; indeed, the two are blurring into each other. Although we may live in a complicated interregnum between Centralized Media and distributed media, the future is likely to favor those creators and businesses who build on open platforms. As Dan Hunter and F. Gregory Lastowka write: "It is clear that two parallel spheres of information production exist today. One is a traditional, copyright-based and profit-driven model that is struggling with technological change. The second is a newly enabled, decentralized amateur production sphere, in which individual authors or small groups freely release their work." [47]

Hunter and Lastowka liken copyright law today to the Roman Empire in decline: "It is meaningless to ask whether the unitary might of imperial Rome was preferable to the distributed, messy agglomeration of tribes and states that eventually emerged after Rome fell. It was not better, just different." That is certainly a debatable conclusion, depending upon one's cultural tastes and sense of history. But the Rome metaphor does capture the fragmentation and democratization of creativity that is now under way. And that, in fact, is something of the point of the CC licenses: to make access and use of culture more open and egalitarian. For all his commitment to law and the CC licenses, Lessig ultimately throws his lot in with social practice: "Remember, it's the *activity* that the licenses make possible that matters, not the licenses themselves. The point is to change the existing discourse by growing a new discourse." [48]

7

THE MACHINE AND THE MOVEMENT

An infrastructure of code gives rise to a movement for free culture.

When the CC licenses were first launched, many regarded them as a boring legal license that may or may not really matter. The real surprise was how the CC licenses became a focal object for organizing a movement. As more users began to adopt the licenses in 2003 and 2004, they ceased being just a set of legal permissions and became a cool social brand. The CC licenses and logo became symbols of resistance against the highly controlled, heavily marketed, Big Brother worldview that Hollywood and the record industry seem to embody. The CC licenses offered a way to talk about one's legal and creative rights in the Internet age, and to cite to a positive alternative—the sharing economy. With no paid advertising to speak of, the CC logo came to symbolize an ethic and identity, one that stood for artistic integrity, democratic transparency, and innovation.

Glenn Otis Brown recalls how people spontaneously took up the license to express their anger at the media establishment and their yearning for a more wholesome alternative: "If you're frustrated with the way the world works now, frustrated with the way the media is becoming more democratized but all these laws aren't really facilitating that," said Brown, "you can just cast a little virtual vote for a different sort of copyright system by putting the 'Some Rights Reserved' tag on your Web page. But also, practically, you can help create pools of content that people can work with and make it so much easier to participate." Without really planning it, the Creative Commons became much more than a system of free licenses for sharing. It became a symbol for a movement. Communities of social practice began to organize themselves around the CC project.

"Inside of the organization, we always talked about how we really had *two* organizations," said Brown. "One was Creative Commons, the *movement*; and one was Creative Commons, the *machine*."[1] The machine was about meeting utilitarian needs through licenses and software; the movement was about motivating people and transforming culture. Just as the GPL had given rise to the free software community and a hacker political philosophy (which in turn inspired the Creative Commons's organizers), so the CC licenses were spontaneously igniting different pockets of the culture: Web designers, bloggers, musicians, book authors, videographers, filmmakers, and amateurs of all stripes. The viral spiral was proceeding apace.

The tension between the machine and the movement has been an animating force in the evolution of the Creative Commons. "You want to have something that's actually useful to people," said Brown, "but you also have to get people excited about it, and build up your constituency."[2] Some CC initiatives have had strong symbolic resonances but little practical value, while other initiatives were quite useful but not very sexy. For example, embedding CC metadata into software applications and Web services is complicated and technical—but highly effective in extending the practices of free culture. On the other hand, the Creative Commons's release of specialty licenses for music sampling, developing nations, and a CC version of the General Public License for software (as discussed below) were discretionary moves of some utility that were probably more important as gestures of solidarity to allies.

This has been a recurrent motif for the organization—pragmatic, improvisational outreach to distinct constituencies as part of a larger attempt to build a movement. There has always been a corresponding pull, however, "not to put 'the machine' at risk by incorporating the new licenses into every last one of our software tools," said Brown. The integrity of "the machine" ultimately needs to be respected.

Even as the machine was getting built, Lessig was taking steps to stoke up a movement. In 2004, Lessig published his third book in five years, *Free Culture*. The book described, as the subtitle put it, "how big media uses technology and the law to lock down culture and control creativity." Lessig's earlier books, *Code* and *The Future of Ideas*, had critiqued the alarming trends in copyright law, explained the importance of the commons, and set forth a philosophical rationale for what became the CC licenses. Now *Free Culture* provided a wide-ranging survey of how incumbent industries with old business models—for recorded music, film, broadcasting, cable television—were (and are) curbing traditional creative freedoms and technological innovations. Drawing explicitly on the ideas of freedom developed by Richard Stallman in the 1980s, and upon legal history, politics, and colorful stories, Lessig argued that industry protectionism poses a profound harm to creators, business, and democratic culture—and that action needed to be taken.

Although *Free Culture* repeats many of the fundamental arguments made in his earlier books, Lessig's arguments this time did not sound like a law professor's or academic's, but more like an activist trying to rally a social movement. "This movement must begin in the streets," he writes. "It must recruit a significant number of parents, teachers, librarians, creators, authors, musicians, filmmakers, scientists—all to tell their story in their own words, and to tell their neighbors why this battle is so important. . . . We will not reclaim a free culture by individual action alone. It will take important reforms of laws. We have a long way to go before the politicians will listen to these ideas and implement these reforms. But that also means that we have time to build awareness around the changes that we need." [3] The preeminent challenge for this would-be movement, Lessig wrote, is "rebuilding freedoms previously presumed" and "rebuilding free culture."

Lessig had reason to think that his analysis and exhortations would find receptive ears. He was now a leading voice on copyright and Internet issues, and well known through his earlier books, public speaking, and *Eldred* advocacy. The launch of the Creative Commons was thrusting him into the spotlight again. Adoption of the CC licenses was steadily growing in 2003 and 2004 based on the most comprehensive sources at the time, search engines. Yahoo was reporting in September 2004 that there were 4.7 million links to CC licenses on the Web. This number shot up to 14 million only six months later, and by August 2005 it had grown to 53 million.[4] These numbers offer only a crude estimate of actual license usage, but they nonetheless indicated a consistent trend. Usage was also being propelled by new types of Web 2.0 sites featuring user-generated content. For example, Flickr, the photo-sharing site, had 4.1 million photos tagged with CC licenses at the end of 2004, a number that has soared to an estimated 75 million by 2008.

The decisive choice, four years earlier, to build a suite of licenses that could propagate themselves via open networks was bearing fruit.

Building the CC Machine

It was a pleasant surprise for the organization to learn that a great deal of individual usage of the CC licenses was fairly spontaneous. Persuading large companies and respected institutions to use the CC licenses was a more difficult proposition. Lessig therefore spent a fair amount of time trying to get prominent institutions to adopt the licenses and give them some validation. Among the early converts were MIT, Rice University, Stanford Law School, and Sun Microsystems, supplemented by some relatively new organizations such as Brewster Kahle's Internet Archive and the Public Library of Science, a publisher of open-access journals.

Personal diplomacy can accomplish only so much, however, and in any case the Internet itself needed to be leveraged to disseminate the licenses and educate the public. One challenge, for example, was to introduce the CC licenses—which are not, after all, a self-evident need for most people—in a clear, compelling way. Most authors and artists have little idea what licenses they may want to choose, and their implications for how they might be able to sell or share works in the future. People needed a quick and easy way to make intelligent choices. It fell to Lisa Rein, the first technical director at CC, in late 2001, to develop a license-generating interface for the Web site. The quandary she faced was how to maximize user choice in selecting licenses while minimizing complexity.

The Web interface for the licenses has steadily improved over the years, but in a sense, those improvements have been offset by a growing complexity and number of CC licenses. Some critics have complained that the whole CC scheme can be a bit daunting. Yes, the licenses can ensure certain freedoms without your having to hire an attorney, which is clearly an improvement over relying on the fair use doctrine. But that does not mean that anyone can immediately understand the implications of using a NonCommercial or Share-Alike license for a given work. Any lurker on a CC listserv soon encounters head-scratching questions like "Can I use a BY-NC photo from Flickr on my blog if the blog is hosted by a company whose terms of service require me to grant them a worldwide, nonexclusive license to use any work hosted by their service, in-cluding for commercial use?"

By far the more important vehicle for promoting usage of the CC licenses has been software code. Lessig and the CC team real-ized that if the licenses could become an embedded element of leading search engines, Web publishing tools, and Web 2.0 plat-forms, it could powerfully promote license use. Integrating the code into existing Web sites and software can pose some serious technical challenges, however. Figuring out how to integrate the CC licenses with popular software applications, Web services, and digital file formats has fallen chiefly to Nathan Yergler, the chief technology officer of Creative Commons. Over the years, he and other CC de-velopers have come up with a variety of applications to help make software infrastructures more friendly. One program that was devel-oped, ccHost, is a content management system that has licensing and remix tracking built into its core. JsWidget is a simple javascript widget that developers can easily integrate into their sites to enable users to choose a license without leaving the site. Creative Com-mons has made it a standard practice to coordinate its work with technology volunteers, startup companies, and nonprofits with a stake in digitally enabling open licensing. It does this work through a CC development wiki, the cc-devel mailing list, Internet Relay Chat, World Wide Web Consortium working groups, and partici-pation in Google's annual "Summer of Code" program for student programmers.

Lessig and top CC staff have worked hard at convincing executives at major software enterprises to incorporate the CC licenses into a software application or Web site. One early triumph came when the makers of Movable Type, a blogging platform, agreed to make it easy for users to tack a CC license onto their blogs. Two months later, the O'Reilly empire of software blogs adopted the CC licenses. Then programmer Dave Winer embedded the licenses in his new Web log software in 2003. Blogs may not be core infrastructure for the Internet, but they are plentiful and popular, and have given Creative Commons enormous visibility and a high adoption curve.

It had always been Lessig's ambition that the major search engines would be reengineered to help people find CC-tagged content. To help prove that it could be done, Creative Commons built its own jerry-rigged search engine that retrieved content tagged with CC metadata. Lessig and Brown, meanwhile, made numerous diplomatic overtures to Google and Yahoo executives and software engineers. After two years of off-and-on conversations, both search engine companies agreed in 2005 to incorporate changes into their advanced searches so that users could locate CC-licensed content. (The Google advanced search does not use the Creative Commons name, but simply asks users if they want content that is "free to use or share," among other options.) The search engine exposure was a serious breakthrough for Creative Commons's visibility and legitimacy.

After a few years, the CC licenses were integrated into a number of other software platforms. It became possible to search for CC-licensed images (Flickr), video programs (blip.tv), music (Owl), and old Web content (Internet Archive, SpinXpress). With these search tools, Internet users had a practical way to locate blues tunes that could be remixed, photos of the Eiffel Tower that could be modified and sold, and articles about flower arrangements that could be legally republished. Advertisers, publishers, and other companies could search for images, songs, and text that could be licensed for commercial use.

Lessig and Brown worked hard to get other major Web and soft-

ware companies to make it easy for users to tag content with CC licenses. The ultimate goal was to make it easy for users to automate
their preferences. Joi Ito, a Japanese venture capitalist and democratic reformer who became the chair of the Creative Commons's
board of directors in 2006, put it this way: "Every input device that
you have, whether it's a camera phone, a digital camera or Power-
Point software, should allow you to automatically set it to the CC license that you want. And the minute you take that picture, you've
already expressed how you would want that picture to be used."

Creative Commons also urged open-source software communities to incorporate CC-made software into their applications so that
users can more easily tag content with the licenses or find licensed
works. Firefox, for example, has integrated a Creative Commons
search function into the drop-down menu of its browser search interface. It also has a plug-in module called MozCC that scans for
any CC metadata as you browse Web pages, and then reports on the
browser status bar how content is licensed. CC licenses have been
integrated into other software as well, such as Songbird, a free software media player, and Inkscape, a free vector-graphics program
similar to Adobe Illustrator.

Application by application, Web site by Web site, the Creative
Commons board and staff have tried to insinuate the licenses into as
many software applications and Web services as they could, in a kind
of behind-the-scenes enactment of Lessig's book *Code*. If code is
law, then let's write it ourselves! The diffusion of the licenses has
tended to occur through personal connections of Lessig, CC board
members, and friendly tech entrepreneurs and programmers. Joi Ito
used his contacts at Sony to persuade it to develop a video remix
Web site in Japan that uses CC licenses as the default choice. For
Sony, the licenses help the company avoid any whiff of legal impro-
priety because users must stipulate whether their video remixes may
be shared or not.

In 2006, Microsoft went so far as to come out with a plug-in
module for its Word program, enabling writers to tag their text
documents with CC licenses. At the time, many CC fans grumbled
at the hypocrisy of Microsoft, the five-hundred-pound gorilla of

proprietary software, embracing the Creative Commons, even in such a modest way. But for Lessig and CC board members, any business that chooses to advance the reach of free culture—in this case, by accessing the 400 million users of Microsoft Office—is welcomed. While this ecumenical tolerance has made the Creative Commons a big-tent movement with an eclectic assortment of players, it has also provoked bitter complaints in free software and Wikipedia circles that the Creative Commons promotes a fuzzy, incoherent vision of "freedom" in the digital world (an issue to which I return in chapter 9).

One vexing problem that CC developers confronted was how to digitally tag stand-alone files as CC-licensed work if they are not on the Web. How could one tag an MP3 file, for example, to show that the music is under a CC license? One problem with just inserting a CC tag onto the MP3 file is that anyone could fraudulently mark the file as CC-licensed. To prevent scams, Neeru Paharia, then CC assistant director, and other developers came up with a solution that requires any stand-alone digital files that are embedded with CC licenses to include a URL (Uniform Resource Locator) that links to a Web page verifying the assertions made on the file.

The practice of embedding CC license information on digital files has been called *digital rights expression*—a kind of benign analogue to digital rights management. The purpose is to embed information about the copyright status of a work *in* the digital file. Unlike DRM, the goal is not to try to build an infrastructure for enforcing those rights or controlling how people may use a work. "Instead of using technology to ensure that the consumer can't do anything with it," said Mike Linksvayer, CC vice president and former chief technology officer, "we're trying to use technology to ensure that people can find a CC-licensed work. If they're looking, for instance, for music that can remixed, then this information will help a search engine locate that information."[5]

Perhaps the neatest self-promotional trick that the Creative Commons has devised is to rely upon companies whose very business plans revolve around CC licenses. We will examine "open business" enterprises in chapter 10, but for now it is worth noting that a number of innovative companies use the licenses as a core element of their business strategy. These enterprises include Flickr (photo sharing), Magnatune (an online record label), Jamendo (a Luxembourg-based music site), and Revver (a video-sharing site that shares advertising revenues with creators).

Infrastructure grows old and occasionally needs to be updated and improved. The CC licenses have been no exception. As users have incorporated them into one medium after another, the unwitting omissions and infelicitous legal language of some parts of the licenses needed revisiting. After many months of discussions with many parts of the CC world, the Creative Commons issued a new set of 2.0 licenses in May 2004.[6] They did not differ substantially from the original ones, and in fact the changes would probably bore most nonlawyers. For example, version 2.0 included a provision that allows a licensor to require licensees to provide a link back to the licensor's work. The 2.0 licenses also clarify many complicated license options affecting music rights, and make clear that licensors make no warranties of title, merchantability, or fitness for use. Perhaps the biggest change in version 2.0 was the elimination of the choice of Attribution licenses. Since nearly 98 percent of all licensors chose Attribution, the Creative Commons decided to drop licenses without the Attribution requirement, thereby reducing the number of CC licenses from eleven to six.

Another set of major revisions to the licenses was taken up for discussion in 2006, and agreed upon in February 2007.[7] Once again, the layperson would care little for the debates leading to the changes, but considerable, sometimes heated discussion went into the revisions. In general, the 3.0 tweaks sought to make the licenses clearer, more useful, and more enforceable. The issue of "moral rights" under copyright law—an issue in many European countries—is explicitly addressed, as are the complications of the CC licenses and collecting societies. New legal language was introduced to ensure that people who remix works under other licenses, such as the GNU Free Documentation License (FDL), would be able to also use CC-licensed materials in the same work—an important provision for preventing free culture from devolving into "autistic islands" of legally incomptabile material. Besides helping align the CC world with Wikipedia (which uses the GNU FDL license), the 3.0 revisions also made harmonizing legal changes to take account of MIT and the Debian software development community.

By getting the CC licenses integrated into so many types of software and Web services, and even leveraging market players to embrace the sharing ethic, Creative Commons has managed to kill at least three birds with one stone. It has enlarged the universe of shareable Internet content. It has educated people to consider how copyright law affects them personally. And it has given visibility to its larger vision of free culture.

In one sense, the CC "machine" composed of the licenses, the CC-developed software, and the CC-friendly protocol was the engine for change. In another sense, the influence that Creative Commons has acquired derives from the social communities that gradually began to use its infrastructure. The social practice infused power into the "machine" even as the machine expanded the social practice. A virtuous cycle took hold, as the CC community used its self-devised legal and technological infrastructure to advance their shared cultural agenda.

Driving this cycle was an ever-growing staff and new managers working out of offices in downtown San Francisco. Although Lessig has been the chief executive officer and chairman of the board of Creative Commons for most of its existence, most day-to-day operating responsibilities fell to executive director Glenn Otis Brown until his departure in 2005, and then to general counsel Mia Garlick, who left in 2007. (Both took jobs at Google.) Key executives at Creative Commons in 2008 included Mike Linksvayer, vice president; Eric Steuer, creative director; Diane Peters, general counsel; Nathan Yergler, chief technology officer; and Jennifer Yip, operations manager. The annual budget, which was $750,000 in 2003, had grown to $3.6 million in 2008 (a sum that included the Science Commons project). Much of this funding came from foundations such as the John D. and Catherine T. MacArthur Foundation, the

William and Flora Hewlett Foundation, the Rockefeller Foundation, and Omidyar Network.

Once the CC machine had secured its footing, Lessig and the CC staff paid close attention to the movement—the social communities that find utility and meaning through Creative Commons—and to developing new software and projects that these early adopters would welcome. In 2006, the organization hit upon the idea of hosting a series of "salons" in major cities. The gatherings have become a big success, and are now replicated in cities throughout the world. Artists talk about how they use CC licenses; entrepreneurs explain how their business models work; remix artists perform their work. The events, free and open to the public, combine testimonials about free culture, personal networking, entrepreneurial idea-mongering, live performances, and partying. The CC crowd seems to enjoy partying; they do it well. Every December, there are gala anniversary parties in groovy San Francisco hot spots. There have been virtual parties in the immersive online world, Second Life. Because CC users tend to include some of the most adventurous artistic talent and eclectic innovators around—people who know where the truly cool night spots are—CC parties tend to be lively, good times. The parties in Rio and Dubrovnik, at the iCommons Summits, were memorable international happenings, for example—occasions, as one self-styled Lothario boasted to me, "where a guy could dance with a woman from every continent of the world in a single evening."

Add to the mix tech-oriented college students, another key sector of free culture activism, and there is even more youthful energy. Hundreds of college students participate in a nationwide student organization, FreeCulture.org, later renamed Students for Free Culture. The group got its start in 2004 when some students at Swarthmore College began investigating the reliability of Diebold electronic voting machines; the company invoked copyright law in an attempt to keep the problems secret, leading to a public confrontation that Diebold lost. Nelson Pavlosky and Luke Smith, who were also inspired by Lessig's advocacy, co-founded the group, which has since spawned over thirty quasi-autonomous chapters on campuses across the United States and a few foreign nations. The organization tries to be a grassroots force on Internet, digital technology, and copyright issues. It has mounted protests against CDs with digital rights management, for example, and hosted film remixing contests and exhibits of CC-licensed art at NYU and Harvard. Students for Free Culture also organized a "no-profit record company/recording collective," the Antenna Alliance, which gave bands free recording space and distributed their CC-licensed music to college radio stations.

We have looked at the machine and many parts of the movement, but not at one of the most significant forces fueling Creative Commons—the dozens of national projects to adapt the licenses to legal systems around the world. The long-term reverberations of this movement—which includes activists in Brazil, Croatia, South Africa, Egypt, Peru, Scotland, and dozens of other countries—are only beginning to be felt.

8

FREE CULTURE GOES GLOBAL

*The commoners mount a transnational mobilization
to build their own digital commons.*

It is a measure of Lessig's ambition for Creative Commons that only
five months after the release of the licenses, in April 2003, he instigated a move to take the idea global. Glenn Brown remembers ob-
jecting, "I don't know how we're going to get this done! Larry was
like, 'We have no other choice. We *have* to do this. This needs to be
an international organization.' "[1]

Professor James Boyle, a board member, was aghast. "That's the
stupidest thing I've ever heard," he said upon hearing the idea. "I
was practically foaming at the mouth," he recalled, noting that it was
"just insane" to try to adapt the licenses to the mind-boggling complexities of copyright laws in scores of nations.[2] But Lessig, determined to make the Creative Commons an international project,
proceeded to hire Christiane Asschenfeldt (now Christiane
Henckel von Donnersmarck), a Berlin-based copyright lawyer
whom he had met the previous summer at an iLaw (Internet Law)
conference in Cambridge, Massachusetts. He charged her with
helping project leaders in different countries adapt the licenses (or,
in computerese, "port" them) to their respective national legal
codes.

Asschenfeldt set about inventing a system for gathering teams
of volunteers, usually associated with a law school or technology
institute, to become CC affiliates. Once an affiliate institution and
project lead are chosen, the project lead produces a first draft of
the licenses, which then undergoes public discussion, rewriting,
and a final review by the new international arm of Creative Commons, CC International.[3] (Confusingly, this project was originally
called "iCommons," a name that in 2006 was reassigned to a new

CC spinoff group that convenes the international free culture movement.)

In a pre-Internet context, the whole idea of a creating a new international license architecture and network of legal experts might seem ridiculously unrealistic. But by 2003 there were enough examples of "distributed intelligence" popping up that it no longer seemed so crazy to think that a passionate corps of dispersed volunteers could collaborate as catalysts for change. In any case, following the *Eldred* defeat, Lessig and Brown came to believe, as discussed earlier, that the Creative Commons needed to be both a machine and a movement.

Going international with the licenses offered an appealing way to grow both simultaneously without forcing unpleasant trade-offs between the two, at least initially. Drafting the licenses for a country, for example, helps convene top lawyers committed to the idea of legal sharing and collaboration while also mobilizing diverse constituencies who are the potential leaders of a movement.

According to Jonathan Zittrain, an early collaborator on the project and a board member, Creative Commons at the international level is more of a "persuasive, communicative enterprise than a legal licensing one."[4] It is a vehicle for starting a process for engaging public-spirited lawyers, law scholars, and all manner of creators. The licenses do have specific legal meanings in their respective legal jurisdictions, of course, or are believed to have legal application. (Only three courts, in the Netherlands and Spain, have ever ruled on the legal status of the CC licenses. In two instances the courts enforced the licenses; in the other case, in which the defendant lost, the validity of the licenses was not at issue.)[5] Apart from their legal meaning, the licenses' most important function may be as a social signaling device. They let people announce, "I participate in and celebrate the sharing economy." The internationalization of the CC licenses has also been a way of "localizing" the free culture movement.

The first nation to port the CC licenses was Japan. This was partly an outgrowth of a five-month sabbatical that Lessig had spent in Tokyo, from late 2002 through early 2003. There were already stirrings of dissatisfaction with copyright law in Japan. Koichiro Hayashi, a professor who had once worked for the telecom giant NTT, had once proposed a so-called d-mark system to allow copyright owners to forfeit the statutory term of copyright protection and voluntarily declare a shorter term for their works. In the spring of 2003, a team of Japanese lawyers associated with a technology research institute, the Global Communications Center (GLOCOM), working with CC International in Berlin, set about porting the licenses to Japanese law.

Yuko Noguchi, a former Lessig student and lawyer who later became the legal project lead, explained that the CC licenses are a culturally attractive way for Japanese to address the structural problems of copyright law. Japan is a country that prizes harmony and dislikes confrontation. The licenses offer a way to promote legal sharing without forcing bitter public policy conflicts with major content industries.[6] (Partly for such reasons, CC Japan shifted its affiliation to the University of Tokyo in 2006.) In a culture that enjoys the sharing of comics, animation, haiku, and other works, the CC Japan licenses, launched in January 2004, have been used by a diverse range of artists and companies.

During his sojourn in Japan, Lessig had a fateful meeting with Joichi Ito, who in many ways embodies the tech sophistication, democratic zeal, and cosmopolitan style of the international Creative Commons movement. Widely known as Joi (pronounced "Joey"), Ito, forty-two, was born in Japan and educated in the United States. Disaffected with formal education in the U.S., where he studied computer science and physics, he dropped out and began his highly unusual career in Japan as an activist, entrepreneur, and venture capitalist. He has worked as a nightclub disc jockey, and brought industrial music and the rave scene to Japan, but he has also become a talented venture capitalist and early stage investor in such companies as Six Apart, Technorati, Flickr, SocialText, Dopplr, and Rupture. Lessig and Ito became close friends; Ito later joined the Creative Commons board. He was appointed chairman of the board in 2007 and then, in 2008, he became chief executive officer when

Lessig left to start a congressional reform project. Duke law professor James Boyle, a board member, replaced Ito as chairman.

Once it went public, the very idea of Creative Commons attracted many other people like Ito to its ranks: educated, tech-savvy,
culturally fluent, activist-minded. In fact, following the American
launch of Creative Commons, volunteers from many countries
began to approach the organization, asking if they could port the
licenses to their own legal systems. Finland became the second nation to adopt the licenses, in May 2004, followed a month later by
Germany. In Europe, the early adopters included Denmark, Hungary, Scotland, Slovenia, Sweden, and Malta. In South America, CC
licenses were introduced in Argentina, Chile, and Peru. In Asia,
Malaysia and China ported the licenses, as did Australia. Israel was
the first Middle Eastern country to port the licenses.

As each jurisdiction introduces its licenses, it typically hosts a
gala public event to celebrate and publicize free culture. News
media and government officials are invited. There are panel discussions about copyright law and digital culture; performances by musicians who use the licenses; and endorsements by prominent
universities, cultural institutions, and authors. Lessig has made it a
practice to fly in and deliver an inspirational speech. Few international launches of CC licenses have been more spectacular or con-
sequential than the one staged by Brazil in March 2004.

Brazil, the First Free Culture Nation

Luiz Inácio Lula da Silva had just been elected president of Brazil,
and he was eager to stake out a new set of development policies
to allow his nation to plot its own economic and cultural future.
His government, reflecting his electoral mandate, resented the coercive effects of international copyright law and patent law. To tackle
some of these issues on the copyright front, President Lula appointed Gilberto Gil, the renowned singer-songwriter, as his minister of culture.

Gil became a revered cultural figure when he helped launch a new musical style, *tropicalismo*, in the late 1960s, giving Brazil a fresh, international cachet. The music blended national styles of music with pop culture and was inflected with political and moral themes. As one commentator put it, *tropicalismo* was "a very '60s attempt to capture the chaotic, swirling feel of Brazil's perennially uneven modernization, its jumble of wealth and poverty, of rural and urban, of local and global. . . . They cut and pasted styles with an abandon that, amid today's sample-happy music scene, sounds up-to-the-minute."[7] The military dictatorship then running the government considered *tropicalismo* sufficiently threatening that it imprisoned Gil for several months before forcing him into exile, in London. Gil continued writing and recording music, however, and eventually returned to Brazil.[8]

This history matters, because when Gil was appointed culture minister, he brought with him a rare political sophistication and public veneration. His moral stature and joyous humanity allowed him to transcend politics as conventionally practiced. "Gil wears shoulder-length dreadlocks and is apt to show up at his ministerial offices dressed in the simple white linens that identify him as a follower of the Afro-Brazilian religion *candomblé*," wrote American journalist Julian Dibbell in 2004. "Slouching in and out of the elegant Barcelona chairs that furnish his office, taking the occasional sip from a cup of pinkish herbal tea, he looks—and talks—less like an elder statesman than the posthippie, multiculturalist, Taoist intellectual he is."[9]

As luck had it, Dibbell—author of the article on cyber-rape that had enticed Lessig to investigate digital culture in the first place (see chapter 3)—was living in Rio at the time. He was friendly with Hermano Vianna, a prominent intellectual who knew Gil and was deeply into the music scene and digital technology. Between Dibbell and Vianna, a flurry of introductions was made, and within months Larry Lessig, John Perry Barlow, and Harvard law professor William Fisher were sitting with Gil, Vianna, and Dibbell in Gil's Rio de Janeiro penthouse across from the beach.[10] Lessig's mission was to pitch the Creative Commons licenses to Gil, and in particular, get Gil's thoughts about a new CC Sampling license that would let musicians authorize sampling of their songs.

"Gil knew that sampling was a central driving power for contemporary creativity well before digital instruments came along," recalled Vianna. "*Tropicalismo* was all about sampling different ideas and different cultures. *Tropicalismo* was about juxtapositions, not fusions, and in this sense was heir to a long tradition of Brazilian modern thought and art that began with the cultural anthropology of the early modernists, in the 1920s and 1930s, and can be traced back to all debates about Brazilian identity in the 20th century."[11]

Lessig did not need to argue his case. Gil immediately understood what Creative Commons was trying to accomplish culturally and politically. He was enthusiastic about CC licenses, the proposed Sampling license, and the prospect of using his ministry to advance a vision of free culture.

By further coincidence, Ronaldo Lemos da Silva, then a Brazilian law student who has been described as a "Lessig of the Southern Hemisphere," had just completed his studies at Harvard Law School. He was well acquainted with Creative Commons and was considering his future when friends at the Fundação Getulio Vargas (FGV), a Rio de Janeiro university, urged him to join them in founding a new law school. The school would host a new Center for Technology and Society to study law and technology from the perspective of developing nations like Brazil. Lemos accepted, and the center soon became the host for CC Brazil and myriad free culture projects.

This alignment of intellectual firepower, artistic authority, and political clout was extraordinary—and a major coup for Creative Commons. The culture minister of the world's fifth-largest country and tenth-largest economy—whose own forty-year career was based on a remix sensibility—became a spirited champion of the CC licenses and free culture. Unlike most culture ministers, who treat culture chiefly as an aesthetic amenity, Gil took the economic and technological bases of creativity seriously. He wanted to show

how creativity can be a tool for political and cultural emancipation, and how government can foster that goal. It turned out that Brazil, with its mix of African, Portuguese, and indigenous cultures and its colorful mix of vernacular traditions, was a perfect laboratory for such experimentation.

One of the first collaborations between Creative Commons and the Brazilian government involved the release of a special CC-GPL license in December 2003.[12] This license adapted the General Public License for software by translating it into Portuguese and putting it into the CC's customary "three layers"—a plain-language version, a lawyers' version compatible with the national copyright law, and a machine-readable metadata expression of the license. The CC-GPL license, released in conjunction with the Free Software Foundation, was an important international event because it gave the imprimatur of a major world government to free software and the social ethic of sharing and reuse. Brazil has since become a champion of GNU/Linux and free software in government agencies and the judiciary. It regards free software and open standards as part of a larger fight for a "development agenda" at the World Intellectual Property Organization and the World Trade Organization. In a related vein, Brazil has famously challenged patent and trade policies that made HIV/AIDS drugs prohibitively expensive for thousands of sick Brazilians.

When the full set of CC Brazil licenses was finally launched—at the Fifth International Free Software Forum, in Port Alegre on June 4, 2004—it was a major national event. Brazilian celebrities, government officials, and an enthusiastic crowd of nearly two thousand people showed up. Gil, flying in from a cabinet meeting in Brasília, arrived late. When he walked into the auditorium, the panel discussion under way immediately stopped, and there was a spontaneous standing ovation.[13] "It was like a boxer entering the arena for a heavyweight match," recalled Glenn Otis Brown. "He had security guards on both sides of him as he walked up the middle aisle. There were flashbulbs, and admirers trailing him, and this wave of people in the audience cresting as he walked by."[14]

Gil originally planned to release three of his songs under the new CC Sampling license—dubbed the "Recombo" license—but his record label, Warner Bros., balked. He eventually released one song, "Oslodum," that he had recorded for an indie label. "One way to think about it," said Brown, "is that now, anybody in the world can jam with Gilberto Gil." [15]

As culture minister, Gil released all materials from his agency under a CC license, and persuaded the Ministry of Education as well as Radiobrás, the government media agency, to do the same. He also initiated the Cultural Points (Pontos de Cultura) program, which has given small grants to scores of community centers in poor neighborhoods so that residents can learn how to produce their own music and video works. Since industry concentration and payola make it virtually impossible for newcomers to get radio play and commercially distribute their CDs, according to many observers, the project has been valuable in allowing a fresh wave of grassroots music to "go public" and reach new audiences.

For developing countries, the real challenge is finding ways to tap the latent creativity of the "informal" economy operating on the periphery of formal market systems. Brazil is rich with such creative communities, as exemplified by the flourishing *tecnobrega* music scene in the northeast and north regions of Brazil. Ronaldo Lemos says that *tecnobrega*—"a romantic sound with a techno-beat and electronica sound" [16]—arose on the fringes of the mainstream music marketplace through "sound system parties" attended by thousands of people every weekend. Local artists produce and sell about four hundred new CDs every year, but both the production and distribution take place outside the traditional music industry. The CDs can't be found in retail stores but are sold entirely by street vendors for only $1.50. The CDs serve as advertising for the weekend parties. The music is "born free" in the sense that the *tecnobrega* scene doesn't consider copyrights as part of its business model and does not enforce copyrights on their CDs; it invites and authorizes people to share and reuse the content. [17] (The *tecnobrega* business model is discussed at greater length in chapter 10.)

Lemos believes the CC licenses are an important tool for help-ing grassroots creativity in Brazil to "go legitimate." He explains, "Creative Commons provides a simple, non-bureaucratic structure for intellectual property that might help to integrate the massive marginal culture that is arising in the peripheries, with the 'official,' 'formal' structures of the Brazilian economy." [18] Freed of the block-buster imperatives of the current music market, the CC licenses allow creativity in the informal "social commons" to flow—yet not be appropriated by commercial vendors. People can experiment, generate new works, and learn what resonates with music fans. All of this is a predicate for building new types of open markets, says Lemos. *Tecnobrega* is just one of many open-business models that use the free circulation of music to make money.

Since its launch in June 2004, Lemos and the CC Brazil office have instigated a number of projects to demonstrate how sharing and collaboration can spur economic and cultural development. They have promoted free software and open business models for music and film and started collaborations with allies in other devel-oping nations. Nigerian filmmakers inspired the People's Cinema in Brazil, a project to help people use audio-video technology to pro-duce their own films and develop audiences for them. The *culture-livre* (free culture) project, a joint effort of Creative Commons in Brazil and South Africa, is using the ccMixter software to encourage young musicians to mix traditional African instruments with con-temporary sensibilities, and launch their careers. [19]

In Brazil, there are open-publishing projects for scientific jour-nals; [20] a Web site that brings together a repository of short films; [21] and Overmundo, a popular site for cultural commentary by Internet users. [22] TramaVirtual, an open-platform record label that lets musi-cians upload their music and fans download it for free, now features more than thirty-five thousand artists. [23] (By contrast, the largest commercial label in Brazil, Sony-BMG, released only twelve CDs of Brazilian music in 2006, according to Lemos.)

"Cultural production is becoming increasingly disconnected from traditional media forms," said Lemos, because mass media in-stitutions "are failing to provide the adequate incentives for culture to be produced and circulated. . . . Cultural production is migrating to civil society and/or the peripheries, which more or less already operate in a 'social commons' environment, and do not depend on intellectual property within their business models."[24]

As more people have adopted legal modes of copying and sharing under CC licenses, it is changing the social and political climate for copyright reform. Now that CC Brazil can cite all sorts of successful free culture ventures, it can more persuasively advocate for a Brazilian version of the fair use doctrine and press for greater photocopying privileges in educational settings (which are legally quite restrictive).

Although the CC licenses are now familiar to many Brazilians, they have encountered some resistance, mostly from lawyers. "Among all other audiences—musicians, artists, writers—they were extremely well received," said Lemos. When he presented the CC licenses to an audience of three hundred lawyers, however, he recalls that a famous law professor publicly scoffed: "You're saying this because you're young, foolish, and communist." Three years later, Lemos discovered that the professor was using his intellectual property textbook in her class.

As a unique global ambassador of creative sharing, Gilberto Gil did a lot to take the CC licenses to other nations and international forums such as the World Intellectual Property Organization. The day before his 2004 benefit concert for the Creative Commons in New York City with David Byrne, Gil delivered a powerful speech explaining the political implications of free culture:

A global movement has risen up in affirmation of digital culture. This movement bears the banners of free software and digital inclusion, as well as the banner of the endless expansion of the circulation of information and creation, and it is the perfect model for a Latin-American developmental cultural policy (other developments are possible) of the most anti-xenophobic, anti-authoritarian, anti-bureaucratizing, anti-centralizing, and for the very reason, profoundly democratic and transformative sort.[25]

The Brazilian government was making digital culture "one of its strategic public policies," Gil said, because "the most important political battle that is being fought today in the technological, economic, social and cultural fields has to do with free software and with the method digital freedom has put in place for the production of shared knowledge. This battle may even signify a change in subjectivity, with critical consequences for the very concept of civilization we shall be using in the near future." [26]

To advance this new paradigm, Gil, who left his post as culture minister in 2008, called for the rise of "new creative *mestizo* [hybrid] industries" that break with the entrenched habits of the past. Such businesses "have to be flexible and dynamic; they have to be negotiated and re-negotiated, so that they may contemplate the richness, the complexity, the dynamism and the speed of reality itself and of society itself, without becoming impositions." [27]

National Variations of a Global Idea

When it comes to free culture, Brazil is clearly a special case. But citizens in more than seventy nations have stepped forward to build a CC presence in their societies. Each has shown its own distinctive interests.

Tomislav Medak, a philosopher by training and a copyfighter by circumstance, runs the Multimedia Institute in Zagreb, Croatia, a cultural center that consists mostly of a performance space, a lounge, and a café. The organization survives on donations from the likes of George Soros's Open Society Institute, but it thrives because it is the gathering place for an avant-garde corps of electronic music-makers, publishers, performers, and hackers. Mainstream Croats would probably describe the community as a bunch of "cyber-Serbian-gay-Communists," said Medak, which he concedes is not inaccurate. [28] But the institute is not just a coalition of minority interests; it is also broad-spectrum champion of cultural freedom. It sees free software, civil liberties, and artists' rights as core elements of a democratic society that it would like to build.

The Multimedia Institute was understandably excited when it

learned about Creative Commons and Lessig's vision of free culture. With help from some lawyer friends, the institute in January 2004 ported the CC licenses to Croatian law, primarily as a way to empower artists and counteract the dominance of corporate media and expansive copyright laws. "We are a country where the IP framework is very young, and most of the policies are protection-driven. Most policies are dictated by official institutions that just translate international documents into local legislation," Medak said.[29] This commercial/copyright regime tends to stifle the interests of emerging artists, amateurs, consumers and local culture.

"In the post-socialist period," said Medak, "our society has been hugely depleted of the public domain, or commons. The privatization process and the colonizing of cultural spaces have been blatant over the last couple of years, especially in Zagreb. So the Creative Commons has fit into a larger effort to try to recapture some of those public needs that were available, at least ideologically, in socialist societies. Now they are for real."[30] Medak has since gone on to become a leader of iCommons and the host of the international iCommons Summit in 2007, which brought several hundred commoners from fifty nations to Dubrovnik.

In Scotland, government and other public-sector institutions have been huge fans of the CC licenses. In fact, museums, archives, and educational repositories have been the primary advocates of the CC Scotland licenses, says Andrés Guadamuz, a law professor at the Research Centre for Studies in Intellectual Property and Technology Law at the University of Edinburgh. "People who want to try to share information in the public sector are turning to Creative Commons because they realize that here is a license that is already made."[31]

The BBC was a pioneer in making its archived television and radio programs available to the public for free. In 2003, inspired by the CC licenses, the BBC drafted its own "Creative Archive" license as a way to open up its vast collection of taxpayer-financed television and radio programs.[32] The license was later adopted by Channel 4, the Open University, the British Film Institute, and the Museum, Libraries and Archives Council. Although the Creative

Archive license has similar goals as the CC licenses, it contains several significant differences: it restricts use of video programs to
United Kingdom citizens only, and it prohibits use of materials for
political or charitable campaigns and for any derogatory purposes.

The CC licenses have proven useful, also, to the British Museum
and National Archives. In 2004, these and other British educational
institutions were pondering how they should make their publicly
funded digital resources available for reuse. A special government
panel, the Common Information Environment, recommended
usage of the CC licenses because they were already international in
scope. The panel liked that the licenses allow Web links in licensed
materials, which could help users avoid the complications of formal
registration. The panel also cited the virtues of "human readable
deeds" and machine-readable metadata.[33]

As it happened, a team of Scottish legal scholars led by a private
attorney, Jonathan Mitchell, successfully ported the licenses and released them a few months later, in December 2005. The Scottish effort had been initiated a year earlier when Mitchell and his
colleagues objected that the U.K. CC licenses then being drafted
were too rooted in English law and not sufficiently attuned to Scottish law. Since the introduction of the CC Scotland licenses, public-
sector institutions have enthusiastically embraced them. Museums
use the licenses on MP3 files that contain audio tours, for example,
as well as on Web pages, exhibition materials, and photographs of
artworks. Interestingly, in England and Wales, individual artists and
creative communities seem to be more active than public-sector institutions in using the licenses.

The use of CC licenses for government information and
publicly funded materials is inspiring similar efforts in other countries. Governments are coming to realize that they are one of the
primary stewards of intellectual property, and that the wide dissemination of their work—statistics, research, reports, legislation,
judicial decisions—can stimulate economic innovation, scientific
progress, education, and cultural development. Unfortunately, as
Anne Fitzgerald, Brian Fitzgerald, and Jessica Coates of Australia
have pointed out, "putting all such material into the public domain

runs the risk that material which is essentially a public and national asset will be appropriated by the private sector, without any benefit to either the government or the taxpayers."[34] For example, the private sector may incorporate the public-domain material into a value-added proprietary model and find other means to take the information private. The classic instance of this is West Publishing's dominance in the republishing of U.S. federal court decisions. Open-content licenses offer a solution by ensuring that taxpayer-financed works will be available to and benefit the general public.

In the United States, the National Institutes of Health has pursued a version of this policy by requiring that federally funded research be placed in an open-access archive or journal within twelve months of its commercial publication. The European Commission announced in 2007 that it plans to build a major open-access digital repository for publicly funded research.[35] In Mexico, the Sistema Internet de la Presidencia, or Presidency Internet System (SIP), decided in 2006 to adopt CC licenses for all content generated by the Mexican presidency on the Internet—chiefly the president's various Web sites, Internet radio station, and documents.[36] In Italy, CC Italy is exploring legislation to open up national and local government archives. It also wants new contract terms for those who develop publicly funded information so that it will automatically be available in the future.[37]

Laboratories of Free Culture

In 2005, about two years after the launch of CC International, twenty-one jurisdictions around the world had adopted the licenses. (A legal jurisdiction is not necessarily the same as a nation because places like Scotland, Puerto Rico, and Catalonia—which have their own CC licenses—are not separate nations.) Under a new director of CC International, copyright attorney Catharina Maracke, who took over the license-porting project in 2006, the pace of license adoption has continued. By August 2008, forty-seven jurisdictions had ported the CC licenses, and a few dozen more had their projects under way. The CC affiliates have now reached a sufficient critical mass that they represent a new sort of international constituency for the sharing economy. The CC network of legal scholars, public institutions, artistic sectors, and Internet users is not just a motivated global community of talent, but a new sort of transnational cultural movement: a digital republic of commoners.

To be sure, some nations have more institutional backing than others, and some have more enthusiastic and active projects than others. CC Poland reported in 2006 that its biggest challenge was "a complete lack of financial and organizational support, in particular from our partner organization." [38] (This was remedied in 2008 when CC Poland entered into a partnership with an interdisciplinary center at the University of Warsaw and with a law firm.) CC affiliates in smaller developing countries with fewer resources—especially in Africa—often have to beg and scrape to pull together resources to supplement the work of volunteers.

Not surprisingly, the American CC licenses—a version of which was spun off as a generic license, as opposed to jurisdiction-specific licenses—are the most used. In a pioneering study of license usage in January 2007, Giorgos Cheliotis of Singapore Management University and his co-authors conservatively estimated that there were 60 million distinct items of CC content on the Internet—a sum that rose to 90 million by the end of 2007. Over 80 percent of these items use a license that is not jurisdiction-specific; the remaining 20 percent are spread among the thirty-three nations included in the study. [39] The highest volume of license usage per capita can be found in European nations—particularly Spain, Germany, Belgium, France, Italy, and Croatia—which were among the earliest adopters of the licenses. In absolute terms, the heaviest usage can be seen in Spain, Germany, France, South Korea, Italy, and Japan. [40] Overall, however, CC usage outside of the United States is still fairly new, and usage and growth rates vary immensely from country to country.

As a fledgling network, the international CC community is a rudimentary platform for change. Its members are still groping toward a shared understanding of their work and devising new systems of communication and collaboration. But a great deal of cross-border collaboration is occurring. A variety of free culture advocates have constituted themselves as the Asia Commons and met in Bangkok to collaborate on issues of free software, citizen access to government information, and industry antipiracy propaganda. CC Italy has invited leaders of neighboring countries— France, Switzerland, Austria, Croatia, and Slovenia—to share their experiences and work together. A CC Latin America project started *Scripta*, a new Spanish-language journal based in Ecuador, to discuss free software and free culture issues affecting the continent.

CC leaders in Finland, France, and Australia have published books about their licensing projects.[41] CC Brazil and CC South Africa have collaborated on a project about copyright and developing nations. CC Canada is working with partners to develop an online, globally searchable database of Canadian works in the Canadian public domain. CC Salons have been held in Amsterdam, Toronto, Berlin, Beijing, London, Warsaw, Seoul, Taipei, and Johannesburg.

In the Netherlands, CC project lead Paul Keller engineered a breakthrough that may overcome the persistent objections of European collecting societies to CC-licensed content. Collecting societies in Europe generally insist that any musician that they represent transfer all of their copyrights to the collective. This means that professional musicians cannot distribute their works under a CC license. Artists who are already using CC licenses cannot join the collecting societies in order to receive royalties for commercial uses of their works. In this manner, collecting societies in many European nations have effectively prevented many musicians from using the CC licenses.

In 2007, however, CC Netherlands negotiated a one-year pilot program with two Dutch collecting societies, Buma and Stemra, to let artists use CC NonCommercial licenses for parts of their repertoire.[42] As a result, artists will have greater choice in the release of their works and the ability to easily manage their rights via a Web site. Other European CC affiliates hope that this Dutch experiment will break the long stalemate on this issue and persuade their collecting societies to be more flexible.

The Developing Nations License

One of the boldest experiments in the CC world was the creation of the Developing Nations license, launched in September 2004. A year earlier, Lessig had approached James Love, the director of Knowledge Ecology International (previously the Consumer Project on Technology), to ask him to craft a CC license that might help developing countries. Love proposed that the CC offer a "rider" at the end of its existing licenses so that people using the licenses could exempt developing nations from, say, the NonCommercial or NoDerivatives license restrictions. So, for example, if a textbook author wanted to let developing nations copy her book for either commercial or noncommercial purposes, she could add a rider authorizing this practice.

Love was trying to do for books and journal articles what is already possible for drugs—the legalization of a commercial market for generic equivalents. Love had seen how generic drugs could reach people only because for-profit companies were able to produce and sell the drugs; nonprofit or philanthropic distribution is just not powerful enough. But the market for generic drugs is possible only because of laws that authorize companies to make legal knockoffs of proprietary drugs once the patent terms expire. Love hoped to do the same via a Developing Nations license for copyrighted works: "It would create an opportunity for the publishing equivalent of generic drug manufacturers who make 'generic' books. In developing countries, you have whole libraries full of photocopied books. You would not have libraries there if people didn't engage in these practices." [43]

In the end, Creative Commons offered the Developing Nations license as a separate license, not a rider. It had simple terms: "You must attribute the work in the manner specified by the author or licensor (but not in any way that suggests that they endorse you or your use of the work)"—and the license was valid only in non–high income nations, as determined by United Nations' statistics. Although the release of the license got considerable press coverage, actual usage of the license was extremely small. The most prominent use was totally unexpected—for architectural designs. Architecture for Humanity, a California nonprofit, used the license for its designs of low-cost housing and health centers. The organization wanted to give away its architectural plans to poor countries while not letting its competitors in the U.S. use them for free.[44]

The expected uses of the Developing Nations license never materialized. In 2006, Love said, "The license is there, but people who might be willing to use it are not really aware of it." He worried that the license "hasn't really been explained in a way that would be obvious to them," and ventured that there may be "a need for a re-marketing campaign." By this time, however, the license had attracted the ire of Richard Stallman for its limitations on "freedom."[45] It prohibited copying of a work in certain circumstances (in high-income countries) even for noncommercial purposes, and so authorized only a partial grant of freedom, not a universal one. "Well, the whole point was *not* to be universal," said Love. "The license is for people that are unwilling to share with high-income countries, but are willing to share with developing countries. So it actually expands the commons, but only in developing countries."[46]

The controversy that grew up around the Developing Nations license illuminates the different approaches to movement building that Lessig and Stallman represent. Lessig's advocacy for free culture has been an exploratory journey in pragmatic idealism; Stallman's advocacy for free software has been more of a crusade of true believers in a core philosophy. For Stallman, the principles of "freedom" are unitary and clear, and so the path forward is fairly self-evident and unassailable. For Lessig, the principles of freedom are more situational and evolving and subject to the consensus of key creative communities. The flexibility has enabled a broad-spectrum movement to emerge, but it does not have the ideological coherence of, say, the free software movement.

Several factors converged to make it attractive for Creative

Commons to revoke the Developing Nations license. Some people in the open-access publishing movement disliked the license because it did not comply with its stated standards of openness. In addition, Richard Stallman's increasingly strident objections to Creative Commons licenses were starting to alarm some segments of the "free world." What if Internet content became Balkanized through a series of incompatible licenses, and the movement were riven with sectarian strife? Stallman objected not only to the Developing Nations license, but to attempts by Creative Commons to get Wikipedia to make its content, licensed under the GNU Free Documentation license, compatible with the CC licenses. By 2007 this dispute had been simmering for four years (see pages 212–217).

Finally, many CC staff members regarded the Developing Nations and Sampling licenses as misbegotten experiments. Fewer than 0.01 percent of uses of CC licenses at the time involved the Developing Nations license, and the Sampling license was used by a relatively small community of remix artists and musicians. If eliminating two little-used niche licenses could neutralize objections from the open access and free software movements and achieve a greater philosophical and political solidarity in the "free world," many CC partisans regarded a rescission of the licenses as a modest sacrifice, if not a net gain.

In June 2007, Creative Commons announced that it was officially retiring the two licenses.[47] In a formal statement, Lessig explained, "These licenses do not meet the minimum standards of the Open Access movement. Because this movement is so important to the spread of science and knowledge, we no longer believe it correct to promote a standalone version of this license."[48] The Creative Commons also revoked the Sampling license because it "only permits the remix of the licensed work, not the freedom to share it." (Two other sampling licenses that permit noncommercial sharing—SamplingPlus and NonCommercial SamplingPlus—were retained.)

Anyone could still use the Sampling or Developing Nations license if they wished; they still exist, after all. It's just that the Creative Commons no longer supports them. While the actual impact of the license revocations was minor, it did have major

symbolic and political significance in the commons world. It sig-
naled that the Creative Commons was capitulating to objections
by free software advocates and the concerns of open access publishing activists.

The iCommons Network

As an international network of CC affiliates grew, it naturally
spawned new pockets of activism. Lessig explained: "Once a country gets launched, it becomes a cell of activism. Sometimes it is very
traditional—Creative Commons Korea is made up of a bunch of
federal judges—and sometimes it is very radical—Creative Commons Croatia is made of up a bunch of real activists who want to
change copyright. Creative Commons Poland, too, is a bunch of
really smart law graduates. But then there is the artist community,
on the other side, many of whom want to blow up copyright; they
just think it is ridiculous.

"So the opportunity and problem we faced at that point," said
Lessig, "was, 'Well, what are we going to do with these activists?' Because Creative Commons wanted to facilitate activism, of course,
but it wasn't as if we could bring activism into our core because it
would make it more suspect."[49]

The first steps toward organizing this protocommunity of activists came in March 2005, when eighty people from the various
international licensing projects convened in Boston to talk about
their shared challenges.[50] It quickly became clear that everyone
wanted a forum in which to learn from one another, coordinate
their work, and see themselves as something larger . . . perhaps a
new sort of movement.

Here again was the tension between "the movement" and "the
machine." As neutral stewards of the licenses, the CC affiliates could
not become full-throated advocates of a new international free culture movement. Their mission was preserving the integrity and utility of the licenses for all users, not advocacy. To avoid this problem,
the Creative Commons, with an infusion of seed money and CC
leaders, in 2006 started a new nonprofit organization, iCommons.

iCommons, a registered charity in the United Kingdom, is led by Heather Ford, a South African who met Lessig at Stanford and went back to her country to evangelize the Creative Commons licenses. Working out of Johannesburg, Ford is the activist counterpart to her Berlin licensing colleagues. She is a gregarious, spirited organizer who keeps tabs on activist gambits in dozens of nations and pulls together annual iCommons "summits."

The iCommons conferences are something of a staging area for a new type of global citizenship in the digital "free world." The first conference, in Rio de Janeiro in June 2006, attracted more than three hundred commoners from fifty nations.[51] The second one, in Dubrovnik, Croatia, drew a somewhat larger and still more diverse crowd, and a third was held in Sapporo, Japan, in 2008. The free and open-source software community and the Creative Commons network are two of the largest, most influential blocs participating in iCommons, although Wikipedians represent a growing sector. But there are many other factions. There are musicians from the indie music, netlabels, and the remix scene. Filmmakers trying to reform fair use legal norms and video artists who are into mashups. Bloggers and citizen-journalists and social-networking fans. Gamers and participants in immersive environments like Second Life and World of Warcraft. Open business entrepreneurs who regard free software and CC licenses as key elements of their competitive, profit-making strategies.

From Japan, there were anime artists who are into remixes. From South Africa, print-on-demand research publishers. A bare-chested Brazilian guitarist traded thoughts about copyright law with a Zagreb performer. An Amsterdam hacker with a punk t-shirt shared a smoke with an American academic. From India, there was Lawrence Liang, founder of the Alternative Law Forum, a leading intellectual about copyright law and economic and social inequality. From Syria, there was Anas Tawileh, who is working to produce the Arab Commons, a directory of Arabic works released under any of the CC licenses. He hopes it will counteract "the weak representation of the Arabic language on the Internet, the shallow nature of Arabic content currently available and the consumption rather than the production of knowledge." From the United States, there was Michael Smolens, an entrepreneur who started dotSUB, a captioning system to make any film available in any language.

The convergence of so many players in the nascent sharing economy, assembled in the flesh, was a bracing glimpse into a new kind of cosmopolitan, democratic sensibility. The program organizers stated their aspirations this way: "How do we help one another to build a commons that nurtures local communities while respecting the needs of others? How can we move towards the growth of a 'Global Commons Community'?"[52]

Although most international commoners seem to be culturally progressive and politically engaged, they cannot be situated along a left-right ideological spectrum. This is because commoners tend to be more pragmatic and improvisational than ideological. They are focused on building specific projects to facilitate sharing and creativity, based on open-source principles. Their enthusiasm is for cool software, effective legal interventions, and activist innovations, not sectarian debate.

It is not as if politics has been banished. For example, some critics have questioned the "elite" origins and governance structure of iCommons, which was hatched by CC board members and leaders. David Berry, a free culture advocate who teaches at the University of Sussex, complained on a listserv that iCommons was "creating a corporate machine rather than a democratic one."[53] He cited ambiguity in the powers of the organization, the murky process by which the iCommons code of conduct was adopted, and the board's selection of community council members. Still other critics have grumbled at the Creative Commons's collaboration with Microsoft in developing a licensing feature within the Word application.

When pressed at the 2006 iCommons Summit to develop more formal organizational structure, Lessig begged off for the time being, saying that "trust and faith in each other" was a better approach than rigid rules and system. "We need a recognition that we have a common purpose. Don't tell me that I need to tell you what that is, because we'll never agree, but we do have a common purpose."[54] This provoked Tom Chance, a free software and free culture advocate, to complain that "Lessig's call to base the organization on 'trust and faith in each other' is too idealistic and undemocratic."

The encounter nicely captures the quandaries of leadership and governance in the networked environment. How can the effectiveness and clarity of leadership be combined with networked participation and the legitimacy that it provides? How should an organization draw philosophical boundaries to define itself while remaining open to new ideas? How should participation in online collectives be structured to generate collective wisdom and legitimacy and avoid collective stupidity and bureaucratic paralysis? In this case, iCommons diversified its governance in late 2007. It invited the Free Software Foundation Europe, Computer Professionals for Social Responsibility, and Instituto Overmundo, a Brazilian nonprofit dedicated to cultural diversity, to join Creative Commons as full-fledged partners in managing the organization. Despite its broadened leadership, iCommons remains more of a convener of annual forums and discussion host than the democratically sanctioned voice of an international movement.

This is not surprising. The international commons community is still a fledgling enterprise trying to forge an identity and agenda. The resources for many CC affiliates are quite modest and the bonds of cooperation remain rudimentary. That said, the international explosion of free culture projects, above and beyond the CC licenses themselves, is nothing short of remarkable. It represents a "vast, transnational mobilization in favor of digital freedom," as Gilberto Gil put it. In the early stages of the viral spiral, no one could have imagined that a corps of passionate, self-selected volunteers cooperating through the Internet could accomplish so much. And it continues, unabated.

9

THE MANY FACES OF THE COMMONS

As the "free world" grows and diversifies, so does debate
over how to build the commons.

As the Creative Commons insinuated itself into one creative sector after another, and throughout dozens of nations, the variety of licenses proliferated. By one count in 2006, there were once eighteen distinct CC licenses, not counting version changes.* In the meantime, other parties were offering their own licenses. While the Creative Commons licenses had become the most-used licenses on the Internet, many people were choosing to use Free Software Foundation licenses for text (the GNU Free Documentation License, or FDL), the European Art Libre license, and special licenses that various institutions have devised for the arts, music, and educational works.

In theory, a proliferation of licenses is not a bad thing. By the lights of free-market economics and complexity theory, in fact, the best way to identify the most useful licenses is to introduce a variety of them and then let them compete for supremacy. Let natural selection in an ecosystem of licenses cull the losers and elevate the most useful ones.

---

* The eighteen licenses once offered include the core six licenses; a non-attribution version of five of those six licenses (now retired); three sampling licenses (one of which has been retired); the Developing Nations license (now retired); and a public domain dedication (which is otherwise not possible under copyright statutes). There was also a "Music Sharing license," which was just another name for the Attribution-NonCommercial-No Derivatives license, and a "Founders' Copyright," which is not a license but a contract between an author and Creative Commons to place a particular work in the public domain after fourteen years (or twenty-eight years, if the author opts for a fourteen-year extension).

Unfortunately, this libertarian vision of diverse licenses competing for supremacy in the cultural ecosystem can run up against a
harsh reality of the Internet. Too many disparate licenses may make
it *harder* for people to share content in an easy, interoperable way. It
is not the proliferation of licenses per se that is problematic, it is the
absence of a mechanism to enable differently licensed works to
"play together" so that they can commingle and be used to produce
new things. If bodies of works released under a CC license cannot
be combined with works licensed under other licenses, it defeats
one of the key value propositions of the Internet, easy interoperability and facile sharing and reuse. Despite its best intentions, license
proliferation has the effect of "fencing off the commons," because
the different license terms keep different bodies of work in separate
ghettos.

Incompatibility is a problem both within the suite of CC licenses
and between CC licenses and other licenses. Within the CC suite
of licenses, for example, a work licensed under the Attribution-
NonCommercial-ShareAlike license (BY-NC-SA) cannot legally
be combined with a work licensed under the Attribution–No
Derivatives license (BY-ND) or an Attribution–NonCommercial
(BY-NC). The former license requires that any derivative works be
licensed under the same license, period.

Some observers are not disturbed by the internal incompatibilities of the CC suite of licenses. They regard the different licenses as
tools for various communities to build their own "subeconomies"
of content, based on their own distinct needs and priorities. A scientist may not want his research articles altered or combined with
other material. A musician may want to promote noncommercial
usage on the Internet but retain commercial rights so that he can
benefit from any CD sales. Not all creative sectors want to distribute
their work in the same ways.

The incompatibility between CC-licensed work and other free-
content licenses is arguably more problematic. At a conference in
Spain in the summer of 2005, Lessig recalls having a "Homer Simp-
son moment"—*D'oh!*—when he realized where license proliferation was heading. The incompatibility of licenses, and therefore

bodies of content, could lead to an irretrievably fragmented universe of content. Lessig saw license proliferation as analogous to the Balkanization of technical standards that once plagued mainframe computing. IBM computers couldn't communicate with DEC, which couldn't communicate with Data General.[1] "The legal framework of the licensing world is basically a pre-Internet framework," said Lessig in 2007. "We don't have interoperability at the layer of legal infrastructure."[2]

> In my view [said Lessig], there's a critical need for the free culture movement to achieve interoperability. And until it achieves interoperability, there's a huge problem—because we're creating these kinds of autistic islands of freedom. Basically, the stuff produced in the Wikimedia world is free, but can only be used in the Wikimedia world; the stuff created in the Creative Commons world is free, but can only be used in the Creative Commons world—and never the two will meet. That's very destructive, because what we want is a kind of invisible platform of freedom that everybody can then build on. It's been my objective from the very beginning to find the way to assure that we would get that platform.[3]

A critic might call it "the revenge of choice"—the inevitable outcome of a neoliberal philosophy that privileges individualism and choice, rather than a collective concern for the commons. This is the view of Niva Elkin-Koren, a law professor at the University of Haifa (which coincidentally is the host of CC Israel). Elkin-Koren argues that the Creative Commons is replicating and reinforcing property rights discourse and failing to advance the cause of copyright reform. Because the Creative Commons is plagued by an "ideological fuzziness" that does not adequately set forth a philosophical vision of freedom or the commons, Elkin-Koren believes the CC project threatens to "spread and strengthen the proprietary regime in information."[4]

This critique was at the heart of one of the most serious internecine squabbles in the movement, the struggle to make Wikpedia content—licensed under the Free Software Foundation's GNU Free Documentation License—compatible with CC-licensed con- tent. The failure to find a solution, after four years of negotiation, threatened to keep two great bodies of Internet content from legally commingling and cause further fragmentation of open content.

There are other controversies. Anticapitalist leftists periodically take the Creative Commons to task for being too politically re- spectable. Friendly voices from underdeveloped nations of the Southern Hemisphere have raised alarms that the public domain is just another excuse for corporate exploitation of their resources. Others from the South argue that the informal, social commons inhabited by poor people—the "nonlegal commons"—deserve respect, too. And then there are copyright traditionalists, who be- lieve that a redoubled effect to fortify the fair use doctrine should be a top priority.

For the most part, the general public is oblivious to these in- ternecine disputes. Who cares about the relative merits of using a GNU Free Documentation License for Wikipedia entries instead of a Creative Commons license? The layperson may not understand the long-term implications of vesting individual authors with the choice of how to share a work (in the style of the Creative Com- mons) as opposed to vesting communities of practice with those rights (in the style of the Free Software Foundation's General Pub- lic License). Yet tech sophisticates realize that, in the context of the Internet, uninformed choices today can have serious practical con- sequences tomorrow. The terms of a license or the design of a soft- ware application or digital appliance can prevent people from sharing or reusing works. Bodies of content may become legally in- compatible. Consumer freedoms to innovate and distribute may be limited. And then there are second-order questions that have great symbolic importance within the movement, such as, Whose vision of "freedom" in digital spaces shall we endorse? What is philosoph- ically desirable and consistent?

For a movement that aspires to simplify copyright law, the free culture movement has gotten embroiled in knotty debates that might give lawyers headaches. It is not easy to tell if the disputants are persnickety zealots who have spent too much time in front of their screens or latter-day Jeffersons, Madisons, and Hamiltons— brilliant thinkers who are astute enough to understand the long-term implications of some difficult issues and passionate enough to take a stand. One person's arcana can be another person's foundational principle, and one person's quest for intellectual clarity is another person's distraction from the messy challenges of building a movement.

That is the basic problem of the crazy-quilt network that constitutes the free world. There are, in fact, so many divergent, sometimes competing, sometimes congruent agendas that it can be difficult to orchestrate them into a single, harmonious song. For better or worse, the passions that animate culture jammers, copyright reformers, hackers, law scholars, artists, scientists, and countless others in seventy-plus countries are widely divergent. Although the intra-movement disagreements may sometimes seem gratuitous, sectarian, and overblown, they are, in fact, understandable. The commoners tend to see their projects as part of a larger, ennobling enterprise— the construction of a new democratic polity and cultural ecology. It makes sense to fret about the technical, legal, and philosophical details when so much is potentially at stake.

Individual Choice Versus the Commons

It turns out that overcoming license incompatibilities is not such an easy task. Any attempt to bridge differences immediately runs into mind-bending legal complexities. Crafting new licensing language can trigger philosophical disagreements, some of which may be proxies for turf issues and personal control. One of the major philosophical disagreements involves the one raised by Elkin-Koren: the merits of individual choice versus the commons. Should individuals be allowed to choose how their work may circulate in the wider world, or is such legal partitioning of culture an affront to the value proposition of the commons and its sharing ethic? Why should the choices of individual creators be privileged over the creative needs of the general culture?

The question is a divisive one. The answer that you give, Yochai Benkler of Harvard Law School told me, "depends on whether you think that what you're doing is building a political movement or whether you're building a commons that has narrower appeal, but is potentially, more functionally unitary."[5] A movement is about building a "big tent," he said—a vision that accommodates many different types of people with different preferences. If you are building a movement, then you will use terminologies that are attractive to a very broad range of liberal and illiberal conceptions of choice, he said.

But a commons—of the sort that Richard Stallman's GPL enables for software code—requires that its members honor a community's social and moral priorities. A commons does not cater to individual preferences; its first priority is to advance the shared goals and relationships of the community. A commons is not oblivious to the self-interest of individuals. It just fulfills that self-interest in a different way. A commons does not confer benefits through individual negotiations or transactions, but instead through an individual's good-faith participation in an ongoing, collective process. There is no individual quid pro quo, in other words. A person's contributions accrue to the collective—and benefits flow from belonging to that collective. This is not an exotic or communistic model; it more or less resembles a scientist's relationship with his research discipline. In the style of a gift economy, a scientist's articles and lectures are gifts to the discipline; in return, he enjoys privileged access to his colleagues and their research.

It is worth noting that a commons does not necessarily preclude making money from the fruit of the commons; it's just that any commercial activity cannot interfere with the integrity of social relationships within the commons. In the case of GPL'd software, for example, Red Hat is able to sell its own versions of GNU/Linux only because it does not "take private" any code or inhibit sharing within the commons. The source code is always available to everyone. By contrast, scientists who patent knowledge that they glean from their participation in a scientific community may be seen as "stealing" community knowledge for private gain. The quest for individual profit may also induce ethical corner-cutting, which undermines the integrity of research in the commons.

Ironically, the Creative Commons is not itself a commons, nor do its licenses necessarily produce a commons in the strict sense of the term. The licenses are *tools* for creating commons. But the tools do not require the creation of a commons (unlike the GPL). In this sense, a commons of CC-licensed content may be a "lesser" type of commons because it may have restrictions on what content may be shared, and how. The choices of individual authors, not the preexisting claims of the community, are considered paramount.

Is one type of commons superior to the others? Does one offer a superior vision of "freedom"? This philosophical issue has been a recurrent source of tension between the Free Software Foundation, the steward of the GPL, and the Creative Commons, whose licenses cater to individual choice.

Strictly speaking, a commons essentially offers a binary choice, explained Benkler: "You're in the commons or you're out of the commons." By broadening that binary choice, the CC licenses make the commons a more complicated and ambiguous enterprise. This is precisely what some critics like Stallman have found objectionable about certain CC licenses. They don't necessarily help forge a community of shared values and commitments. Or as two British critics, David Berry and Giles Moss, have put it, the CC licenses create "commons without commonality."[6]

Inviting authors to choose how their work may circulate can result in different types of "commons economies" that may or may not be interoperable. ShareAlike content is isolated from NoDerivatives content; NonCommercial content cannot be used for commercial purposes without explicit permission; and so on. CC-licensed works may themselves be incompatible with content licensed under other licenses, such as the GNU Free Documentation License.

Freedom, the Commons, and Movement Building

The slightly confused layperson may ask, Why does all of this matter? The answer may depend on your commitment to the commons as a different (better?) way of creating value. Do you believe in individual freedom and choice, as conceived by contemporary liberal societies? Or do you believe in the *different type of freedom* that comes through participation in a community of shared values?

Does this state the choice too starkly, as an either/or proposition? Some believe that it does. Perhaps a broader taxonomy of commons is possible. Perhaps a commons can accommodate some measure of individual choice. Or is that an oxymoron?

These are pivotal questions. The answers point toward different visions of free culture and different strategic ideas about movement building. Is it enough to put forward a demanding, utopian ideal of the commons, and hope that it will attract a corps of true believers willing to toil away in the face of general indifference or hostility? This is essentially what Stallman has done. Or is it better to build a "coalition of the reasonable," so that a more accessible, practical vision can gain widespread social acceptance and political traction in a relatively short period of time? This is the vision that drives Larry Lessig and his allies.

Some critics accuse Creative Commons of betraying the full potential of the commons because its licenses empower individual authors to decide how "shareable" their works can be. The licenses do not place the needs of the general culture or the commons first, as a matter of universal policy, and some licenses restrict how a work may be used. The lamentable result, say critics like Niva Elkin-Koren, is a segmented body of culture that encourages people to think of cultural works as property. People internalize the norms, such as "This is *my work* and *I'll* decide how it shall be used by others."

This can be seen in the actual choices that CC licensors tend to use. Some 67 percent of CC-licensed works do not allow commercial usage.[7] Arguments go back and forth about whether the NC restriction enhances or shrinks freedom. Many musicians and writers want to promote their works on the Internet while retaining the possibility of commercial gain, however remote; this would seem a strike for freedom. Yet critics note that the NC license is often used indiscriminately, even when commercial sales are a remote possibility. This precludes even modest commercial reuses of a work, such as reposting of content on a blog with advertising.[8]

The larger point of criticism is that the Creative Commons licenses do not "draw a line in the sand" about what types of freedoms are inherent to the commons. In the interest of building a broad movement, Creative Commons does not insist upon a clear standard of freedom or prescribe how a commons should be structured.

"While ideological diversity may be crucial for the successes of a social movement," observed Elkin-Koren, "it may impair attempts to make creative works more accessible. The lack of a core perception of freedom in information, may lead to ideological fuzziness. This could interfere with the goal of offering a workable and sustainable alternative to copyright."[9] In an essay that offers "a skeptical view of a worthy pursuit," Elkin-Koren says that the CC regime encourages narrow calculations of self-interest and the same attitudes toward property and individual transactions as the market economy; it does not promote a coherent vision of "freedom" that fortifies the commons as such.

"The normative message that we communicate by using Creative Commons licenses is the strategy of choice," Elkin-Koren told me. "You're the owner, you're the author, and therefore, you are entitled to govern your work. . . . No one tells you that maybe it's wrong; maybe you should allow people to use your work." By using the CC licenses, she continued, we internalize these norms. "We are teaching ourselves and others that our works are simply commodities, and like every other commodity, everyone has to acquire a license in order to use it."[10]

But champions of the Creative Commons licenses celebrate their approach as a pragmatic and effective way to break free from the stifling "all rights reserved" ethic of copyright law. Historically, of course, not much else has been successful in challenging copyright norms—which is precisely why Lessig and others find the CC strategy attractive. "If I believed that there was a different discourse that had political purchase in someplace other than tiny corners of law faculty commons rooms, I'd be willing to undertake it," said Lessig. He concedes that his viewpoint may be affected by his living in the United States instead of Israel (where Elkin-Koren lives) but, in the end, he considers the Creative Commons as "just my judgment about what's going to be effective."[11]

The Splintering of the Free World?

At one point, the philosophical disagreements between the Creative Commons and its critics did not matter so much. There was enough shared purpose and common history that everyone could agree to disagree. And since the project was still young, the stakes were not so high. But then it became clear that the CC licenses would be quite popular indeed. When the Creative Commons issued its Developing Nations and Sampling licenses in 2003, it brought Richard Stallman's simmering dissatisfaction with the organization to a boil, threatening a serious schism. Pointing to the "four freedoms" that define the free software movement, Stallman criticized the new CC licenses as "not free" because they do not allow universal copying of a work.

Stallman objected to the Sampling license because, while it allowed a remix of a licensed work, it did not allow the freedom to share it. The Developing Nations license was objectionable because its freedoms to copy are limited to people in the developing world, and do not extend to everyone. Stallman also disliked the fact that the CC tag that licensors affix to their works did not specify *which* license they were using. With no clear standard of "freedom" and now a mix of licenses that included two "non-free" licenses, Stallman regarded the CC tag as meaningless and the organization itself problematic.

"I used to support Creative Commons," said Stallman on his blog in July 2005, "but then it adopted some additional licenses which do not give everyone that minimum freedom, and now I no longer endorse it as an activity. I agree with Mako Hill that they are taking the wrong approach by not insisting on any specific freedoms for the public."[12]

Mako Hill is a brilliant young hacker and Stallman acolyte who wrote a 2005 essay, "Towards a Standard of Freedom: Creative

Commons and the Free Software Movement,"[13] a piece that shares Elkin-Koren's complaint about the CC's "ideological fuzziness." Then enrolled in a graduate program at the MIT Media Lab, Hill has written a number of essays on the philosophy and social values of free software. (When he was an undergraduate at Hampshire College, I was an outside advisor for his senior thesis and remain friends with him.)

In his "Freedom's Standard" essay, Hill wrote: "[D]espite CC's stated desire to learn from and build upon the example of the free software movement, CC sets no defined limits and promises no freedoms, no rights, and no fixed qualities. Free software's success is built on an ethical position. CC sets no such standard." While CC prides itself on its more open-minded "some rights reserved" standard, Hill says that a real movement for freedom must make a bolder commitment to the rights of the audience and other creators— namely, that "essential rights are unreservable."[14]

By this, Hill means that certain essential freedoms should not be restricted by copyright law or any license. The problem with the CC licenses, argued Hill, is that they cannot commit to any "*defined spirit of sharing*" (emphasis in original). This is not the way to build a transformative, sustainable movement, said Hill.[15]

But what, then, about the choice of authors? Doesn't that freedom count for anything? CC partisans have responded. Joi Ito, the chair of the Creative Commons, wrote in 2007, "CC is about providing choice. FSF is mostly about getting people to make *their* choice. I realize it's not THAT clear-cut, but I think the point of CC is to provide a platform for choice. . . . I realize that we are headed in the same general free culture direction and many of us debate what choices should be allowed, but I think we are more 'tolerant' and support more diverse views than the FSF."[16]

Lessig has argued many times that, just as the free software community decided for itself how its content ought to be distributed, so other artistic sectors—musicians, photographers, filmmakers, etc.— must make such decisions themselves. If they can't have certain choices, then they will have little interest in joining a movement for free culture, said Lessig at the 23rd Chaos Communication Congress in Berlin. "We don't have the standing to tell photographers or musicians what 'freedom' is." Why should the Free Software Foundation, or any other group, be able to dictate to an artistic community how their works should circulate?

Elkin-Koren is not so sure we can segment the world according to creative sectors and let each determine how works shall circulate. "I don't think we can separate the different sectors, as if we work in different sectors," she told me. "We all work in the production of information. My ideas on copyright are really affected by the art that I use and the music that I listen to. . . . Information is essential not only for creating something functional or for selling a work of art, but for our citizenship and for our ability to participate in society. So it's not as if we can say, 'Well, this sector can decide for themselves.' "[17]

As Wikipedia began to take off in popularity, what might have been an unpleasant philosophical rift grew into a more serious fissure with potentially significant consequences. All Wikipedia content is licensed under the Free Software Foundation's GNU Free Documentation License, or FDL,[18] largely because the CC licenses did not exist when Wikipedia was launched in 2001. The FDL, originally intended for the documentation manuals that explicate software applications, is essentially the same as the CC ShareAlike license (any derivative works must also be released under the same license granting the freedom to share). But using the FDL can get cumbersome, especially as more video, audio, and photos are incorporated into a text; each artifact would require that the license be posted on it. As more content is shared, the potential for misuse of the content, and lawsuits over violations of licensing agreements, would grow.[19]

Unfortunately, as a legal matter, the FDL is incompatible with the CC licenses. This means that all content on Wikipedia and its sister Wikimedia projects (Wikispecies, Wikiquote, Wikinews, among other projects) cannot legally be combined with works licensed under CC licenses. Angered by the two "non-free" CC licenses, Stallman dug in his heels and defended Wikipedia's use of the FDL. He also made it clear that he would remain a critic of Creative Commons unless it revoked or changed its licenses to conform with the Free Software Foundation's standards of "freedom."

Thus began a four-year search for a resolution. Lessig recalled, "We started to think about a way that Wikimedia could migrate to a license that we would then deem as compatible to a Creative Commons license. That took two years of negotiation, basically." One proposed solution was for Wikimedia projects to offer both licenses, the FDL and CC BY-SA, for the same work. However, it was determined that derivative works licensed under one license would still be incompatible with dual-licensed works, resulting in "project bleed" (new works would migrate away the existing corpus of works). Another approach was for a "one-way compatibility" of licenses, so that people creating works under the FDL could use CC-licensed content.

But Lessig realized that these solutions dealt only with the issue at hand; the real challenge was finding a more systemic solution. As various players engaged with the FDL/CC controversy, it grew from a licensing squabble into an intertribal confrontation. It became a symbol for everything that Stallman found politically unacceptable about the Creative Commons's vision of freedom.

From 2005 to 2007, the issue roiled many factions within the free culture/free software communities. The debate and invective flew back and forth in various venues, and there were proposals, negotiations, and political maneuvers. MIT computer scientist (and CC board member) Hal Abelson rejoined the FSF board. Lessig and other CC staff entered into talks with the FSF general counsel, Eben Moglen. Wikipedia co-founder Jimmy Wales joined the Creative Commons board. Yet Stallman continued to resist, and the Wikimedia board would not approve any proposed solutions.

The stalemate was broken in June 4, 2007, when Lessig made a surprise announcement that the Creative Commons was "retiring" the Developing Nations and Sampling licenses.[20] One reason was a lack of interest in the licenses: only 0.01 percent of CC licensors were using each license. But, without alluding to the Free Software Foundation or Stallman, Lessig also noted that the two licenses did not ensure a minimal freedom to share a work noncommercially—

a standard met by all other CC licenses. In addition, Lessig pointed out to me, some publishers were beginning to see the Developing Nations license as a subterfuge to avoid meeting open-access publishing standards.

For Creative Commons, the revocation of the two licenses was at least a shrewd political move; it also affirmed a stricter standard of "freedom" in the ability to use digital materials. In return for sacrificing two little-used licenses, the organization gained Stallman's eventual support for a deal that would let the FDL be treated as compatible with the CC ShareAlike license. This was a major triumph because it could avoid the contorted, legalistic solutions that had been previously proposed and rejected. It was also a breakthrough because it averted a major rift between two growing bodies of open content and avoided a slow drift into a wider Balkanization of content across the Internet. "I kind of thought that no matter what we did, Richard would find a reason to object," recalled Lessig, "but he didn't. He stuck to his principles, so I give credit to him." [21]

The debates about "freedom" produced several specific results. In November 2006, when Creative Commons released an updated legal version of its licenses, version 3.0, it formally recognized other licenses as legally compatible with the ShareAlike license if they have the same purpose, meaning, and effect, and if the other license recognizes the CC license. The move should help avoid future strife over interoperability.

A few months later, the Creative Commons also adopted a "Free Cultural Works" definition and seal as a way to recognize works that are "free," as understood by the Free Software Foundation. The definition declares that works with either the CC Attribution or Attribution-ShareAlike licenses should be considered "free" because they give people the freedom to modify works without any discrimination against specific uses or users. The definition and seal *exclude* the CC NonCommercial and NoDerivatives licenses, however, because those licenses do not allow this sort of freedom. The purpose of the seal is not to denigrate use of the NC and ND licenses, but to educate users about the less restrictive licenses and to assert a philosophical solidarity with the free software community.

As part of this larger effort, the Creative Commons also issued a draft statement in April 2008 declaring the special importance of the ShareAlike license in the free culture movement and the organization's intentions in its stewardship of the license. The statement amounted to a diplomatic peace treaty, to be finalized in the months ahead.

By May 2008 the details of the agreement to make Wikipedia's entries, licensed under the FDL, legally compatible with materials licensed under the CC ShareAlike license had not been consummated. But it was expected that the legal technicalities would be ironed out, and two great bodies of open content would no longer be legally off-limits to each other.

Criticism from the Left and from the South

As the Creative Commons has grown in popularity, a longer line has formed to take issue with some of its fundamental strategies. One line of criticism comes from anticapitalist ideologues, another from scholars of the underdeveloped nations of the South.

British academics Berry and Moss apparently hanker for a more bracing revolution in culture; they object to the commodification of culture in any form and to the role that copyright law plays in this drama. To them, Lessig is distressingly centrist. He is "always very keen to disassociate himself and the Creative Commons from the (diabolical) insinuation that he is (God forbid!) anti-market, anti-capitalist, or communist," Berry and Moss complain.[22] The gist of their objection: Why is Lessig collaborating with media corporations and neoclassical economists when there is a larger, more profound revolution that needs to be fought? A new social ethic and political struggle are needed, they write, "not lawyers exercising their legal vernacular and skills on complicated licenses, court cases and precedents."

Dense diatribes against the antirevolutionary character of Creative Commons can be heard in various hacker venues and cultural blogs and Web sites. The argument tends to go along the lines sketched here by Anna Nimus of Berlin, Germany:

Creative Commons preserves Romanticism's ideas of originality, creativity and property rights, and similarly considers
"free culture" to be a separate sphere existing in splendid
isolation from the world of material production. Ever since
the 18th century, the ideas of "creativity" and "originality"
have been inextricably linked to an anti-commons of
knowledge. Creative Commons is no exception. There's no
doubt that Creative Commons can shed light on some of the
issues in the continuing struggle against intellectual property. But it is insufficient at best, and, at its worst, it's just another attempt by the apologists of property to confuse the
discourse, poison the well, and crowd out any revolutionary
analysis.[23]

To ensure that her revolutionary analysis gets out, Nimus released
her piece under a self-styled "Anticopyright" notation, with the
added phrase, "All rights dispersed."

A more penetrating brand of criticism has come from the South,
which fears that the West's newfound enthusiasm for the commons
may not necessarily benefit the people of developing nations; indeed, it could simply legitimate new thefts of their shared resources.
In an important 2004 law review article, "The Romance of the
Public Domain," law professors Anupam Chander and Madhavi
Sunder argue that "public domain advocates seem to accept that
because a resource is open to all by force of law, that resource will indeed be exploited by all. In practice, however, differing circumstances—including knowledge, wealth, power and ability—render
some better able than others to exploit a commons. We describe this
popular scholarly conception of the commons as 'romantic.' . . . It is
celebratory, even euphoric, about the emancipatory potential of the
commons. But it is also naïve, idealistic and removed from reality."[24]

If genes, seeds, indigenous medicines, agricultural innovations,
artistic designs, music, and the various ecological and cultural resources of the South are not treated as private property, but instead
as elements of the public domain, then anyone can exploit them
freely. This can lead to serious injustices, as powerful corporations

swoop in to exploit resources that are available to all in the public domain.

Chander and Sunder write: "By presuming that leaving information and ideas in the public domain enhances 'semiotic democracy'—a world in which all people, not just the powerful, have the ability to make cultural meanings—law turns a blind eye to the fact that for centuries the public domain has been a source for exploiting the labor and bodies of the disempowered—namely, people of color, the poor, women and people from the global South."[25] Chander and Sunder argue that the binary logic of copyright law—something is either private property or in the public domain—"masks the ways in which the commons often functions more in the interests of traditional property owners than in the interests of commoners."

This critique makes clear why the distinction between the public domain and the commons matters. The public domain is an open-access regime available to all; it has no property rights or governance rules. The commons, however, is a legal regime for ensuring that the fruits of collective efforts remain under the control of that collective. The GPL, the CC licenses, databases of traditional knowledge, and sui generis national statutes for protecting biological diversity all represent innovative legal strategies for protecting the commons. The powerful can exploit and overwhelm the public domain, but they are not likely to overwhelm a commons that has a legal regime to protect a collective's shared resources.

A more radical and profound critique of the commons came in an open letter to "inhabitants of the 'legal' Commons" from "Denizens of Non Legal Commons, and those who travel to and from them." The three-page letter, drafted by Shuddhabrata Sengupta, a filmmaker and writer with the Raqs Media Collective in New Delhi, is a plea for recognizing the informal sharing economy that flourishes beneath the oblivious gaze of mainstream society, and certainly beyond the reach of property rights and law.

"Greetings!" the letter opens. "This missive arrives at your threshold from the proverbial Asiatic street, located in the shadow of an improvised bazaar, where all manner of oriental pirates and other

dodgy characters gather to trade in what many amongst you consider to be stolen goods." To this *other* commons, stolen goods are really "borrowed," because nothing is really "owned"—and therefore
nothing can be "stolen." This is the realm of "the great circulating
public library of the Asiatic street." The letter continues:

> We appreciate and admire the determination with which
> you nurture your garden of licenses. The proliferation and
> variety of flowering contracts and clauses in your hothouses
> is astounding. But we find the paradox of a space that is
> called a commons and yet so fenced in, and in so many ways,
> somewhat intriguing. The number of times we had to ask
> for permission, and the number of security check posts we
> had to negotiate to enter even a corner of your commons
> was impressive. . . . Sometimes we found that when people
> spoke of "Common Property" it was hard to know where
> the commons ended and where property began . . .
>
> Strangely, the capacity to name something as "mine,"
> even if in order to "share" it, requires a degree of attainments
> that is not in itself evenly distributed. Not everyone comes
> into the world with the confidence that anything is "theirs"
> to share. This means that the "commons," in your parlance,
> consists of an arrangement wherein only those who are in
> the magic circle of confident owners effectively get a share in
> that which is essentially, still a configuration of different bits
> of fenced in property. What they do is basically effect a series
> of swaps, based on a mutual understanding of their exclusive
> property rights. So I give you something of what I own, in
> exchange for which, I get something of what you own. The
> good or item in question never exits the circuit of property,
> even, paradoxically, when it is shared. Goods that are not
> owned, or those that have been taken outside the circuit of
> ownership, effectively cannot be shared, or even circulated.[26]

The letter invites a deeper consideration of how humans form commons. However ingenious and useful the jerry-rigged legal mecha-

nisms of the GPL and Creative Commons, the disembodied voice of the Non Legal Commons speaks, as if through the sewer grate, to remind us that the commons is about much more than law and civil society. It is part of the human condition. Yet the chaotic Asiatic street is not likely to yield conventional economic development without the rule of law, civil institutions, and some forms of legal property. The question posed by the informal commons remains a necessary one to ponder: What balance of commons and property rights, and in what forms, is best for a society?

Fair Use and the Creative Commons

Walk through the blossoming schools of commons thought and it quickly becomes clear that the commons is no monolithic ideal but a many-splendored mosaic of perspectives. To the befuddlement of conventional observers, the perspectives are not necessarily adversarial or mutually exclusive. More often than not, they are fractal— interesting variations of familiar commons themes. In our fascination with newfangled commons, it is easy to overlook a more traditionally minded defender of the commons: the champion of fair use. It is all well and good to promote works that are "born free" under CC licenses, say these friendly critics. But the hard fact of the matter is that for the foreseeable future, creators will still need access to copyrighted content—and this requires a strong fair use doctrine and aggressive public education.

It is a compelling argument, but in fact only an indirect criticism of Creative Commons. For filmmakers who need to use film clips from existing films and musicians who want to use a riff from another performer, the fair use doctrine is indeed more important than any CC license. Peter Jaszi, the law professor at American University's Washington School of Law, believes that even with growing bodies of CC-licensed content, "teachers, filmmakers, editors, freelance critics and others need to do things with proprietary content." As a practical matter, they need a strong, clear set of fair use guidelines.

Jaszi and his colleague Pat Aufderheide, a communications professor who runs the Center for Social Media at American University, have dedicated themselves to clarifying the scope and certainty of fair use. They have launched a major fair use project to get specific creative communities to define their "best practices in fair use." If filmmakers, for example, can articulate their own artistic needs and professional interests in copying and sharing, then the courts are more likely to take those standards into consideration when they rule what is protected under the fair use doctrine.[27] A set of respectable standards for a given field can help stabilize and expand the application of fair use.

Inspired in part by a professional code developed by news broadcasters, some of the nation's most respected filmmakers prepared the Documentary Filmmakers' Statement of Best Practices in Fair Use, which was released in November 2005. The guidelines have since been embraced by the film industry, television programmers, and insurance companies (who insure against copyright violations) as a default definition about what constitutes fair use in documentary filmmaking.[28] Aufderheide and Jaszi are currently exploring fair use projects for other fields, such as teaching, as a way to make fair use a more reliable legal tool for sharing and reuse of works.

Lessig has been highly supportive of the fair use project and, indeed, he oversees his own fair use law clinic at Stanford Law School, which litigates cases frequently. "It's not as if I don't think fair use is important," said Lessig, "but I do think that if the movement focuses on fair use, we don't attract the people we need. . . . From my perspective, long-term success in changing the fundamental perspectives around copyright depends on something like Creative Commons as opposed to legal action, and even quasi-legal action, like the Fair Use Project."

For Lessig, fair use is deeply flawed as the basis for building a political movement to reform copyright law. He argues that its advocates are dogged by the (unfair) perception that they are "just a bunch of people who want to get stuff for free, without paying for it. . . . It's too easy to dismiss that movement." Lessig recalled the time that the head of a major record label snorted, "Fair use is the last refuge of the scoundrel." Fair use defenders obviously take issue with this characterization, but the accusation nonetheless pushes fair use champions into a rhetorical corner from which it is difficult to escape.

A more appealing alternative, Lessig argues, is to use the credibility of copyright ownership to argue the point in a different way. He cited the successful campaign by European software engineers in the 1980s to fight attempts to expand patent protection for software. Their campaign did not resemble "a bunch of peer-to-peer downloaders who are saying, 'Yeah, I want my music for free,' " said Lessig. "It was a bunch of people who are the *beneficiaries* of patent rights saying, 'Look, we *don't want* these rights.' That creates a kind of credibility." From a moral and political standpoint, Lessig argued, a movement based on copyright owners declaring that they want to forfeit certain rights in order to *share* and promote creativity, has greater credibility than a campaign seeking to "balance" the public's rights against private copyright privileges.

"I imagine a world where there are one hundred million Creative Commons–licensed artists out there, creating works according to Creative Commons views," he said. Then, when Hollywood pressures Congress for stronger copyright protections, he said, "there would be all these people out there who are creating according to a radically different model. [Hollywood's] claims about extremism would just not be true for a large number of creators." Instead of a copyright debate that pits "creators" against "pirates," Lessig said, "I want to create this world where there is a third category of people who are creators, but who create according to different values, values that emphasize the importance of sharing and building upon the past." [29]

In the larger scheme of things, the tensions between the fair use and free culture advocates are not mutually exclusive. In the end, the two approaches complement each other with different contributions. Both seek to promote sharing and reuse, but the former works within the traditional framework of copyright law; the latter is trying to build a whole new body of culture and discourse. There is a kind of gentleman's agreement between the fair use and free culture communities to work on different sides of the street, while traveling a parallel path down the same road.

For Lessig, there is little advantage in shirking the property rights discourse of copyright law, as Elkin-Koren and the "Non Legal Commons" urge. Indeed, he sees a distinct strategic advantage in *embracing* that discourse—and then trying to turn it to different ends. This, in a way, is what Stallman succeeded in doing with the GPL, a license based on copyright law. Yet, while Stallman attracted a somewhat homogeneous community of programmers to his movement, Creative Commons has attracted a sprawling community of eclectic interests, diverse priorities, and no agreed-upon philosophical core.

By choosing a middle path that embraces but seeks to transform property discourse, Creative Commons may avoid the marginalization of ardent leftists and the modest agenda of fair use activism. It remains an open question whether the ideological fuzziness at the core of Creative Commons, or the limitations of its licenses, is offset by its success in popularizing a new cultural vision. Yochai Benkler, the great commons theorist, understands the legal criticisms, and agrees with them to an extent. But ultimately, the significance of Creative Commons, he believes, has been "in galvanizing a movement, in symbolizing it and in providing a place to organize around. From my perspective, if I care about Creative Commons, it is as a cultural icon for a movement, more than as a set of licenses. Which is why I am less bothered than some, about the people who are beginning to criticize Creative Commons and how good the licenses really are, and how compatible they are."[30]

For Cory Doctorow, the copyfighter and sci-fi writer, the eclectic viewpoints within the free culture movement is a decisive strength: "The difference between a movement and an organization," he wrote on the iCommons listserv, "is that an organization is a group of people who want the same thing for the same reason. A movement is a collection of groups of people who want the same thing for different reasons. Movements are infinitely more powerful than organizations."

The reason the environmental movement is so powerful,

Doctorow continued, is the very fact that it encompasses "anti-capitalists, green investors, spiritualists, scientists, hunters and fishers, parents worried about environmental toxins, labor reformers, pro-globalists, anti-globalists, etc. . . . . Denuding the ideological land-scape of the environmental movement in a purge to eliminate all those save the ones who support environmentalism *qua* environ-mentalism would be the worst setback environmentalism could suf-fer. Likewise copyfighters: there are Marxists, anarchists, Ayn Rand objectivists, economists, artists, free marketeers, libertarians, liberal democrats, etc., who see copyright liberalization as serving their agenda. If we insist that copyright reform is about copyright reform and nothing else, there will be no copyright reform movement."[31]

There is a price to be paid for all this diversity, however. Diver-sity means constant debate. Debate can escalate into strife and sec-tarianism. And in the free culture movement, where so many people are feverishly improvising and inventing, nearly everything is open for debate. It turns out that this business of inventing the commons is complicated stuff; there are many ways to construct a commons. It is only natural for people to have their own ideas about how to build the digital republic.

The fundamental question may be whether the existing frame-work of copyright law and property discourse can be adequately reformed—or whether its very categories of thought are the prob-lem. The late poet and activist Audre Lorde, in the context of femi-nist struggle, declared that the prevailing discourse must be overthrown, not reformed, because, in her words, "the master's tools will never dismantle the master's house." Within the free software and free culture movements, however, there are those who believe that copyright law can be sufficiently adapted to build a sharing economy, a more competitive marketplace, and a more humane democratic culture. Others are convinced that the legal discourse of property rights, however modified, will simply entrench the very principles that they wish to transcend. As the movement grows and diversifies, debates over what constitutes the most strategic, morally honorable path forward are likely to intensify.

PART III

A Viral Spiral of New Commons

By 2008 the viral spiral had come a long way. Richard Stallman's fringe movement to build a commons for code became an enormous success, partly inspiring Lawrence Lessig and his compatriots to develop the Creative Commons licenses and a larger vision of free culture. Empowered by these tools, ordinary people began to develop some exciting new models for creativity and sharing. New types of commons arose. Soon there was a popular discourse about the sharing economy, a politics of open networks, and a new international social movement. The movement was so successful at diversifying itself that it was able to engage in serious internecine squabbles.

As the commons movement matured, and people came to understand the sensibilities of open networks, the viral spiral seemed to acquire new speed and powers. Over the past few years, it has advanced into all sorts of new arenas. Part III examines three of the most exciting ones—business, science, and education. Each has taken the tools and insights developed by the commons movement—free software, CC licenses, collaborative models—and adapted them to its own special needs.

These spin-off movements of entrepreneurs, scientists, and educators recognize their debt to the free software and CC licenses, but none feels confined by that history or beholden to its leaders. Each is too intent on adapting the tools to its own circumstances. Just as CC licenses have been used in some ways by musicians, and in other ways by filmmakers, and in still other ways by bloggers, so the commoners in the worlds of business, science, and education are forging their own paths. Development requires differentiation. It is fascinating to watch how the principles of the commons are being crafted to meet the distinctive needs of the marketplace, the academy, the research lab, and the classroom.

What may be most notable about these developments is the blurring of these very categories. On open platforms, social communities are becoming sites for market activity. Scientists are increasingly collaborating with people outside their disciplines, including amateurs. Formal education is becoming more focused on learning, and learning is moving out of the classroom and into more informal and practice-driven venues.

If there is a common denominator in each of the domains examined in Part III, it is the use of distributed networks, social community, and digital technologies to enhance the goals at hand. The new open business models seek to bring consumer and seller interests into closer alignment. The new science commons seek to create more powerful types of research collaboration. The open educational resources movement wants knowledge to circulate more freely and students to direct their own learning.

For the short term, the fledgling models in these fields are likely to be seen as interesting novelties on the periphery of the mainstream. In time, however, given what we know about network dynamics, the new models are likely to supplant or significantly transform many basic parameters of business, science, and education. The participatory practices that open networks enable are showing that knowledge is more about socially dynamic relationships than about fixed bodies of information. These relationships are also spawning new challenges to institutional authority and expertise. If one looks closely enough, the matrix for a very different order of knowledge, institutional life, and personal engagement can be seen.

10

THE NEW OPEN BUSINESS MODELS

*The commons and the market can be great partners if each shows
respect for the other and ingenuity in working together.*

Entrepreneur John Buckman concedes that his Internet record
label, Magnatune, amounts to "building a business model on top of
chaos."[1] That is to say, he makes money by honoring open networks
and people's natural social inclinations. The company rejects the
proprietary muscle games used by its mainstream rivals, and instead
holds itself to an ethical standard that verges on the sanctimonious:
"We are not evil." In the music industry these days, a straight shooter
apparently has to be that blunt.

Magnatune is a four-person enterprise based in Berkeley, California, that since 2003 has been pioneering a new open business
model for identifying and distributing high-quality new music. It
does not lock up the music with anticopying technology or digital
rights management. It does not exploit its artists with coercive, unfair contracts. It does not harass its customers for making unauthorized copies. Internet users can in fact listen to all of Magnatune's
music for free (not just music snippets) via online streaming.[2]

Buckman, a former software programmer turned entrepreneur
in his thirties, previously founded and ran Lyris Technologies, an
e-mail list management company that he sold in 2005. In deciding
to start Magnatune, he took note of the obvious realities that the
music industry has tried to ignore: radio is boring, CDs cost too
much, record labels exploit their artists, file sharing is not going to
go away, people love to share music, and listening to music on the
Internet is too much work. "I thought, why not make a record label
that has a clue?" said Buckman.[3]

Well before the band Radiohead released its *In Rainbows* album
with a "pay what you want" experiment, Magnatune was inviting its

customers to choose the amount they would be willing to pay, from $5 to $18, for any of Magnatune's 547 albums. Buckman explains that the arrangement signals a respect for customers who, after all, have lots of free music choices. It also gives them a chance to express their appreciation for artists, who receive 50 percent of the sales price. "It turns out that people are quite generous and they pay on average about $8.40, and they really don't get anything more for paying more other than feeling like they're doing the right thing," said Buckman.[4] About 20 percent pay more than $12.[5]

"The reality is today nobody really needs to pay for music at all," he acknowledges. "If you choose to hit the 'buy' button at Magnatune then you're one of the people who has decided to actually pay for music. Shouldn't we reflect that honest behavior back and say, well, if you're one of the honest people how much do you want to pay?"[6] The set-your-own-price approach is part of Magnatune's larger strategy of building the business by cultivating open, interactive relationships with its customers and artists. "If you set up a trusting world," explains Buckman, "you can be rewarded."

Magnatune's business model embraces the openness of the Internet and makes it a virtue, rather than treating it as a bothersome liability that must be elaborately suppressed. All of Magnatune's music is released as MP3 files, with no digital rights management, under a CC Attribution-NonCommercial-ShareAlike license. This means that customers can legally make their own remixes and covers of songs, and take samples, so long as the uses are noncommercial and carry the same CC license. Magnatune also invites customers to give free downloads of purchased music to three friends. Podcasters have free access to the entire Magnatune catalog.

By using a CC license, Magnatune saves a bundle by not having to oversee complex terms and conditions for usage of music. Nor does it have to maintain a DRM system and police the behavior of its customers, both of which squander a key marketing asset: consumer goodwill. Instead, the music circulates freely and, in so doing, expands public awareness of Magnatune's 244 artists.

Two-thirds of Magnatune's revenues comes from licensing its music to films, ads, television, and shops. Like so many open business models, it has carved out a mid-tier niche between "expensive and proprietary" and "cheap and crummy." Most mainstream music licensing involves either expensive, highly lawyered deals with record labels or insipid stock music from royalty-free CDs. Magnatune's innovation is to offer high-quality music in multiple genres at flat-rate licenses for sixteen different usage scenarios. The deals can be easily consummated via the Web; artists share in half the proceeds. No accounting flimflam. To date, Magnatune has licensed its music to more than one thousand indie films and many commercials.

Magnatune is a small, fledgling enterprise in the $4 billion music industry. It does not have all the answers, and it may be sideswiped by bigger players at some point. But Magnatune is lean, nimble, profitable, and growing. It has shown how innovative business models can flourish in the open environment of the Internet. Unlike its bloated, besieged competitors, Magnatune is willing to listen closely to its customers, artists, and licensing clients. It is fair-minded and straightforward; it wants to share the wealth and let the music flow.

Open Networks Spur New Business Models

Openness does not come intuitively to many businesses. Competitive advantage has long been associated with exclusive control and secrecy. But as the Internet's power expands, conventional businesses are feeling pressures to rethink their "closed" business models. A new breed of "open businesses" is demonstrating that a reliance on open-source software, open content, and an ethic of transparency in dealings with all corporate stakeholders can be tremendously competitive.

Open businesses understand the Great Value Shift discussed in chapter 5—that working through open networks and commons is likely to generate greater consumer attention, engagement, and loyalty—and thus sales—and may outperform a more exclusive regime of control. Working on an open network is also the best way for a company to get smarter faster, and to stay alert to changing market conditions. It bears noting that business models are not an either/or choice—that is, all open or all closed. There is a continuum of choices, as we will see below. Sometimes there are heated strategic and moral debates about what level of openness to adopt, yet the general trend in business today is clear: toward openness.

Even as broadcast networks decry the posting of copyrighted television programs on YouTube, they clearly welcome the ratings spikes that ensue. Wireless telephony is fragmented among many proprietary systems, but pressures are now growing to make them compete on an open platform.[7] European regulators are calling for "open document format" standards to prevent Microsoft from abusing its proprietary standards in its Office suite of software. There are even calls for open standards for avatars in virtual worlds like Second Life, The Lounge, and Entropia Universe, so that our digital alter egos can glide from one virtual community to another.[8]

Why this inexorable trend toward openness? Because on open networks, excessive control can be counterproductive. The overall value that can be created through interoperability is usually greater than the value that any single player may reap from maintaining its own "walled network."[9] For a company to reap value from interoperability, however, it must be willing to compete on an open platform and it must be willing to share technical standards, infrastructure, or content with others. Once this occurs, proprietary gains come from competing to find more sophisticated ways to add value in the production chain, rather than fighting to monopolize basic resources. Advantage also accrues to the company that develops trusting relationships with a community of customers.

Free software was one of the earliest demonstrations of the power of online commons as a way to create value. In his classic 1997 essay "The Cathedral and the Bazaar," hacker Eric S. Raymond provided a seminal analysis explaining how open networks make software development more cost-effective and innovative than software developed by a single firm.[10] A wide-open "bazaar" such as the global Linux community can construct a more versatile operating system than one designed by a closed "cathedral" such as Microsoft. "With enough eyes, all bugs are shallow," Raymond famously declared. Yochai Benkler gave a more formal economic reckoning of the value proposition of open networks in his pioneering 2002 essay "Coase's Penguin, or, Linux and the Nature of the Firm."[11] The title is a puckish commentary on how GNU/Linux, whose mascot is a penguin, poses an empirical challenge to economist Ronald Coase's celebrated "transaction cost" theory of the firm. In 1937, Coase stated that the economic rationale for forming a business enterprise is its ability to assert clear property rights and manage employees and production more efficiently than contracting out to the marketplace.

What is remarkable about peer production on open networks, said Benkler, is that it undercuts the economic rationale for the firm; commons-based peer production can perform certain tasks more efficiently than a corporation. Those tasks must be modular and divisible into small components and capable of being efficiently integrated, Benkler stipulated. The larger point is that value is created on open networks in very different ways than in conventional markets. Asserting proprietary control on network platforms may prevent huge numbers of people from giving your work (free) social visibility, contributing new value to it, or remixing it. "The only thing worse than being sampled on the Internet," said Siva Vaidhyanathan, with apologies to Oscar Wilde, "is *not* being sampled on the Internet."

The *New York Times*'s experience with its paid subscription service, TimesSelect, offers a great example. The *Times* once charged about fifty dollars a year for online access to its premier columnists and news archives. Despite attracting more than 227,000 subscribers and generating about $10 million a year in revenue, the *Times* discontinued the service in 2007.[12] A *Times* executive explained that lost subscription revenues would be more than offset by advertising to a much larger online readership with free access. The *Financial Times* and the *Economist* have dropped their paywalls, and the *Wall Street Journal* in effect has done so by allowing free access via search engines and link sites. From some leading citadels of capitalism, a rough consensus had emerged: exclusivity can *decrease* the value of online content.[13]

While enormous value can be created on open networks, it can take different forms, notes David P. Reed, who studies information architectures.[14] One of the most powerful types of network value is what Reed calls "Group-Forming Networks," or GFNs—or what Benkler might call commons-based peer production and I would call, less precisely, the commons. Reed talks about "scale-driven value shifts" that occur as a network grows in size. Greater value is created as a network moves from a broadcast model (where "content is king") to peer production (where transactions dominate) and finally, to a group-forming network or commons (where jointly constructed value is produced and shared).

It is unclear, as a theoretical matter, how to characterize the size and behavior of various "value networks" on the Web today. For simplicity's stake—and because Web platforms are evolving so rapidly—I refer to two general value propositions, Web 2.0 and the commons. Web 2.0 is about creating new types of value through participation in distributed open networks; the commons is a subset of Web 2.0 that describes fairly distinct, self-governed communities that focus on their own interests, which usually do not involve moneymaking.

The rise of Web 2.0 platforms and the commons clearly has some serious implications for business strategy and organization. Just consider how Craigslist is displacing millions of dollars of classified newspaper ads; how open-access journals are threatening the economic base of commercial academic journals; and how user-generated content is competing with network television. At the same time, activities that once occurred through informal social means (finding a date, organizing a gathering, obtaining word-of-mouth recommendations) are increasingly becoming commercial endeavors on the Web. Especially when the commons has strong mechanisms to preserve its value-creating capacity, such as the GPL, open networks are helping to convert more market activity into commons-based activity, or at least shifting the boundary between commodity markets and proprietary, high-value-added markets. As this dynamic proceeds, the social and the commercial are blurring more than ever before.

Many "value chains" that have long sustained conventional businesses are being disrupted. As described in chapter 5, more efficient types of distributed media are disrupting the production/distribution chain that sustains Centralized Media. The Long Tail lets online consumers "pull" niche products that they want rather than enduring a relentless marketing "push" of products they don't want. Commons-based peer production is a nonmarket version of the Long Tail: dispersed communities of people with niche interests can find one another, form social communities, bypass the market, and collaborate to create the niche resources that they want.

The question facing many businesses is how to develop stable, long-term business models that can coexist with productive commons, if not leverage them for market gain. Their goal is to find ingenious ways to "monetize" the social relationships of online communities (by selling targeted advertising, personal data, niche products, etc.). Open businesses aim to do this in a respectful, public-spirited way; other, more traditional firms may have fewer scruples because, for them, "it's all about the money."

But here's the rub: a company can go only so far in monetizing the value-generating capacities of a commons without enclosing it or enraging the commoners. A company may consider itself shrewd for acquiring the copyrights for user-generated content, for example, or for blocking user access to third-party widgets that it disapproves of.[15] But participants in Web 2.0 communities will protest or simply leave if a corporate host starts to dictate obnoxious policies. A company can try to run its Web 2.0 platform as a feudal fiefdom, but it risks inciting users to revolt and start their own (nonmarket) online communities, reinventing themselves as commoners. Although there is an implicit social ethic to Web 2.0 platforms, none is necessarily "free" in the Stallman sense of "freedom."

Unfortunately, there is no clear consensus about how exactly to define an "open business." Accordingly, assessments of their social, political, or economic virtue can be slippery. Some analysts such as Henry Chesbrough regard a business as "open" if it relaxes or modifies its intellectual property controls, or changes its organizational practices, as a way to reap value from open networks.[16] Others believe that an open business should use open-source software, and support the copying and sharing of works through CC or other open-content licenses. Sometimes the idea of open business is yoked to a vaguely defined notion of "social responsibility." It is not always clear whether this ethic is a moral gloss or a structural feature, but in general open businesses strive to practice a more open, accountable, and socially enlightened vision of commerce.

One champion of this vision is OpenBusiness, a Web site jointly created by Creative Commons UK in partnership with CC Brazil and the FGV Law School in Rio de Janeiro, Brazil. The mission of OpenBusiness is to "analyze and explain models by which people can share their knowledge and creativity with others whilst at the same time enjoying the more traditional incentives of profit, individual success and societal advancement."[17] By its lights, an open business is commons-friendly if it is committed to "transparency," "sustainable systems," and to putting "the health and welfare of people above everything else." An open business also tries to generate as many "positive externalities" as possible—knowledge, social relationships, revenues—which it is willing to share with its stakeholders.

It is perhaps best to approach open businesses as an eclectic social phenomenon in search of a theory. As it has been said about Wikipedia, "It works in practice, but not in theory."[18] It is risky to overtheorize phenomena that are still fluid and emerging. Still, specific examples of open business can help us understand some basic principles of open networks, and how some businesses are using CC licenses to build innovative sorts of enterprises.

Share the Wealth, Grow a Commercial Ecosystem

The idea that a company can make money by giving away something for free seems so counterintuitive, if not ridiculous, that conventional business people tend to dismiss it. Sometimes they protesteth too much, as when Microsoft's Steve Ballmer compared the GNU GPL to a "cancer" and lambasted open-source software as having "characteristics of communism."[19] In truth, "sharing the wealth" has become a familiar strategy for companies seeking to develop new technology markets. The company that is the first mover in an emerging commercial ecosystem is likely to become the dominant player, which may enable it to extract a disproportionate share of future market rents. Giving away one's code or content can be a great way to become a dominant first mover.

Netscape was one of the first to demonstrate the power of this model with its release of its famous Navigator browser in 1994. The free distribution to Internet users helped develop the Web as a social and technological ecosystem, while helping fuel sales of Netscape's Web server software. (This was before Microsoft arrived on the scene with its Internet Explorer, but that's another story.) At a much larger scale, IBM saw enormous opportunities for building a better product by using GNU/Linux. The system would let IBM leverage other people's talents at a fraction of the cost and strengthen its service relationships with customers. The company now earns more than $2 billion a year from Linux-related services.[20]

Today, sharing and openness are key to many business strategies. "Open Source: Now It's an Ecosystem," wrote *BusinessWeek* in 2005, describing the "gold rush" of venture capital firms investing in startups with open-source products. Most of them planned to give away their software via the Web and charge for premium versions or for training, maintenance, and support.[21]

The pioneers in using open platforms to develop commercial ecosystems on the Internet are Amazon, Google, Yahoo, and eBay. Each has devised systems that let third-party software developers and businesses extend their platform with new applications and business synergies. Each uses systems that dynamically leverage users' social behaviors and so stimulate business—for example, customer recommendations about books, search algorithms that identify the most popular Web sites, and reputation systems that enhance consumer confidence in sellers. Even Microsoft, eager to expand the ecology of developers using its products, has released 150 of its source code distributions under three "Shared Source" licenses, two of which meet the Free Software Foundation's definition of "free."[22]

More recently, Facebook has used its phenomenal reach—more than 80 million active users worldwide—as a platform for growing a diversified ecology of applications. The company allows software developers to create custom software programs that do such things as let users share reviews of favorite books, play Scrabble or poker with others online, or send virtual gifts to friends. Some apps are just for fun; others are the infrastructure for independent businesses that sell products and services or advertise. In September 2007, Facebook had more than two thousand software applications being used by at least one hundred people.[23]

Open Content as a Gateway to Commercial Opportunities

Of course, not every business can own a major platform, as Google, eBay, and Facebook do. Still, there are many other opportunities. One of the most popular is to use open platforms to attract an audience, and then strike a deal with an advertiser or commercial distributor, or sell premium services ("get discovered"). Another approach is to use open content to forge a spirited community to which things may be sold ("build a market on a commons").

Get discovered. This dynamic has been played out countless times on YouTube, MySpace, Facebook, and other high-traffic social networking sites. An unknown remix artist suddenly becomes famous when his track is discovered by a network swarm: the story of DJ Danger Mouse that we saw in chapter 6. A band attracts a huge following through viral word of mouth: the story of Jake Shapiro and Two Ton Shoe's stardom in South Korea. There are even calculated scams to get discovered, like the lonelygirl15 series of videos purportedly shot by a teenage girl in her bedroom, which became a huge Internet sensation in 2006.[24]

As any television network will tell you, the capacity to aggregate audiences is worth a lot of money. The customary way of monetizing this talent is to sell advertising. Or one can parlay newfound name recognition into side deals with the mass media, which have always depended upon "star power" as a draw. Thus, Ana Marie Cox was able to parley her notoriety as a political gossip on her Wonkette blog into a job as Washington editor of *Time* magazine. Perez Hilton, a Hollywood blogger who attracted a following, was offered a lucrative perch at the *E!* cable television channel. We saw in chapter 6 how producer Samuli Torssonen's *Star Wreck* attracted millions of Internet viewers, enabling him to strike a deal with Universal Studios to distribute a DVD version. With the same visions of stardom, or at least paying gigs, in mind, thousands of bands now have fan sites, music downloads, and banner ads on MySpace and other sites to promote themselves.[25]

The CC NonCommercial license is one way to help pursue the "get discovered" business strategy. The license allows authors to seek a global Internet audience without having to cede rights to any commercial opportunities. It is not, however, a terribly reliable way to make money, which is why some artists, especially musicians, find fault with the implicit promise of the NC license. Many serious artists regard the NC license as too speculative a mechanism to get paid for one's creative work. It is a fair complaint, as far as it goes. The real problem is the closed, highly concentrated music industry, which has a hammerlock on marketing, radio play, and distribution. Newcomers and mid-tier talent cannot get past the corporate gatekeepers to reach an audience, let alone make money.

In an attempt to bridge the sharing economy with the market, and thereby open up some new channels of commercial distribution for commoners, the Creative Commons in late 2007 introduced a new protocol, CC+. The new project aims to make it easier for the owners of NC-licensed content to signal that agreements, products, or services beyond the scope of the CC licenses are on offer—for example, commercial licensing, warranties, or higher-quality copies. A photographer who has hundreds of NC-licensed photos on Flickr would be able to continue to let people use those photos for noncommercial purposes—but through CC+, he could also sell licensing rights to those who want to use the photos for commercial purposes. CC+ is a metadata architecture and standard that allows third-party intermediaries to develop services for consummating commercial transactions. People can use CC+ as a simple "click-through" mechanism for acquiring commercial rights for music, photos, text, and other content.

One of the earliest "copyright management" companies to take advantage of the CC+ standard was RightsAgent, a Cambridge, Massachusetts, company founded by Rudy Rouhana. RightsAgent essentially acts as a go-between for people who create NC-licensed works on the Web and those who wish to buy rights to use them for commercial purposes. Just as PayPal facilitates the exchange of money on the Internet, so RightsAgent aspires to be a paid intermediary for facilitating the sale of user-generated content.

The rise of CC+ and associated companies brings to mind Niva Elkin-Koren's warning that the Creative Commons licenses can be a slippery slope that merely promotes a property-oriented, transactional mentality—the opposite of the commons. On the other hand, many people operating in the noncommercial sharing economy, such as musicians and photographers, have long complained that, as much as they enjoy participating in the commons, they still need to earn a livelihood.

Revver is another company that has developed an ingenious way to promote the sharing of content, yet still monetize it based on the scale of its circulation. Revver is a Los Angeles–based startup that hosts user-generated video. All videos are embedded with a special tracking tag that displays an ad at the end. Like Google's Ad-Words system, which charges advertisers for user "click-throughs" on ad links adjacent to Web content, Revver charges advertisers for every time a viewer clicks on an ad. The number of ad views can be tabulated, and Revver splits ad revenues 50-50 with video creators. Key to the whole business model is the use of the CC Attribution-NonCommercial-No Derivatives license. The license allows the videos to be legally shared, but prohibits anyone from modifying them or using them for commercial purposes.

One of the most-viewed videos on Revver sparked a minor pop trend. It showed kids dropping Mentos candies into bottles of Coca-Cola, which produces an explosive chemical reaction. The video is said to have generated around $30,000.[26] So is new media going to feature silly cat videos and stupid stunts? Steven Starr, a co-founder of Revver, concedes the ubiquity of such videos, but is quick to point to "budding auteurs like Goodnight Burbank, Happy Slip, Studio8 and LoadingReadyRun, all building audiences." He also notes that online, creators "can take incredible risks with format and genre, can grow their own audience at a fraction of network costs, can enjoy free syndication, hosting, audience-building and ad services at their disposal."[27]

Blip.tv is another video content-sharing Web site that splits ad revenues with video creators (although it is not automatic; users must "opt in"). Unlike many videos on YouTube and Revver, blip.tv tends to feature more professional-quality productions and serialized episodes, in part because its founders grew out of the "video-blogging" community. Blip.tv espouses an open business ethic, with shout-outs to "democratization, openness, and sustainability." While there is a tradition for companies to spout their high-minded principles, blip.tv puts some bite into this claim by offering an open platform that supports many video formats and open metadata standards. And it allows content to be downloaded and shared on other sites. Users can also apply Creative Commons licenses to their videos, which can then be identified by CC-friendly search engines. For all these reasons, Lessig has singled out blip.tv as a "true sharing site," in contrast to YouTube, which he calls a "faking sharing site" that "gives you tools to make it *seem* as if there's sharing, but in fact, all the tools drive traffic and control back to a single site."[28]

Lessig's blog post on blip.tv provoked a heated response from blogger Nicholas Carr, a former executive editor of the *Harvard Business Review*. The contretemps is worth a close look because it illuminates the tensions between Web 2.0 as a business platform and Web 2.0 as a commons platform. In castigating YouTube as a "fake sharing site," Carr accused Lessig of sounding like Chairman Mao trying to root out counterrevolutionary forces (that is, capitalism) with "the ideology of digital communalism."

Like Mao, Lessig and his comrades are not only on the wrong side of human nature and the wrong side of culture; they're also on the wrong side of history. They fooled themselves into believing that Web 2.0 was introducing a new economic system—a system of "social production"—that would serve as the foundation of a democratic, utopian

model of culture creation. They were wrong. Web 2.0's economic system has turned out to be, in effect if not intent, a
system of exploitation rather than a system of emancipation.
By putting the means of production into the hands of the
masses but withholding from those same masses any ownership over the product of their work, Web 2.0 provides an incredibly efficient mechanism to harvest the economic value
of the free labor provided by the very, very many and con-
centrate it into the hands of the very, very few.

The Cultural Revolution is over. It ended before it even
began. The victors are the counterrevolutionaries. And they
have $1.65 billion [a reference to the sale price of YouTube
to Google] to prove it.[29]

Lessig's response, a warm-up for a new book, *Remix*, released in
late 2008, pointed out that there are really *three* different economies
on the Internet—commercial, sharing, and hybrid. The hybrid
economy now emerging is difficult to understand, he suggested, because it "neither gives away everything, nor does it keep everything." The challenge of open business models, Lessig argues, is to
discover the "golden mean."

It can be hard to conceptualize a "hybrid sector" when we are
accustomed to dividing the world into "private" and "public" sectors, and "profit-making" and "nonprofit" enterprises. Open business models quickly run up against deep-seated prejudices that
associate property with "freedom" and sharing with "communism."
How can there be a middle ground? Although some like Nicholas
Carr seem to hanker for the predatory enterprises of an earlier capitalism, only this time on Web 2.0 platforms, that is not likely to
happen in a world of distributed computing. Power is too dispersed
for predators to survive very long, and besides, the commoners are
too empowered.

Build a market on a commons. A number of online business models
are based on building communities of deep social affection and respect, and then using the community as a platform for selling mer-

chandise, advertising, or products. Interestingly, some of the most successful "customer relationship" models revolve around music. The Grateful Dead's strategy of building a business around a rabid fan base (discussed in chapter 6) occurred well before the Internet became prevalent. It is paradigmatic of the digital age, nonetheless. If the band had locked up its music and prohibited free taping of its concert performances and sharing of homemade tapes, it would have effectively weakened the fan base that sustained its business model. Sharing concert tapes actually made Deadheads more inclined to buy t-shirts, official music releases, and concert tickets because the tape sharing deepened the community's identity and quasi-spiritual ethic. The Grateful Dead's focus on touring as opposed to studio albums not only intensified the sharing ethic of its fan base, it obliged the band to "keep on truckin' " in order to keep earning money.

The Brazilian *tecnobrega* music scene discussed briefly in chapter 7 is another example of artists making money through respectful, in-person relationships with their fans. In the town of Belém, Brazil, *tecnobrega* artists release about four hundred CDs every year, but none are sold in stores; street vendors sell them for $1.50 apiece. The CDs function mostly as advertising for live "sound system" parties on the outskirts of town that attract as many as five thousand people and use state-of-the-art audio technology. Immediately following the performances, some artists also sell a significant number of "instant CDs" that are of better quality (and more expensive) than those sold in the streets. (Interestingly, street sales do not compete with after-concert sales.)

"In their live presentations, the tecnobrega DJ's usually acknowledge the presence of people from various neighborhoods, and this acknowledgement is of great value to the audience, leading thousands of buy copies of the recorded live presentation," said Ronaldo Lemos of CC Brazil, who has studied Brazil's record industry.[30] The same basic model is also at work in other grassroots musical genres in Brazil, such as baile funk, which originated in the shantytowns of Rio de Janeiro.

Artists make most of their money from these live performances, not from CDs, said Lemos. Bands earn an average of $1,100 per solo performance at these events, and $700 when playing with other bands—this, in a region where the average monthly income is $350. Altogether, Lemos estimates that the sound system parties as a business sector earn $1.5 million per month, on fixed assets of $8 million.

"The band Calypso has been approached several times by traditional record labels," said Lemos, "but they turned down all the offers. The reason is that they make more money by means of the existing business model. In an interview with the largest Brazilian newspaper, the singer of the band said, 'We do not fight the pirates. We have become big *because* of piracy, which has taken our music to cities where they would never have been.'" Calypso has sold more than 5 million albums in Brazil and is known for attracting as many as fifty thousand people to its concerts, Lemos said.[31]

Another highly successful open business model in the Brazilian music scene is TramaVirtual, an open platform on which more than 15,000 musicians have uploaded some 35,000 albums. Fans can then download the music for free. While this does not sound like a promising business proposition, it makes a lot of sense in the context of Brazil's music marketplace. Major record labels release a minuscule number of new Brazilian music CDs each year, and they sell for about $10 to $15.[32] Only the cultured elite can afford music CDs, and the native musical talent—which is plentiful in Brazil—has no place to go. With such a constricted marketplace, TramaVirtual has become hugely popular by showcasing new and interesting music.

TramaVirtual's artistic and social cachet—itself the product of open sharing in a commons—has enabled it to develop a highly respected brand identity. "By exploiting the trademark," said Lemos, "Trama has been able to create parallel businesses that work with music, but not in the same way that a record label does."[33] For instance, Trama created a business that sponsors free concerts at universities under its trademark sponsorship. It then sells marketing rights at the concerts to cosmetic makers and car companies. Musicians have gained wide public exposure through Trama, and then used that association to negotiate international record and marketing deals for themselves. CSS (Cansei de Ser Sexy) won a record contract with the American label Sub Pop, for example.

For the past five years, a related business model for music on an international scale has been emerging in Luxembourg. In only three years, Jamendo has amassed a huge international following in much the same way as TramaVirtual—by attracting music fans to its open platform for free music sharing. (The name *Jamendo* is a mix of the words *jam* and *crescendo*.) The site is not a music retailer but a repository for free music—with a business model overlay to pay the bills. Jamendo's purpose is not to maximize returns to shareholders, in other words, but to service musicians and fans in a self-sustaining way. It makes most of its money from "tip jar" donations from fans and from advertising on the Web pages and streamed music. Ad revenues are shared 50-50 with artists, and any donations are passed along to individual artists, minus a small transaction fee.

The Jamendo community is sizable and growing. By 2008 it had more than 357,000 active members from around the world. Part of the draw is the catalog of more than 10,000 albums, all free. Unlike Magnatune, Jamendo does not select the artists that are featured on its site; everyone is welcome to upload his or her music. To help fans identify music they like, the site offers many sophisticated tools. There are some 60,000 member-written reviews, custom playlists, community ratings of albums, and "folksonomy" tags for albums and songs.* Fans are *urged* to download music through peer-to-peer networks such as BitTorrent and eMule because it reduces Jamendo's bandwidth expenses.

"Users can listen, download, review, remix, and 'widgetize,'" said Sylvain Zimmer, the founder and chief technology officer of Jamendo. As part of its commitment to musicians, the site has a forum

---

* Folksonomies, a cross of *taxonomy* and *folk,* are essentially user-generated tags attached to each song and album, which enables categories of music to emerge from the "bottom up," as fans regard the music, rather than through top-down marketing categories.

for artists and listings of concerts, as well as open APIs* so the Jamendo ecosystem can be integrated into other software.

What's striking about Jamendo is its nonchalant international feel, as if it were only natural to browse for "deathmetal," "power-pop," "hypnotique," "ambient," "psytrance," and "jazzrock" on the same site. (These are just a few of the scores of folksonomy tags that can be used to browse the catalog.) "We are a Babel, not a label," said Zimmer, who reports that India and Japan are heavy downloaders of Jamendo music. Complete, official versions of the site are available in French, the original language for the site, and now English and German. Incomplete versions of the site are available in Spanish, Polish, Portuguese, Russian, Turkish, Italian, Swedish, Czech, and Ukrainian.

Virtually all the albums on Jamendo use one or more of the six basic CC licenses. The CC ethic is a perfect match for the company's community-driven business model, said Zimmer. "The best way of detecting CC-incompatible content and commercial uses of NC-licensed work is the community. The Creative Commons makes the community feel more confident and active."[34] He adds that if the site's managers run too many ads, "the community will tell you."

Commoners as Co-creators of Value

For businesses operating on open networks, it is a mistake to regard people merely as customers; they are collaborators and even co-investors. As more companies learn to interact closely with their customers, it is only natural that conversations about the product or service become more intimate and collaborative. The roles of the

---

* An API is an "application programming interface," a set of protocols that enable a software application to operate on a computer operating system, library, or service. Many companies use proprietary APIs to retain control over who may develop applications that will interoperate with their software. Other companies that wish to encourage development of compatible applications—and thus promote a software ecosystem entwined with the operating system or service—use open APIs.

"consumer" and "producer" are starting to blur, leading to what some business analysts call the "prosumer"[35] and the "decentralized co-creation of value."[36] The basic idea is that online social communities are becoming staging areas for the advancement of business objectives. Businesses see these communities as cost-effective ways to identify promising innovations, commercialize them more rapidly, tap into more reliable market intelligence, and nurture customer goodwill.

Amateurs who share with one another through a loose social commons have always been a source of fresh ideas. Tech analyst Elliot Maxwell (citing Lessig) notes how volunteers helped compile the *Oxford English Dictionary* by contributing examples of vernacular usage; how the Homebrew Computer Club in the San Francisco Bay area developed many elements of the first successful personal computer; and how sharing among auto enthusiasts helped generate many of the most important early automotive innovations.[37] In our time, hackers were the ones who developed ingenious ways to use unlicensed electromagnetic spectrum as a commons, which we now know as Wi-Fi. They tinkered with the iPod to come up with podcasts, a new genre of broadcasting that commercial broadcasters now emulate.[38] Numerous self-organized commons have incubated profitable businesses. Two movie buffs created the Internet Movie Database as separate Usenet newsgroups in 1989; six years later they had grown so large that they had merged and converted into a business that was later sold to Amazon.[39] The Compact Disc Database was a free database of software applications that looks up information about audio CDs via the Internet. It was originally developed by a community of music fans as a shared database, but in 2000 it had grown big enough that it was sold and renamed Gracenote.[40]

A commons can be highly generative because its participants are tinkering and innovating for their own sake—for fun, to meet a challenge, to help someone out. Amateurs are not constrained by conventional business ideas about what may be marketable and profitable. They do not have to meet the investment expectations of venture capitalists and Wall Street. Yet once promising new ideas do surface in the commons, market players can play a useful role in supplying capital and management expertise to develop, improve, and commercialize an invention.

Because online commons are such a rich source of new ideas, the most farsighted companies are trying to learn how they might be harnessed to help them innovate and compete more effectively. MIT professor Eric von Hippel is one of the foremost researchers of this process. His 2005 book *Democratizing Innovation* describes how the leading participants in high-performance sports—extreme skiing, mountain biking, skateboarding, surfing, and hot-rodding—are forming "innovation communities" that work closely with manufacturers.[41] The most active practitioners of these sports are intimately familiar with the equipment and have their own imaginative ideas about what types of innovations the sport needs. Indeed, many of them have already jerry-rigged their own innovations—better cockpit ventilation in sailplanes, improved boot and bindings on snowboards, a method for cutting loose a trapped rope used by canyon climbers. For companies willing to listen to and collaborate with users, says von Hippel, "communities of interest are morphing into communities of creation and communities of production."

"Users that innovate can develop exactly what they want, rather than relying on manufacturers to act as their (often very imperfect) agents," von Hippel writes. "Moreover, individuals users do not have to develop everything they need on their own: they can benefit from innovations developed and freely shared by others."[42] Besides finding empirical examples of this trend, von Hippel has developed a theoretical vocabulary for understanding how collaborative innovation occurs. He probes the user motivations for "free revealing" of their knowledge, the attractive economics that fuel "users' low-cost innovation niches," and the public policies that sometimes thwart user-driven innovation (patent rights for a field may be fragmented, anticopying restrictions such as the Digital Millennium Copyright Act may prevent user tinkering, etc.).

User-driven innovation is not as esoteric as the "extreme sports" examples may suggest. It is, in fact, a growing paradigm. In one of the more celebrated examples, Lego, the Danish toymaker, invited some of its most fanatic users to help it redesign its Mindstorms robotics kit. The kits are meant to let kids (and adults) build a variety of customized robots out of a wild assortment of plastic Lego pieces, programmable software, sensors, and motors.[43] In 2004, when some Lego users reverse-engineered the robotic "brain" for the Mindstorms kit and put their findings on the Internet, Lego at first contemplated legal action. Upon reflection, however, Lego realized that hackers could be a valuable source of new ideas for making its forthcoming Mindstorms kit more interesting and cool.

Lego decided to write a "right to hack" provision into the Mindstorms software license, "giving hobbyists explicit permission to let their imaginations run wild," as Brendan I. Koerner wrote in *Wired* magazine. "Soon, dozens of Web sites were hosting third-party programs that help Mindstorms users build robots that Lego had never dreamed of: soda machines, blackjack dealers, even toilet scrubbers. Hardware mavens designed sensors that were far more sophisticated than the touch and light sensors included in the factory kit."[44] It turns out that not only are Lego fans happy to advise the company, the open process "engenders goodwill and creates a buzz among the zealots, a critical asset for products like Mindstorms that rely on word-of-mouth evangelism," said Koerner. In the end, he concluded, the Mindstorm community of fanatics has done "far more to add value to Lego's robotics kit than the company itself."

Another improbable success in distributed, user-driven innovation is Threadless, a Chicago-based t-shirt company. Threadless sells hundreds of original t-shirt designs, each of which is selected by the user community from among more than eight hundred designs submitted every week. The proposed designs are rated on a scale of one to five by the Web site's more than 600,000 active users. Winners receive cash awards, recognition on the Web site, and their names on the t-shirt label. Every week, Threadless offers six to ten new t-shirts featuring the winning designs.

In 2006, the company sold more than 1.5 million t-shirts without any traditional kind of marketing. Its business model is so rooted in the user community that Threadless co-founders Jake Nickell and Jacob DeHart have declined offers to sell their t-shirts through conventional, big-name retailers. Threadless's business model has helped it overcome two major challenges in the apparel industry, write Harvard Business School professor Karim R. Lakhani and consultant Jill A. Panetta—the ability "to attract the right design talent at the right time to create recurring fashion hits," and the ability "to forecast sales so as to be better able to match production cycles with demand cycles."[45]

A number of companies have started successful enterprises based on the use of wikis, the open Web platforms that allow anyone to contribute and edit content and collaborate. Evan Prodromou, the founder of Wikitravel, a free set of worldwide travel guides, has identified four major types of wiki businesses: service providers who sell access to wikis (Wikispace, wetpaint, PBwiki); content hosters of wikis (wikiHow, Wikitravel, Wikia); consultants who advise companies how to run their own wikis (Socialtext); and content developers (WikiBiz, an offshoot of Wikipedia).

Since the success of a wiki-based business depends upon honoring the integrity of wiki users, Prodromou scorns what he sees as the backhanded strategies of business models based on "wikinomics" and "crowdsourcing." He sees such models as sly attempts to get "suckers" to do free work for the entrepreneur owning the business. A sustainable commercial wiki, said Prodromou at a conference, respects the community of users and does not try to exploit them. It strives to fulfill a "noble purpose" for users and demonstrate in a transparent way that it offers value. Any hint of trickery or calculation begins to sow distrust and erode the community. Yet any wiki-based business must be able to set boundaries that allow the owners to make responsible business decisions; those decisions, however, must respect the wiki community's values.[46]

It is hard to predict what new models of "decentralized cocreation of value" will take root and flourish, but the experiments are certainly proliferating. Staples, the office supplies store, now hosts a contest inviting the public to suggest inventions that Staples can develop and sell under the its brand name.[47] A number of mass-market advertisers have hosted competitions inviting users to create ads for their products. One of the more interesting frontiers in user-driven innovation is tapping the audience for investment capital.

SellaBand ("You are the record company") is a Web site that invites bands to recruit five thousand "Believers" to invest $10 apiece in their favorite bands; upon reaching the $50,000 mark, a band can make a professional recording, which is then posted on the Sella-Band site for free downloads. Bands and fans can split advertising revenues with SellaBand.[48] Robert Greenwald, the activist documentary filmmaker, used e-mail solicitations, social networks, and the blogosphere to ask ordinary citizens to help finance his 2006 film *Iraq for Sale: The War Profiteers*.[49]

Reintegrating the Sharing and Commercial Economies

If there is persistent skepticism about the very idea of open business models, from both business traditionalists focused on the bottom line and commoners committed to sharing, it is because the commons and the commercial economy seem to represent such divergent moral values and social orders. One depends upon reciprocal exchanges of monetary value, with the help of individual property rights and contracts; the other depends upon the informal social circulation of value, without individual property rights or quid pro quos. A market is impersonal, transactional, and oriented to a bottom line; a commons tends to be personal and social and oriented to continuous relationships, shared values, and identity.

Yet, as the examples above show, the market and the commons interpenetrate each other, yin/yang style. Each "adds value" to the other in synergistic ways. Historically, this has always been true. Adam Smith, the author of *The Wealth of Nations*, was also the author of *The Theory of Moral Sentiments*, about the moral and social norms that undergird market activity. The market has always depended upon the hidden subsidies of the commons (folk stories, vernacular motifs, amateur creativity) to drive its engine of wealth creation. And the commons builds its sharing regimes amid the material wealth produced by the market (free software is developed on commercially produced computers).

What has changed in recent years is our perceptions. The actual role of the commons in creative endeavors has become more culturally legible. For businesses to function well on Web 2.0 platforms, they must more consciously integrate social and market relationships in functional, sustainable ways. If the results sometimes seem novel, if not bizarre, it is partly because networking technologies are making us more aware that markets are not ahistorical, universal entities; they are rooted in social relationships. Open business models recognize this very elemental truth, and in this sense represent a grand gambit to go back to the future.

11

SCIENCE AS A COMMONS

*Web 2.0 tools, open access, and CC licenses are helping
to accelerate scientific discovery.*

It was one of those embarrassing episodes in science: Two sets of researchers published papers in a German organic chemistry journal, *Angewandte Chemie*, announcing that they had synthesized a strange new substance with "12-membered rings." Then, as blogger and chemist Derek Lowe tells the story, "Professor Manfred Cristl of Wurzburg, who apparently knows his pyridinium chemistry pretty well, recognized this as an old way to make further pyridinium salts, not funky twelve-membered rings. He recounts how over the last couple of months he exchanged awkward emails with the two sets of authors, pointing out that they seem to have rediscovered a 100-year-old reaction. . . ."[1]

In the Internet age, people generally assume that these kinds of things can't happen. All you have to do is run a Web search for "pyridinium," right? But as scientists in every field are discovering, the existence of some shard of highly specialized knowledge does not necessarily mean that it can be located or understood. After all, a Google search for "pyridinium" turns up 393,000 results. And even peer reviewers for journals (who may have been partly at fault in this instance) have the same problem as any researcher: the unfathomable vastness of the scientific and technical literature makes it difficult to know what humankind has already discovered.

Paradoxically, even though academic science played the central role in incubating the Internet (in conjunction with the military), it has not fared very well in developing it to advance research. Most search engines are too crude. Journal articles can be expensive and inaccessible. They do not link to relevant Web resources or invite reader comment. Nor do they contain metadata to facilitate computer-based searches, collaborative filtering, and text mining. Scientific databases are plentiful but often incompatible with one another, preventing researchers from exploring new lines of inquiry. Lab researchers who need to share physical specimens still have to shuffle papers through a bureaucratic maze and negotiate with lawyers, without the help of eBay- or Craigslist-like intermediaries.

"The World Wide Web was designed in a scientific laboratory to facilitate access to scientific knowledge," observed Duke law professor James Boyle in 2007. "In every other area of life—commercial, social networking, pornography—it has been a smashing success. But in the world of science itself? With the virtues of the open Web all around us, we have proceeded to build an endless set of walled gardens, something that looks a lot like Compuserv or Minitel and very little like a world wide web for science."[2]

Therein lies a fascinating, complicated story. To be sure, various scientific bodies have made great progress in recent years in adapting the principles of free software, free culture, and Web 2.0 applications to their research. Open-access journals, institutional repositories, specialty wikis, new platforms for collaborative research, new metatagging systems: all are moving forward in different, fitful ways. Yet, for a field of inquiry that has long honored the ethic of sharing and "standing on the shoulders of giants," academic science has lagged behind most other sectors.

Part of the problem is the very nature of scientific knowledge. While the conventional Web works fairly well for simple kinds of commerce and social purposes, the Research Web for science requires a more fine-grained, deliberately crafted structure.[3] Science involves *practices*, after all; it is not just about information. The "wisdom of the crowds" is not good enough. Scientific knowledge tends to be significantly more specialized and structured than cultural information or product recommendations. The Web systems for organizing, manipulating, and accessing that knowledge, accordingly, need to be more hierarchical and structured, often in quite specific ways depending upon the discipline. A scientist cannot just type "signal transduction genes in pyramidal neurons" into a search engine; she needs to be able to locate specific genes and annotations of them. Data may be strewn across dozens of different data systems, and those are not likely to be interoperable. This means that technical standards need to be coordinated, or some metasystem developed to allow different data reservoirs to communicate with one another. A scientist must be able to use computers to browse and organize a vast literature. And so on.

Much as scientists would like to build new types of Internet-based commons, they have quickly run up against a thicket of interrelated problems: overly broad copyright and patent limitations; access and usage restrictions by commercial journal publishers and database owners; and university rules that limit how cell lines, test animals, bioassays, and other research tools may be shared. In a sense, scientists and universities face a classic collective-action problem. Everyone would clearly be better off if a more efficient infrastructure and enlightened social ethic could be adopted—but few single players have the resources, incentive, or stature to buck the prevailing order. There is no critical mass for instigating a new platform for scientific inquiry and "knowledge management."

Like so many other sectors confronting the Great Value Shift, science in the late 1990s found itself caught in a riptide. The proprietarian ethic of copyright and patent law was intensifying (as we saw in chapter 2), spurring scientists and universities to claim private ownership in knowledge that was previously treated as a shared resource.[4] Yet at the same time the Internet was demonstrating the remarkable power of open sharing and collaboration. Even as market players sought to turn data, genetic knowledge, and much else into private property rights, a growing number of scientists realized that the best ideals of science would be fulfilled by recommitting itself to its core values of openness and sharing. Open platforms could also strengthen the social relationships that are essential to so much scientific inquiry.[5]

Perhaps the most salient example of the power of open science was the Human Genome Project (HGP), a publicly funded research project to map the 3 billion base pairs of the human genome. Many other scientific projects have been attracted by the stunning efficacy and efficiency of the open research model. For example, the

HapMap project is a government-supported research effort to map variations in the human genome that occur in certain clusters, or haplotypes. There is also the SNP Consortium, a public-private partnership seeking to identify single-nucleotide polymorphisms (SNPs) that may be used to identify genetic sources of disease. Both projects use licenses that put the genomic data into the public domain.

A 2008 report by the Committee for Economic Development identified a number of other notable open research projects.[6] There is the PubChem database, which amasses data on chemical genomics from a network of researchers; the Cancer Biomedical Informatics Grid, a network of several dozen cancer research centers and other organizations that shares data, research tools, and software applications; and TDR Targets a Web clearinghouse sponsored by the World Health Organization that lets researchers share genetic data on neglected diseases such as malaria and sleeping sickness. It is telling that Bill Gates, who in his commercial life is a staunch advocate of proprietary control of information, has been a leader, through his Bill & Melinda Gates Foundation, in requiring research grantees to share their data.

There has even been the emergence of open-source biotechnology, which is applying the principles of free software development to agricultural biotech and pharmaceutical development.[7] Richard Jefferson, the founder of Cambia, a nonprofit research institute in Australia, launched the "kernel" of what he calls the first open-source biotech toolkit. It includes patented technologies such as TransBacter, which is a method for transferring genes to plants, and GUSPlus, which is a tool for visualizing genes and understanding their functions.[8] By licensing these patented research tools for open use, Jefferson hopes to enable researchers anywhere in the world—not just at large biotech companies or universities—to develop their own crop improvement technologies.

The Viral Spiral in Science

Sociologist Robert Merton is often credited with identifying the social values and norms that make science such a creative, productive enterprise. In a notable 1942 essay, Merton described scientific knowledge as "common property" that depends critically upon an open, ethical, peer-driven process.[9] Science is an engine of discovery precisely because research is available for all to see and replicate. It has historically tried to keep some distance from the marketplace for fear that corporate copyrights, patents, or contractual agreements will lock up knowledge that should be available to everyone, especially future scientists.[10] Secrecy can also make it difficult for the scientific community to verify research results.

Although scientific knowledge eventually becomes publicly available, it usually flows in semirestricted ways, at least initially, because scientists usually like to claim personal credit for their discoveries. They may refuse to share their latest research lest a rival team of scientists gain a competitive advantage. They may wish to claim patent rights in their discoveries.

So scientific knowledge is not born into the public sphere, but there is a strong presumption that it ought to be treated as a shared resource as quickly as possible. As law scholar Robert Merges noted in 1996, "Science is not so much given freely to the public as shared under a largely implicit code of conduct among a more or less well-identified circle of similarly situated scientists. In other words . . . science is more like a limited-access commons than a truly open public domain."[11] In certain disciplines, especially those involving large capital equipment such as telescopes and particle accelerators, the sharing of research is regarded as a kind of membership rule for belonging to a club.

As Web 2.0 innovations have demonstrated the power of the Great Value Shift, the convergence of open source, open access, and open science has steadily gained momentum.[12] Creative Commons was mindful of this convergence from its beginnings, but it faced formidable practical challenges in doing anything about it. "From the very first meetings of Creative Commons," recalled law professor James Boyle, a CC board member, "we thought that science could be the killer app. We thought that science could be the place where Creative Commons could really make a difference, save lives, and have a dramatic impact on the world. There is massive, unnecessary friction in science and we think we can deal with it. Plus, there's the Mertonian ideal of science, with which Creative Commons couldn't fit more perfectly." [13]

But despite its early interest in making the Web more research-friendly, Creative Commons realized that science is a special culture unto itself, one that has so many major players and niche variations that it would be foolhardy for an upstart nonprofit to try to engage with it. So in 2002 Creative Commons shelved its ambitions to grapple with science as a commons, and focused instead on artistic and cultural sectors. By January 2005, however, the success of the CC licenses emboldened the organization to revisit its initial idea. As a result of deep personal engagement by several Creative Commons board members—computer scientist Hal Abelson, law professors James Boyle and Michael Carroll, and film producer Eric Saltzman—Creative Commons decided to launch a spin-off project, Science Commons. The new initiative would work closely with scientific disciplines and organizations to try to build what it now calls "the Research Web."

Science Commons aims to redesign the "information space"—the technologies, legal rules, institutional practices, and social norms—so that researchers can more easily share their articles, datasets, and other resources. The idea is to reimagine and reinvent the "cognitive infrastructures" that are so critical to scientific inquiry. Dismayed by the pressures exerted by commercial journal publishers, open-access publishing advocate Jean-Claude Guédon has called on librarians to become "epistemological engineers." [14] They need to design better systems (technical, institutional, legal, and social) for identifying, organizing, and using knowledge. The payoff? Speedier research and greater scientific discovery and innovation. It turns out that every scientific discipline has its own special set of impediments to address. The recurring problem is massive, unnecessary transaction costs. There is an enormous waste of time, expense, bureaucracy, and logistics in acquiring journal articles, datasets, presentations, and physical specimens.

If transaction costs could be overcome, scientists could vastly accelerate their research cycles. They could seek answers in unfamiliar bodies of research literature. They could avoid duplicating other people's flawed research strategies. They could formulate more imaginative hypotheses and test them more rapidly. They could benefit from a broader, more robust conversation (as in free software—"with enough eyes, all bugs are shallow") and use computer networks to augment and accelerate the entire scientific process.

That is the vision of open science that Science Commons wanted to address in 2005. It recognized that science is a large, sprawling world of many institutional stakeholders controlling vast sums of money driving incommensurate agendas. In such a milieu, it is not easy to redesign some of the most basic processes and norms for conducting research. Science Commons nonetheless believed it could play a constructive role as a catalyst.

It was fortunate to have some deep expertise not just from its board members, but from two Nobel Prize winners on its scientific advisory panel (Sir John Sulston and Joshua Lederberg) and several noted scholars (patent scholar Arti Rai, innovation economist Paul David, and open-access publishing expert Michael B. Eisen). The director of Science Commons, John Wilbanks, brought a rare mix of talents and connections. He was once a software engineer at the World Wide Web Consortium, specializing in the Semantic Web; he had founded and run a company dealing in bioinformatics and artificial intelligence; he had worked for a member of Congress; and he was formerly assistant director of the Berkman Center at Harvard Law School.

After obtaining free office space at MIT, Wilbanks set off to instigate change within the scientific world—and then get out of the way. "We're designing Science Commons to outstrip ourselves," Wilbanks told me. "We don't want to control any of this; we're designing it to be decentralized. If we try to control it, we'll fail."

With a staff of seven and a budget of only $800,000 in 2008, Science Commons is not an ocean liner like the National Academy of Science and the National Science Foundation; it's more of a tugboat. Its strategic interventions try to nudge the big players into new trajectories. It is unencumbered by bureaucracy and entrenched stakeholders, yet it has the expertise, via Creative Commons, to develop standard licensing agreements for disparate communities. It knows how to craft legal solutions that can work with technology and be understood by nonlawyers.

In 2006, Science Commons embarked upon three "proof of concept" projects that it hopes will be models for other scientific fields. The first initiative, the Scholar's Copyright Project, aspires to give scientists the "freedom to archive and reuse scholarly works on the Internet." It is also seeking to make the vast quantities of data on computerized databases more accessible and interoperable, as a way to advance scientific discovery and innovation.

A second project, the Neurocommons, is a bold experiment that aims to use the Semantic Web to make a sprawling body of neurological research on the Web more accessible. The project is developing a new kind of Internet platform so that researchers will be able to do sophisticated searches of neuroscience-related journal articles and explore datasets across multiple databases.

Finally, Science Commons is trying to make it cheaper and easier for researchers to share physical materials such as genes, proteins, chemicals, tissues, model animals, and reagents, which is currently a cumbersome process. The Biological Materials Transfer Project resembles an attempt to convert the pony express into a kind of Federal Express, so that researchers can use an integrated electronic data system to obtain lab materials with a minimum of legal complications and logistical delays.

In many instances, Science Commons has been a newcomer to reform initiatives already under way to build open repositories of scientific literature or data. One of the most significant is the open-access publishing movement, which has been a diverse, flourishing effort in academic circles since the 1990s. It is useful to review the history of the open access (OA) movement because it has been an important pacesetter and inspiration for the open-science ethic.

The Open-Access Movement

The open-access movement has a fairly simple goal: to get the scientific record online and available to everyone. It regards this task as one of the most fundamental challenges in science. Open-access publishing generally consists of two modes of digital access—open-access archives (or "repositories") and open-access journals. In both instances, the publisher or host institution pays the upfront costs of putting material on the Web so that Internet users can access the literature at no charge.★

The appeal of OA publishing stems from the Great Value Shift described in chapter 5. "OA owes its origin and part of its deep appeal to the fact that publishing to the Internet permits both wider dissemination and lower costs than any previous form of publishing," writes Peter Suber, author of *Open Access News* and a leading champion of OA.[15] "The revolutionary conjunction is too good to pass up. But even lower costs must be recovered if OA is to be sustainable." In most cases, publishing costs are met by scientific and academic institutions and/or by subsidies folded into research grants. Sometimes an OA journal will defray its publishing costs by charging authors (or their grant funders) a processing fee for articles that they accept.

Just as free software and music downloads have disrupted their respective industries, so OA publishing has not been a welcome development among large academic publishers such as Elsevier,

---

★ "Open access" can be a confusing term. In the context of a rivalrous, depletable natural resource like timber or grazing land, an open-access regime means that anyone can use and appropriate the resource, resulting in its overexploitation and ruin. An *open-access regime* is not the same as *a commons*, however, because a commons does have rules, boundaries, sanctions against free riders, etc., to govern the resource. However, in the context of an infinite, nonrivalrous resource like information, which can be copied and distributed at virtually no cost, an open-access regime does not result in overexploitation of the resource. For this reason, open access in an Internet context is often conflated with the commons—even though "open access," in a natural resource context, tends to produce very different outcomes.

Springer, Kluwer, and Wiley. Online publishing usually costs much less than traditional print publishing and it allows authors to retain control over their copyrights. Both of these are a big incentive for disciplines and universities to start up their own OA journals. In addition, OA publishing makes it easier for research to circulate, and for authors to reach larger readerships. This not only augments the practical goals of science, it bolsters the reputation system and open ethic that science depends upon.

Commercial publishers have historically emphasized their shared interests with scholars and scientists, and the system was amicable and symbiotic. Academics would produce new work, validate its quality through peer review, and then, in most cases, give the work to publishers at no charge. Publishers shouldered the expense of editorial production, distribution, and marketing and reaped the bulk of revenues generated. The arrangement worked fairly well for everyone until journal prices began to rise in the early 1970s. Then, as subscription rates continued to soar, placing unbearable burdens on university libraries in the 1990s, the Internet facilitated an extremely attractive alternative: open-access journals. Suddenly, conventional business models for scholarly publishing had a serious rival, one that shifts the balance of power back to scientists and their professional communities.

Publishers have long insisted upon acquiring the copyright of journal articles and treating them as "works for hire." This transfer of ownership enables the publisher, not the author, to determine how a work may circulate. Access to an article can then be limited by the subscription price for a journal, the licensing fees for online access, and pay-per-view fees for viewing an individual article. Publishers may also limit the reuse, republication, and general circulation of an article by charging high subscription or licensing fees, or by using digital rights management. If a university cannot afford the journal, or if a scholar cannot afford to buy individual articles, research into a given topic is effectively stymied.

Open-access champion John Willinsky notes, "The publishing economy of scholarly journals is dominated by a rather perverse property relation, in which the last investor in the research production chain—consisting of university, researcher, funding agency and *publisher*—owns the resulting work outright through a very small investment in relation to the work's overall cost and value." [16] Scientists and scholars virtually never earn money from their journal articles, and only occasionally from their books. Unlike commercial writers, this is no problem for academics, whose salaries are intended to free them to study all sorts of niche interests despite the lack of "market demand." Their works are not so much "intellectual property" that must yield maximum revenues as "royalty-free literature," as Peter Suber calls it. Academics write and publish to contribute to their fields and enhance their standing among their peers.

Not surprisingly, many commercial publishers regard OA publishing as a disruptive threat. It can, after all, subvert existing revenue models for scholarly publishing. This does not mean that OA publishing cannot support a viable business model. Much of OA publishing is sustained through "author-side payments" to publishers. In certain fields that are funded by research grants, such as biomedicine, grant makers fold publishing payments into their grants so that the research can be made permanently available in open-access journals. A leading commercial publisher, BioMed Central, now publishes over 140 OA journals in this manner. Hindawi Publishing Corporation, based in Cairo, Egypt, publishes more than one hundred OA journals and turns a profit. And Medknow Publications, based in Mumbai, India, is also profitable as a publisher of more than forty OA journals.

It remains an open question whether the OA business model will work in fields where little research is directly funded (and thus upfront payments are not easily made). As Suber reports, "There are hundreds of OA journals in the humanities, but very, very few of them charge a fee on the author's side; most of them have institutional subsidies from a university say, or a learned society." [17] Yet such subsidies, in the overall scheme of things, may be more attractive to universities or learned societies than paying high subscription fees for journals or online access.

The tension between commercial publishers and academic authors has intensified over the past decade, fueling interest in OA alternatives. The most salient point of tension is the so-called "serials crisis." From 1986 to 2006, libraries that belong to the Association of Research Libraries saw the cost of serial journals rise 321 percent, or about 7.5 percent a year for twenty consecutive years.[18] This rate is four times higher than the inflation rate for those years. Some commercial journal publishers reap profits of nearly 40 percent a year.[19] By 2000 subscription rates were so crushing that the Association of American Universities and the Association of Research Libraries issued a joint statement that warned, "The current system of scholarly publishing has become too costly for the academic community to sustain."[20] Three years later, the high price of journals prompted Harvard, the University of California, Cornell, MIT, Duke, and other elite research universities to cancel hundreds of journal subscriptions—a conspicuous act of rebellion by the library community.

As journal prices have risen, the appeal of OA publishing has only intensified. Unfortunately, migrating to OA journals is not simply an economic issue. Within academia, the reputation of a journal is deeply entwined with promotion and tenure decisions. A scientist who publishes an article in *Cell* or *Nature* earns far more prestige than she might for publishing in a little-known OA journal.

So while publishing in OA journals may be economically attractive, it flouts the institutional traditions and social habits that scientists have come to rely on for evaluating scientific achievement. The OA movement's challenge has been to document how OA models can help a university, and so it has collaborated with university administrators to showcase exemplary successes and work out new revenue models. It is urging promotion and tenure committees, for example, to modify their criteria to stop discriminating against new journals just because they are new, and hence to stop discriminating against OA journals (which are all new). Much of this work has fallen to key OA leaders like the Open Society Institute, the Hewlett Foundation, Mellon Foundation and the library-oriented SPARC (Scholarly Publishing and Academic Resources Coalition) as well as individuals such as John Willinsky, Jean-Claude Guédon, Stevan Harnad, and Peter Suber. One of the first major salvos of the movement came in 2000, when biomedical scientists Harold E. Varmus, Patrick O. Brown, and Michael B. Eisen called on scientific publishers to make their literature available through free online public archives such as the U.S. National Library of Medicine's PubMed Central. Despite garnering support from nearly 34,000 scientists in 180 countries, the measure did not stimulate the change sought. It did alert the scientific world, governments, and publishers about the virtues of OA publishing, however, and galvanized scientists to explore next steps.

At the time, a number of free, online peer-reviewed journals and free online archives were under way.[21] But much of the momentum for organized OA movement began in 2001, when the Open Society Institute convened a group of leading librarians, scientists, and other academics in Hungary. In February 2002 the group released the Budapest Open Access Initiative, a statement that formally describes "open access" as the freedom of users to "read, download, copy, distribute, print, search or link to the full texts of . . . articles, crawl them for indexing, pass them as data to software, or use them for any other lawful purpose, without financial, legal or technical barriers other than those inseparable from gaining access to the Internet itself."[22] Two subsequent statements, the Bethesda Declaration and the Berlin Declaration, in June 2003 and October 2003, respectively, expanded upon the definitions of open access and gave the idea new prominence. (Suber calls the three documents the "BBB definition" of open access.)[23]

Creative Commons licenses have been critical tools in the evolution of OA publishing because they enable scientists and scholars to authorize in advance the sharing, copying, and reuse of their work, compatible with the BBB definition. The Attribution (BY) and Attribution-Non-Commercial (BY-NC) licenses are frequently used; many OA advocates regard the Attribution license as the preferred choice. The protocols for "metadata harvesting" issued by the Open Archives Initiative are another useful set of tools in OA publishing. When adopted by an OA journal, these standardized protocols help users more easily find research materials without knowing in advance which archives they reside in, or what they contain.

There is no question that OA is transforming the market for scholarly publishing, especially as pioneering models develop. The Public Library of Science announced its first two open-access journals in December 2002. The journals represented a bold, high-profile challenge by highly respected scientists to the subscription-based model that has long dominated scientific publishing. Although Elsevier and other publishers scoffed at the economic model, the project has expanded and now publishes seven OA journals, for biology, computational biology, genetics, pathogens, and neglected tropical diseases, among others.

OA received another big boost in 2004 when the National Institutes for Health proposed that all NIH-funded research be made available for free one year after its publication in a commercial journal. The $28 billion that the NIH spends on research each year (more than the domestic budget of 142 nations!) results in about 65,000 peer-reviewed articles, or 178 every day. Unfortunately, commercial journal publishers succeeded in making the proposed OA policy voluntary. The battle continued in Congress, but it became clear that the voluntary approach was not working. Only 4 percent of researchers published their work under OA standards, largely because busy, working scientists did not consider it a priority and their publishers were not especially eager to help. So Congress in December 2007 required NIH to mandate open access for its research within a year of publication.[24]

What may sound like an arcane policy battle in fact has serious implications for ordinary Americans. The breast cancer patient seeking the best peer-reviewed articles online, or the family of a person with Huntington's disease, can clearly benefit if they can acquire, for free, the latest medical research. Scientists, journalists, health-care workers, physicians, patients, and many others cannot access the vast literature of publicly funded scientific knowledge because of high subscription rates or per-article fees. A freely available body of online literature is the best, most efficient way to help science generate more reliable answers, new discoveries, and commercial innovations.

While large publishers continue to dominate the journal market, OA publishing has made significant advances in recent years. In June 2008, the Directory of Open Access Journals listed more than 3,400 open-access journals containing 188,803 articles. In some fields such as biology and bioinformatics, OA journals are among the top-cited journals. In fact, this is one of the great advantages of OA literature. In the networked environment, articles published in OA journals are more likely to be discovered by others and cited, which enhances the so-called impact of an article and the reputation of an author.

Although journals may or may not choose to honor OA principles, any scientist, as the copyright holder of his articles, can choose to "self-archive" his work under open-access terms. But commercial publishers generally don't like to cede certain rights, and authors usually don't know what rights to ask for, how to assert them in legal language, and how to negotiate with publishers. So it is difficult for most academics to assert their real preferences for open access. To help make things simpler, SPARC and MIT developed what is called an "author's addendum." It is a standard legal contract that authors can attach to their publishing contracts, in which they reserve certain key rights to publish their works in OA-compliant ways.

The Scholar's Copyright Project

In an attempt to help the open-access movement, Science Commons in 2007 developed its own suite of amendments to publishing contracts. The goal has been to ensure that "at a minimum, scholarly authors retain enough rights to archive their work on the Web. Every Science Commons Addendum ensures the freedom to use scholarly articles for educational purposes, conference presentations, in other scholarly works or in professional activities."[25] The ultimate goal is to enable authors "to have the clear and unambiguous freedom to engage in their normal everyday scholarly activities

without contending with complex technology, continuous amendments to contracts or the need for a lawyer."[26]

To make the whole process easier for scientists, Science Commons developed the Scholar's Copyright Addendum Engine. This
point-and-click Web-based tool lets authors publish in traditional,
subscription-based journals while retaining their rights to post
copies on the Internet for download, without most copyright and
financial restrictions. There are also options for "drag and drop"
self-archiving to repositories such as MIT's DSpace and the National Library of Medicine's PubMed Central. Besides making self-
archiving easier and more prevalent, Science Commons hopes to
standardize the legal terms and procedures for self-archiving to
avoid a proliferation of incompatible rights regimes and document
formats. "The engine seems to be generating a dialogue between
authors and publishers that never existed," said John Wilbanks. "It's
not being rejected out of hand, which is really cool. To the extent
that the addendum becomes a norm, it will start to open up the
[contractual] limitations on self-archiving."[27]

Harvard University gave self-archiving a big boost in February
2008 when its faculty unanimously voted to require all faculty to
distribute their scholarship through an online, open-access repository operated by the Harvard library unless a professor chooses
to "opt out" and publish exclusively with a commercial journal.
Robert Darnton, director of the Harvard library, said, "In place of a
closed, privileged and costly system, [the open-access rule] will help
open up the world of learning to everyone who wants to learn."[28]
Harvard's move was the first time that a university faculty, and not
just the administration, initiated action to take greater control of its
scholarly publishing. While some critics complain the new policy
does not go far enough, most OA advocates hailed the decision as
a major step toward developing alternative distribution models for
academic scholarship.

By far, the more ambitious aspect of the Scholar's Copyright
project is the attempt to free databases from a confusing tangle of
copyright claims. In every imaginable field of science—from anthropology and marine biology to chemistry and genetics—databases

are vital tools for organizing and manipulating vast collections of empirical data. The flood of data has vastly increased as computers have become ubiquitous research tools and as new technologies are deployed to generate entirely new sorts of digital data streams—measurements from remote sensors, data streams from space, and much more. But the incompatibility of databases—chiefly for technical and copyright reasons—is needlessly Balkanizing research to the detriment of scientific progress. "There is plenty of data out there," says Richard Wallis of Talis, a company that has built a Semantic Web technology platform for open data, "but it is often trapped in silos or hidden behind logins, subscriptions or just plain difficult to get hold of." He added that there is a lot of data that is "just out there," but the terms of access may be dubious.[29]

Questions immediately arise: Can a database be legally used? Who owns it? Will the database continue to be accessible? Will access require payment later on? Since data now reside anywhere in the world, any potential user of data also has to consider the wide variations of copyright protection for databases around the world.

The question of how data shall be owned, controlled, and shared is a profoundly perplexing one. History has shown the virtue of sharing scientific data—yet individual scientists, universities, and corporations frequently have their own interests in limiting how databases may be used. Scientists want to ensure the integrity of the data and any additions to it; they may want to ensure preferential access to key researchers; companies may consider the data a lucrative asset to be privately exploited. Indeed, if there is not some mechanism of control, database producers worry that free riders will simply appropriate useful compilations and perhaps sell it or use it for their own competitive advantage. Or they may fail to properly credit the scientists who compiled the data in the first place. Inadequate database protection could discourage people from creating new databases in the future.

A National Research Council report in 1999 described the problem this way: "Currently many for-profit and not-for-profit database producers are concerned about the possibility that significant portions of their databases will be copied or used in substantial part by others to create 'new' derivative databases. If an identical or substantially similar database is then either re-disseminated broadly or sold and used in direct competition with the original rights holder's database, the rights holder's revenues will be undermined, or in extreme cases, the rights holder will be put out of business."[30]

In the late 1990s, when the Human Genome Project and a private company, Celera, were competing to map the human genome, the publicly funded researchers were eager to publish the genome sequencing data as quickly as possible in order to prevent Celera or any other company from claiming exclusive control over the information. They wanted the data to be treated as "the common heritage of humanity" so that it would remain openly accessible to everyone, including commercial researchers. When Sir John Sulston of the Human Genome Project broached the idea of putting his team's research under a GPL-like license, it provoked objections that ownership of the data would set a worrisome precedent. A GPL for data amounts to a "reach-through" requirement on how data may be used in the future. This might not only imply that data can be owned—flouting the legal tradition that facts cannot be owned—it might discourage future data producers from depositing their data into public databases.[31]

The International HapMap Project attempted such a copyleft strategy with its database of genotypes; its goal is to compare the genetic sequences of different individuals to identify chromosomal regions where genetic variants are shared.[32] The project initially required users to register and agree to certain contract terms in order to use the database. One key term prohibited users from patenting any genetic information from the database or using patents to block usage of HapMap data.[33] This viral, open-content license for data seemed to provide a solution to the problem of how to keep data in the commons. But in time the HapMap Project found that its license inhibited people's willingness to integrate their own data with the HapMap database. It therefore abandoned its license and now places all of its data into the public domain; it is now available to be used by anyone for any purpose, although it has issued guidelines for the "responsible use and publication" of the data.[34]

The basic problem with applying copyright law to databases is how to draw the line between what is private property and what remains in the commons. "If you try to impose a Creative Commons license or free-software-style licensing regime on a database of uncopyrightable facts," explained John Wilbanks, "you create an enormous amount of confusion in the user about where the rights start and stop."[35] It is not very practical for a working scientist to determine whether copyright protection applies only to the data itself, to the database model (the structure and organization of the data), or to the data entry and output sheet. A scientist might reasonably presume that his data are covered by copyright law, and then use that right to apply a CC ShareAlike license to the data. But in fact, the data could be ineligible for copyright protection and so the CC license would be misleading; other scientists could ignore its terms with impunity. At the other extreme, other scientists may be unwilling to share their data at all lest the data circulate with no controls whatsoever. Data are either overprotected or underprotected, but in either case there is great ambiguity and confusion.

For two years, Science Commons wrestled with the challenge of applying the CC licenses to databases. Ultimately, the project came to the conclusion that "copyright licenses and contractual restrictions are simply the wrong tool, even if those licenses are used with the best of intentions." There is just too much uncertainty about the scope and applicability of copyright—and thus questions about any licenses based on it. For example, it is not entirely clear what constitutes a "derivative work" in the context of databases. If one were to query hundreds of databases using the Semantic Web, would the federated results be considered a derivative work that requires copyright permissions from each database owner? There is also the problem of "attribution stacking," in which a query made to multiple databases might require giving credit to scores of databases. Different CC licenses for different databases could also create legal incompatibilities among data. Data licensed under a CC ShareAlike license, for example, cannot be legally combined with data licensed under a different license. Segregating data into different "legal boxes" could turn out to impede, not advance, the freedom to integrate data on the Web.

After meeting with a variety of experts in scientific databases, particularly in the life sciences, biodiversity, and geospatial research, the Science Commons came up with an ingenious solution to the gnarly difficulties. Instead of relying on either copyright law or licenses, Science Commons in late 2007 announced a new legal tool, CC0 (CC Zero), which creates a legal and technical platform for a scientific community to develop its own reputation system for sharing data.

CC0 is not a license but a set of protocols. The protocols require that a database producer waive all rights to the data based on intellectual property law—copyrights, patents, unfair competition claims, unfair infringement rights—a "quitclaim" that covers everything. Then it requires that the database producer affirmatively declare that it is not using contracts to encumber future uses of the data. Once a database is certified as complying with the protocols, as determined by Science Commons, it is entitled to use a Science Commons trademark, "Open Access Data," and CC0 metadata. The trademark signals to other scientists that the database meets certain basic standards of interoperability, legal certainty, ease of use, and low transaction costs. The metadata is a functional software tool that enables different databases to share their data.

"What we are doing," said John Wilbanks, "is reconstructing, contractually, the public domain. The idea is that with any conforming implementation—any licensed database—you have complete freedom to integrate with anything else. It creates a zone of certainty for data integration." [36] Unlike public-domain data, the databases that Science Commons certifies as meeting open-data protocols cannot be taken private or legally encumbered. To qualify to use the Open Access Data mark, databases must be interoperable with other databases licensed under the protocols. If someone falsely represents that his data are covered by the license, Science Commons could pursue a trademark infringement case.

To develop this scheme, Science Commons's attorney Thinh Nguyen worked closely with Talis, a company that has built a

Semantic Web technology platform for open data and developed its own open database license. Nguyen also worked with the company's legal team, Jordan Hatcher and Charlotte Waelde, and with the Open Knowledge Foundation, which has developed the Open Knowledge Definition.

The CC0 approach to data represents something of a breakthrough because it avoids rigid, prescriptive legal standards for a type of content (data) that is highly variable and governed by different community norms. CC0 abandons the vision of crafting a single, all-purpose copyright license or contract for thousands of different databases in different legal jurisdictions. Instead it tries to create a legal framework that can honor a range of variable *social norms* that converge on the public domain. Each research community can determine for itself how to meet the CC0 protocols, based on its own distinctive research needs and traditions. Different norms can agree to a equivalency of public-domain standards without any one discipline constraining the behaviors of another.

The system is clever because it provides legal reliability without being overly prescriptive. It is simple to use but still able to accommodate complex variations among disciplines. And it has low transaction costs for both producers and users of data. Over time, the databases that comply with the CC0 protocols are likely to grow into a large universe of interoperable open data.

It is still too early to judge how well the CC0 program is working, but initial reactions have been positive. "The solution is at once obvious and radical," said Glyn Moody, a British journalist who writes about open-source software. "It is this pragmatism, rooted in how science actually works, that makes the current protocol particularly important." Deepak Singh, the co-founder of Bioscreencast, a free online video tutorial library for the scientific community, said, "I consider just the announcement to be a monumental moment."[37]

The Neurocommons

Every day there is so much new scientific literature generated that it would take a single person 106 years to read it all.[38] In a single year, over twenty-four thousand peer-reviewed journals publish about 2.5 million research articles.[39] Our ability to generate content has far outstripped our ability to comprehend it. We are suffering from a cognitive overload—one that can only be addressed by using software and computer networks in innovative ways to organize, search, and access information. For many years, Sir Tim Berners-Lee, the celebrated inventor of the World Wide Web, and his colleagues at the World Wide Web Consortium (W3C), based at MIT, have been trying to solve the problem of information overload by developing a "new layer" of code for the Web.

This visionary project, the so-called Semantic Web, aspires to develop a framework for integrating a variety of systems, so they can communicate with one another, machine to machine. The goal is to enable computers to identify and capture information from anywhere on the Web, and then organize the results in sophisticated and customized ways. "If you search for 'signal transduction genes in parameter neurons,'" said John Wilbanks of Science Commons, "Google sucks. It will get you 190,000 Web pages." The goal of the Semantic Web is to deliver a far more targeted and useful body of specialized information.

A key tool is the Unique Resource Identifier, or URI, which is analogous to the Unique Resource Locator, or URL, used by the Web. Affix a URI to any bit of information on the Web, and the Semantic Web will (so it is hoped) let you mix and match information tagged with that URI with countless other bits of information tagged with other URIs. It would not matter if the bit of information resides in a journal article, database, clinical image, statistical analysis, or video; the point is that the URI would identify a precise bit of information. By enabling cross-linking among different types of information, the idea is that scientists will be able to make all sorts of unexpected and serendipitous insights.

For example, geneticists studying Huntington's disease, a rare neurodegenerative disorder, and experts studying Alzheimer's disease are both exploring many of the same genes and proteins of the brain. But because of the specialization of their disciplines, the chances are good that they read entirely different scientific journals and attend different conferences. There is no easy or systematic way for scientists in one specialty to explain the knowledge that has developed in another specialty. The Semantic Web could probably help.

Unfortunately, for a grand dream that has been touted since the 1990s, very little has developed. The W3C has been embroiled in the design challenges of the Semantic Web for so long that many companies and computer experts now scoff at the whole idea of the Semantic Web. There have been too many arcane, inconclusive debates about computer syntax, ontology language, and philosophical design choices that no one is holding their breath anymore, waiting for the Semantic Web to arrive. (Wikipedia defines a computer ontology as "a data model that represents a set of concepts within a domain and the relationships between those concepts. It is used to reason about the objects within that domain.") The vision of the Semantic Web may have the potential to revolutionize science, but few people have seen much practical value in it over the near term, and so it has garnered little support.

Wilbanks, who once worked at the W3C, was frustrated by this state of affairs. Although he has long believed in the promise of the Semantic Web, he also realized that it is not enough to extol its virtues. One must demonstrate its practicality. "The way to herd cats is not to herd cats," he said, citing a colleague, "but to put a bowl of cream on your back stoop and run like hell." For Wilbanks, the bowl of cream is the Neurocommons knowledge base, a project that seeks to integrate a huge amount of neuroscientific research using Semantic Web protocols and is easy to use.

"The way to overcome the inertia that the Semantic Web critics rightly point out, is not to sit down and argue about ontologies," said Wilbanks. "It's to release something that's useful enough that it's worth wiring your database into the commons system. If I want to get precise answers to complicated questions that might be found in my own database, among others, now I can do that. I simply have to wire it into the Neurocommons. You don't need to come to some magical agreement about ontology; you just need to spend a couple of days converting your database to RDF [Resource Description

Framework, a set of Semantic Web specifications], and then—boom!—I've got all of the other databases integrated with mine." By getting the ball rolling, Science Commons is betting that enough neuroscience fields will integrate their literature to the Neurocommons protocols and make the new commons a lively, sustainable, and growing organism of knowledge.

Using the "open wiring" of the Semantic Web, the Neurocommons has already integrated information from fifteen of the top twenty databases in the life sciences and neuroscience. The data have been reformatted to conform to Semantic Web protocols and the scientific literature, where possible, has been tagged so that it can be "text-mined" (searched for specific information via URI tags). "We have put all this stuff into a database that we give away," said Wilbanks. "It's already been mirrored in Ireland, and more mirrors are going up. It's sort of like a 'knowledge server,' instead of a Web server."

Commercial journal publishers already recognize the potential power of owning and controlling metadata in scientific literature and datasets. To leverage this control many are starting to make copyright claims in certain kinds of metadata, and to amend their contracts with libraries in order to limit how they may retrieve electronic information. "There is a lot at stake here," says Villanova law professor Michael Carroll. "What Science Commons wants to do is make sure that metadata is an open resource."[40]

Wilbanks has high hopes that the Neurocommons project, by providing a useful demonstration of Semantic Web tools, will hasten the interoperability of specialized knowledge that is currently isolated from related fields. It comes down to how to motivate a convergence of knowledge. Instead of arguing about which discipline's ontology of specialized knowledge is superior to another's—and making little headway toward a consensus—Wilbanks has a strategy to build a knowledge tool that is useful. Period. His bet is that a useful "knowledge server" of integrated neuroscientific information will be a powerful incentive for adjacent disciplines to adapt their own literature and databases to be compatible. The point is to get the commons going—while allowing the freedom for it to evolve. Then, if people have disagreements or quibbles, they will be free to change the ontologies as they see fit. "The version [of the Neurocommons] that we are building is useful and it is free," Wilbanks said. "That means that if you want to integrate with it, you can. It means that if you want to redo our work your way, you can—as long as you use the right technical formats. You can reuse all of our software."

The problem with a field like neuroscience, which has so many exploding frontiers, is that no single company or proprietary software platform can adequately manage the knowledge. The information is simply too copious and complex. Like so many other fields of knowledge that are large and complicated, it appears that only an open-source model can successfully curate the relevant information sources. A Web-based commons can be remarkably efficient, effective, and scalable. This has been the lesson of free and open-source software, wikis, and the Web itself. Although it is too early to tell how the Neurocommons project will evolve, the initial signs are promising. A number of foundations that support research for specific diseases—Alzheimer's disease, Parkinson's, autism, epilepsy, Huntington's disease—have already expressed interest in the Neurocommons as a potential model for advancing research in their respective fields.

Open Physical Tools

Science is not just about text and data, of course. It also involves lots of tangible *stuff* needed to conduct experiments. Typical materials include cell lines, monoclonal antibodies, reagents, animal models, synthetic materials, nano-materials, clones, laboratory equipment, and much else. Here, too, sharing and collaboration are important to the advance of science. But unlike digital bits, which are highly malleable, the physical materials needed for experiments have to be located, approved for use, and shipped. Therein lies another tale of high transaction costs impeding the progress of science. As Thinh Nguyen, counsel for Science Commons, describes the problem:

The ability to locate materials based on their descriptions in journal articles is often limited by lack of sufficient information about origin and availability, and there is no standard citation for such materials. In addition, the process of legal negotiation that may follow can be lengthy and unpredictable. This can have important implications for science policy, especially when delays or inability to obtain research materials result in lost time, productivity and research opportunities.[41]

To the nonscientist, this transactional subculture is largely invisible. But to scientists whose lab work requires access to certain physical materials, the uncertainties, variations, and delays can be crippling. Normally, the transfer of materials from one scientist to another occurs through a Material Transfer Agreement, or MTA. The technology transfer office at one research university will grant, or not grant, an MTA so that a cell line or tissue specimen can be shipped to a researcher at another university. Typically, permission must be granted for the researcher to publish, disseminate, or use research results, and to license their use for commercialization.

While certain types of transactions involve material that could conceivably generate high royalty revenues, a great many transactions are fairly low-value, routine transfers of material for basic research. Paradoxically, that can make it all the harder to obtain the material because consummating an MTA is not a high priority for the tech transfer office. In other cases, sharing the material is subject to special agreements whose terms are not known in advance.

Corporations sometimes have MTAs with onerous terms that prevent academic researchers from using a reagent or research tool. Individual scientists sometimes balk at sharing a substance because of the time and effort needed to ship it. Or they may wish to prevent another scientist from being the first to publish research results. Whatever the motivation, MTAs can act as a serious impediment to verification of scientific findings. They can also prevent new types of exploratory research and innovation.

Wilbanks describes the existing system as an inefficient, artisanal one that needs to becomes more of a streamlined industrial system. Just as Creative Commons sought to lower the transaction costs for sharing creative works, through the use of standard public licenses, so Science Commons is now trying to standardize the process for sharing research materials. The idea is to reduce the transaction costs and legal risks by, in Nguyen's words, "creating a voluntary and scalable infrastructure for rights representation and contracting."[42] Like the CC licenses, the Science Commons MTAs will consist of "three layers" of licenses—the standard legal agreement, the machine-readable metadata version, and the "human-readable deed" that nonlawyers can understand.

There are already some successful systems in place for sharing research materials, most notably the Uniform Biological Material Transfer Agreement (UBMTA), which some 320 institutions have accepted, as well as a Simple Letter Agreement developed by the National Institutes of Health. The problem with these systems is that they cannot be used for transfers of materials between academic and for-profit researchers. In addition, there are many instances in which UBMTA signatories can opt out of the system to make modifications to the UBMTA on a case-by-case basis.

To help standardize and streamline the whole system for sharing research materials, Science Commons is working with a consortium of ten research universities, the iBridge Network, to develop a prototype system. The hope is that by introducing metadata to the system, and linking that information to standard contracts and human-readable deeds, scientists will be able to acquire research materials much more rapidly by avoiding bureaucratic and legal hassles. Just as eBay, Amazon, and Federal Express use metadata to allow customers to track the status of their orders, so the Science Commons MTA project wants to develop a system that will allow searching, tracking, and indexing of specific shipments. It is also hoped that metadata links will be inserted into journal articles, enabling scientists to click on a given research material in order to determine the legal and logistical terms for obtaining the material.

Wilbanks envisions a new market of third-party intermediaries to facilitate materials transfers: "There's an emerging network of third parties—think of them as 'biology greenhouses'—who are funded to take in copies of research materials and manufacture them on demand—to grow a quantity and mail them out. What Science Commons is trying to do with the Materials Transfer Project is to put together a functional system where materials can go to greenhouses under standard contracts, with digital identifiers, so that the materials can be cross-linked into the digital information commons. Anytime you see a list of genes, for example, you will be able to right-click and see the stuff that's available from the greenhouses under standard contract, and the cost of manufacture and delivery in order to access the tool. Research materials need to be available under a standard contract, discoverable with a digital identifier, and fulfillable by a third party. And there needs to be some sort of acknowledgment, like a citation system."

At one level, it is ironic that one of the oldest commons-based communities, academic science, has taken so long to reengineer its digital infrastructure to take advantage of the Internet and open digital systems. Yet academic disciplines have always clung tightly to their special ways of knowing and organizing themselves. The arrival of the Internet has been disruptive to this tradition by blurring academic boundaries and inviting new types of cross-boundary research and conversation. If only to improve the conversation, more scientists are discovering the value of establishing working protocols to let the diverse tribes of science communicate with one another more easily. Now that the examples of networked collaboration are proliferating, demonstrating the enormous power that can be unleashed through sharing and openness, the momentum for change is only going to intensify. The resulting explosion of knowledge and innovation should be quite a spectacle.

12

OPEN EDUCATION AND LEARNING

*Managing educational resources as a commons can make learning
more affordable and exciting.*

In the late 1990s, as Richard Baraniuk taught electrical engineering
to undergraduates at Rice University, the furthest thing from his
mind was revolutionizing learning. He just wanted to make digital
signal processing a more palatable subject for his students. Baraniuk,
an affable professor with a venturesome spirit, was frustrated that
half of his undergraduate class would glaze over when he taught signal processing, perhaps because it involves a lot of math. But then he
explained the social ramifications of signal processing—for wiretap-
ping, the Internet, the airwaves, radar, and much more. Students got
excited.

"If I wanted to reach a broader class of people, outside of Rice
University," Baraniuk said, "that would be very difficult. The standard thing is to write your own book." But he quickly realized
that writing the 176th book ever written on signal processing
(he counted) would not be very efficient or effective. It would take
years to write, and then additional years to traverse the editorial, production, and distribution process. And even if the book
were successful, it would reach only five thousand readers. Finally,
it would be a static artifact, lacking the timeliness and interactivity of online dialogue. A book, Baraniuk ruefully observed, "re-
disconnects things."[1]

As chance had it, Baraniuk's research group at Rice was just discovering open-source software. "It was 1999, and we were moving
all of our workstations to Linux," he recalled. "It was just so robust
and high-quality, even at that time, and it was being worked on by
thousands of people." Baraniuk remembers having an epiphany:
"What if we took books and 'chunked them apart,' just like soft-

ware? And what if we made the IP open so that the books would be free to re-use and remix in different ways?' "

The vision was exciting, but the tools for realizing it were virtually nonexistent. The technologies for collaborative authoring and the legal licenses for sharing, not to mention the financing and outreach for the idea, would all have to be developed. Fortunately, the Rice University administration understood the huge potential and helped Baraniuk raise $1 million to put together a skunk works of colleagues to devise a suitable software architecture and nonprofit plan. A colleague, Don Johnson, dubbed the enterprise "Connexions."

The group made a number of choices that turned out to be remarkably shrewd. Instead of organizing teaching materials into a "course" or a "textbook," for example, the Connexions planners decided to build an open ecosystem of shared knowledge. Just as the Web is "small pieces loosely joined," as David Weinberger's 2003 book put it, so Connexions decided that the best way to structure its educational content was as discrete modules (such as "signal processing") that could be reused in any number of contexts. The planners also decided to build a system on the open Semantic Web format rather than a simple interlinking of PDF files. This choice meant that the system would not be tethered to a proprietary or static way of displaying information, but could adapt and scale in the networked environment. Modules of content could be more easily identified and used for many different purposes, in flexible ways.

By the summer of 2000, the first version of Connexions went live with two Rice University courses, Fundamentals of Electronic Engineering and Introduction to Physical Electronics. The goal was to let anyone create educational materials and put them in the repository. Anyone could copy and customize material on the site, or mix it with new material in order to create new books and courses. Materials could even be used to make commercial products such as Web courses, CD-ROMs, and printed books. By the end of 2000, two hundred course modules were available on Connexions: a modest but promising start.

It turned out to be an auspicious moment to launch an open

platform for sharing. A wave of Web 2.0 applications and tools was just beginning to appear on the Internet. Innovators with the savvy to take advantage of open networks, in the style of free and open software, could amass huge participatory communities in very short order. For Connexions, the living proof was Kitty Schmidt-Jones, a private piano teacher from Champaign, Illinois. She discovered Connexions through her husband and posted a 276-page book on music theory to the site. "Kitty is not the kind of person who would be a music textbook author," said Baraniuk, "but she thought that music education is important, and said, 'I can do this, too!' By 2007 *Understanding Basic Music Theory* had been downloaded more than 7.5 million times from people around the world. A Connexions staffer attending a conference in Lithuania met an educator from Mongolia who lit up at the mention of Schmidt-Jones. "We use her work in our schools!" he said.

Besides curating a collection of educational content, Connexions has developed a variety of open-source applications to let authors create, remix, share, and print content easily. The project has also developed systems to let users rate the quality of materials. Professional societies, editorial boards of journals, and even informal groups can use a customizable software "lens" to tag the quality of Connexions modules, which can then be organized and retrieved according to a given lens.

It was a stroke of good fortune when Baraniuk and his associates learned, in 2002, that Lawrence Lessig was developing a new licensing project called Creative Commons. As the CC team drafted its licenses, Connexions helped it understand academic needs and then became one of the very first institutional adopters of the CC licenses. Connexions decided to require that its contributors license their works under the least restrictive CC license, CC-BY (Attribution). This was a simple decision because most textbook authors write to reach large readerships, not to make money.

The real expansion of Connexions as a major international repository of teaching materials did not occur until early 2004, when the software platform had been sufficiently refined. Then, with virtually no publicity, global usage of the Connexions site took off. It helped that Rice University has never sought to "own" the project. Although it administers the project, the university has deliberately encouraged grassroots participation from around the world and across institutions. Electrical engineering faculty at ten major universities are cooperating in developing curricula, for example, and diverse communities of authors are adding to content collections in music, engineering, physics, chemistry, bioinformatics, nanotechnology, and history. In 2008, Connexions had 5,801 learning modules woven into 344 collections. More than 1 million people from 194 countries are using the materials, many of which are written in Chinese, Italian, Spanish, and other languages.

One of Connexion's neatest tricks is offering printed textbooks for a fraction of the price of conventional textbooks. Because the content is drawn from the commons, a 300-page hardback engineering textbook that normally sells for $125 can be bought for $25, through a print-on-demand publishing partner, QOOP.com. Ten percent of the purchase price is earmarked to support Connexions, and another 10 percent helps disadvantaged students obtain textbooks for free. Unlike conventional textbooks, which may be a year or two old, Connexions materials are generally up-to-date.

By providing an alternative to the spiraling costs of academic publishing, Connexions's publishing model may actually help a number of academic disciplines pursue their scholarly missions. Over the past decade, some sixty university presses have closed or downsized for economic reasons. "If you're in art history, anthropology, or the humanities, you get tenure based on your monographs published by a university press," Baraniuk said. "The problem is that, as university presses shut down, there's nowhere to publish books anymore." It is often financially prohibitive to publish art history books, for example, because such books typically require high-quality production and small press runs. An overly expensive market structure is blocking the flow of new scholarly publishing.

One solution: a new all-digital hybrid business model for academic publishing. As the Connexions platform has proved itself, Rice University saw the virtue of reopening Rice University Press (RUP), which it had closed ten years earlier.[2] The new RUP retains the editorial structure, high standards, and focus on special fields of a conventional academic press, but it now works within a "branded partition" of Connexions. RUP posts all of its books online as soon as the manuscripts are finalized, and all books are licensed under a CC-BY (Attribution) license. The press does not have to pay for any warehouse or distribution costs because any physical copies of the books are printed on demand. The sales price includes a mission-support fee for RUP and the author's royalty. "Because the RUP has eliminated all the back-end costs," said Baraniuk, "they figure they can run it from five to ten times more cheaply than a regular university press."

The Connexions publishing model has inspired a group of more than twenty community colleges to develop its own public-domain textbooks to compete with expensive commercial textbooks. The Community College Consortium for Open Educational Resources[3]—led by Foothill–De Anza Community College District in Los Altos, California—plans to publish the ten most popular textbooks used in community colleges, and expand from there. The consortium will make the books available for free online and sell hardcover versions for less than thirty dollars. Even if the effort gains only a small slice of the textbook market, it will help hold down the prices of commercial textbooks and demonstrate the viability of a new publishing model. More to the point, by slashing one of the biggest costs facing community college students, the project will help thousands of lower-income students to stay in college.

MIT's OpenCourseWare Initiative

The other pioneering visionary in open education has been MIT. In April 2001, MIT president Charles Vest shocked the world when he announced that MIT would begin to put the materials for all two thousand of its courses online for anyone to use, for free. The new initiative, called OpenCourseWare, would cover a wide array of instructional materials: lecture notes, class assignments, problem sets, syllabi, simulations, exams, and video lectures. Putting the materials online in a searchable, consistent format was expected to take ten years and cost tens of millions of dollars. (The Hewlett and Mellon foundations initially stepped forward with two $5.5 million grants, supplemented by $1 million from MIT.)

The project had its origins two years earlier, in 1999, when President Vest charged a study group with exploring how the university might develop online educational modules for lifelong learning. The assumption was that it would sell MIT-branded course materials to the budding "e-learning" market. At the time, Columbia University was developing Fathom.com, a bold for-profit co-venture with thirteen other institutions, to sell a wide variety of digital content. Publishers and universities alike envisioned a lucrative new market for academic and cultural materials.

OpenCourseWare (OCW) was a startling move because it flatly rejected this ambition, and appeared to be either a foolish or magnanimous giveaway of extremely valuable information. Knowledge was assumed to be a species of property that should be sold for as dear a price as possible; few people at the time recognized that the Great Value Shift on the Internet was reversing this logic. The idea that giving information away might actually yield greater gains— by enhancing an institution's visibility, respect, and influence on a global scale—was not seen as credible. After all, where's the money?

After studying the matter closely, MIT decided that the online market was not likely to be a boon, and that posting course materials online would send a strong message about MIT's values. President Vest conceded that the plan "looks counter-intuitive in a market-driven world." But he stressed that OpenCourseWare would combine "the traditional openness and outreach and democratizing influence of American education and the ability of the Web to make vast amounts of information instantly available."[4] Professor Steven Lerman, one of the architects of the OCW plan, told the *New York Times*, "Selling content for profit, or trying in some ways to commercialize one of the core intellectual activities of the university, seemed less attractive to people at a deep level than finding ways to disseminate it as broadly as possible."[5]

MIT also realized the dangers of propertizing college courses and teaching materials, said computer scientist Hal Abelson, another member of the OCW study group (and a CC board member). Ownership, he said, "can be profoundly destructive to the idea of a university community . . . The more people can stop talking about property and start talking about the nature of a faculty member's commitment to the institution, the healthier the discussion will be. It's not really about what you own as a faculty member; it's about what you do as a faculty member."[6]

School officials stressed that using MIT courseware on the Web is not the same as an MIT education. Indeed, the free materials underscore the fact that what really distinguishes an MIT education is one's participation in a learning community. Unlike the Connexions content, MIT's OpenCourseWare is a fairly static set of course materials; they are not modular or constantly updated. In addition, they are licensed under a CC BY-NC-SA (Attribution-NonCommercial-ShareAlike.) license. While this prevents businesses from profiting from MIT course materials, it also prevents other educational institutions from remixing them into new courses or textbooks.

Despite these limitations, MIT's OCW materials have been profoundly influential. The course Laboratory in Software Engineering, for example, has been used by students in Karachi, Pakistan; the island of Mauritius; Vienna, Austria; and Kansas City, Missouri, among scores of other places around the world.[7] Ten of the leading Chinese universities now use hundreds of MIT courses, leading three noted OER experts, Daniel E. Atkins, John Seely Brown, and Allen L. Hammond, to conclude that MIT's OCW "has had a major impact on Chinese education."[8] Noting the life-changing impact that OCW has had on students in rural villages in China and West Africa, Atkins and his co-authors cite "the power of the OCW as a means for cross-cultural engagement." Over the course of four years, from October 2003 through 2007, the OCW site received nearly 16 million visits; half were newcomers and half were repeat visits.

OCW is becoming a more pervasive international ethic now that more than 120 educational institutions in twenty nations have banded together to form the OpenCourseWare Consortium. Its goal is to create "a broad and deep body of open educational content using a shared model."[9] Although plenty of universities are still trying to make money from distance education courses, a growing number of colleges and universities realize that OCW helps faculty connect with other interested faculty around the world, build a college's public recognition and recruitment, and advance knowledge as a public good.

The Rise of the Open Educational Resources Movement

While Connexions and MIT's OpenCourseWare have understandably garnered a great deal of attention, all sorts of fascinating educational projects, big and small, have popped up on the Internet as Web 2.0 innovations matured. Some of these projects have become celebrated, such as Wikipedia, the Public Library of Science, and the Internet Archive. Others, though less celebrated, represent a dazzling mosaic of educational innovation and new possibilities. In a sense, the Long Tail has come to education; even the most obscure subjects have a sustainable niche on the Internet. The groundswell has even produced its own theorists, conveners, and infrastructure builders. Utah State University hosts the Center for Open Sustainable Learning, which is a clearinghouse for open educational tools. Carnegie Mellon has an Open Learning Initiative that designs educational courses. And so on.

While American institutions and educators have been the first movers in this field, it has quickly taken on an international grassroots flavor. Thousands of commoners from around the world have started their own projects. MathWorld has become the Web's most extensive mathematical resource. Curriki is a wiki that offers lessons plans and guidance for teachers. The British Library's Online Gallery features digitized versions of Mozart's musical diary and sketches by Leonardo da Vinci. U.K. and Australian high school students can now use the Internet to operate the Faulkes Telescope on the island of Maui, Hawaii. Students around the world do much the same with Bugscope, a scanning electronic microscope that can be operated remotely.

It is hard to set a precise date when the practitioners in this area realized that such wildly diverse projects might constitute a coherent movement with a shared agenda. But as more grantees began to discover each other, the movement-in-formation adopted a rather ungainly name to describe itself—"Open Educational Resources," or OER.

Most OER projects share a simple and powerful idea—"that the world's knowledge is a public good and that technology in general and the World Wide Web in particular provide an extraordinary opportunity for everyone to share, use and reuse knowledge." That is how Atkins and his co-authors define OER. It consists of "teaching, learning and research resources that reside in the public domain or have been released under an intellectual property license that permits their free use or re-purposing by others."[10]

The heart of the OER movement is, of course, open sharing and collaboration. OER advocates regard learning as an intrinsically social process, and so they believe that knowledge and learning tools ought to freely circulate. Inspired by the GPL and the CC licenses, OER advocates believe they should be free to copy, modify, and improve their learning tools and pass them forward to others. There is a presumption that artificial barriers to the free flow of information should be eliminated, and that teachers and learners should be empowered to create their own knowledge commons.

The OER movement has a special importance for people who want to learn but don't have the money or resources, which is to say, people in developing nations, low-income people, and people with specialized learning needs. For the 4 billion people who live in the developing world, schooling is a privilege, textbooks are rare, and money is scarce. In many African nations, there would not be libraries if books were not photocopied. The OER movement aspires to address these needs. OER projects can provide important benefits in industrialized nations, too, where subscriptions to research journals are often prohibitively expensive and many community college students drop out because textbooks cost more than tuition.

The OER movement is currently in a formative stage, still trying to make sense of the many players in the movement and understand the complex impediments to its progress. Some of this could be seen at a "speed geeking" session at the iCommons Summit in 2007 in Dubrovnik, Croatia. Speed geeking, a puckish variation on "speed dating," consists of people listening to a short presentation, asking questions and then moving on to the next presentation. After five minutes, a moderator blows a whistle and shouts, "Everyone move—now!" A speed geek can learn about twelve different projects, and meet twelve interesting people, in a single hour.

In this case, the speed geeking took place in a sweltering loft space without air-conditioning, in a medieval building overlooking the Adriatic Sea. At the first station, a group of participants marveled at a sturdy lime-green laptop of a kind that was about to be distributed to millions of children around the world. The One Laptop Per Child project, the brainchild of Nicholas Negroponte of MIT's Media Lab, is an ambitious nonprofit initiative to build a sturdy, kid-friendly laptop filled with open-source software and Wi-Fi capabilities for $100.[11] (The cost turned out to be $188, but is expected to decline as production volume grows.) Hundreds of thousands of the so-called XO laptops have now been distributed to kids in Peru, Uruguay, Mexico and other poor nations.

Tweet! Next stop: the Free High School Science Textbooks project in South Africa is developing a free set of science textbooks for students in grades ten through twelve. The project depends on volunteers to write modules of text about various physics, chemistry, and mathematical topics. Paid editors then craft the text into a coherent, high-quality textbook; printing is funded by donations.

Five minutes later, it was on to Educalibre, a Chilean project that is installing free software on old computers so that they can be reused in classrooms. Educalibre is also trying to integrate free software into high school curricula, especially math. The project seeks to bring open-source software principles into formal education.

Next, Delia Browne of the National Education Access Licence for Schools, or NEALS, explained that some ten thousand Australian schools pay millions of dollars each year to collecting societies in order to reprint materials that the Australian schools themselves have produced. NEALS wants to eliminate this expense, as well as millions of dollars in photocopying expenses, by creating a vast new commons of freely shareable educational materials. Its solution is to persuade Australian schools, as copyright holders, to adopt a special license so that participating schools can copy and share each other's materials.

Tweet! At the next station, Ed Bice of San Francisco explained how his nonprofit group, Meedan.net, is developing a "virtual town square" for Arabic- and English-speaking Internet users. Using real-time translation and social networking tools, the site aspires to open up a new global conversation between Arabs and the rest of the world. It plans to break down cultural barriers while opening up educational opportunities to Arab populations.

Tweet! Tweet! Neeru Paharia, a former executive director of the Creative Commons, introduced her fledgling project, AcaWiki. Paharia is concerned that too many academic articles are locked behind paywalls and are not readily accessible to everyone. AcaWiki plans to recruit graduate students, academics, and citizens to write summaries of academic papers. Since many grad students make abstracts as part of their routine research, it would not be difficult to pool thousands of summaries into a highly useful, searchable Web collection.

The speed geekers in Dubrovnik were sweaty and overstimulated at the end, but gratified to learn that there are a great many OER projects under way throughout the world; they just aren't very well known or coordinated with one another. Two of the participants—J. Philipp Schmidt of the University of the Western Cape and Mark Surman of the Shuttleworth Foundation, both of South Africa—conceded that "there is still a great deal of fuzziness about what this movement includes," and that "we don't yet have a good 'map' of open education." But the significance of grassroots initiatives is unmistakable. "There is a movement afoot here," they concluded, "and it is movement with an aim no less than making learning accessible and adaptable for all."[12] "Education," another participant predicted, "will drive the future of the Commons movement."

In a sign that the OER movement is getting serious as a movement, thirty of its leaders met in Cape Town, South Africa, and in January 2008 issued the Cape Town Open Education Declaration.[13] The declaration is a call to make learning materials more freely available online, and to improve education and learning by making them more collaborative, flexible, and locally relevant. The declaration outlines the challenge: "Many educators remain unaware of the growing pool of open educational resources. Many governments and educational institutions are either unaware or unconvinced of the benefits of open education. Differences among licensing schemes for open resources create confusion and incompatibility. And, of course, the majority of the world does not have access to the computers and networks that are integral to most current open education efforts."

New funding support is materializing from foundations like the Open Society Institute and the Shuttleworth Foundation, and the Creative Commons has instigated a new project, ccLearn, headed by Ahrash Bissell, to help coordinate OER factions and tackle barriers to further progress.

Despite the challenges it faces, the Open Educational Resources movement has a promising future if only because it has such an appealing ethos and practical value. It offers to lower the costs and increase the efficiencies of learning. It helps to generate high-quality materials that address specific learning needs. Where markets are too expensive or unresponsive, collective provisioning through the commons can meet needs effectively and in socially convivial ways.

Such intangible satisfactions may be one of the secrets of the OER movement's success to date. Institutions and individuals take pleasure in contributing to the public good. There is pleasure in helping people who thirst for an education, whether in Africa or in a community college, to acquire the resources they need. For learners, the OER movement offers new, more flexible styles of learning. Over time, it seems likely that OER projects will transform the familiar "information transfer" models of formal education into more informal and participatory learning communities. Passive students will more easily become passionate, self-directed learners.

Finally, at a time of great geopolitical rivalries and cultural animosities, the OER movement holds itself forth as an arena of transnational cooperation. It regards diversity as a strength and social inequity as a challenge to be squarely met. It is a measure of the movement's idealism that Schmidt and Surman, the South African OER commoners, compare open education to "a flock of migratory geese, moving back and forth between North and South. The flock combines birds from all places. Each goose takes a turn leading the flock, taking the strain, and then handing over to their peers. The flock is not confined to just the North, or the South. It flourishes as a global movement." [14]

CONCLUSION:
THE DIGITAL REPUBLIC AND THE FUTURE
OF DEMOCRATIC CULTURE

You never change things by fighting the existing reality. To change
something, build a new model that makes the existing model obsolete.
—R. Buckminster Fuller

Legend has it that, upon leaving Independence Hall on the final day
of the Constitutional Convention in 1787, Benjamin Franklin was
approached by a woman, who asked, "Well, Doctor, what have
we got—a Republic or a Monarchy?" Franklin famously replied,
"A Republic, if you can keep it." The American colonies had imagined and engineered a new constitutional order, but its survival
would depend on countless new struggles and innovations. An
American civic culture had to be invented.

The Franklin vignette might well be applied to the digital republic that the commoners have built. Except that, instead of asking,
"Well, Mr. Stallman and Professor Lessig, what have we got—a free
culture or a proprietary tyranny?" the question might better be
posed to the commoners themselves. Their very existence answers
the question, Tyranny or freedom? Free culture exists. It exists to the
extent that people practice its ideals. It is not pervasive; many people
have no idea what it is; it overlaps in fuzzy ways with the market.
But it is flourishing wherever online communities have devised sat-
isfactory commons structures—through law, software, and social
norms—to capture the value that they create. Or, as the American
Framers put it, to secure the blessings of liberty to ourselves and our
posterity.

As the preceding chapters make clear, the commoners are now a
respected force in culture, politics, and economics. Their influence
can be felt in varying degrees in the worlds of music, video, photography, and books; in software, Web design, and Internet policies; in
social networks and peer-to-peer communities; in business, science,

and education; and in scores of countries that have ported the Creative Commons licenses and developed their own commons-based projects.

Thanks to the Internet, the commons is now a distinct sector of economic production and social experience. It is a source of "value creation" that both complements and competes with markets. It is an arena of social association, self-governance, and collective provisioning that is responsive and trustworthy in ways that government often is not. In a sense, the commons sector is a recapitulation of civil society, as described by Alexis de Tocqueville, but with different capacities.

Yet even with the great advances that the commoners have made in building their own shared platforms, tools, and content, the digital republic is not secure. In most countries, the commoners have less conventional political power than corporations, which means that the interests of citizens, consumers, and users are scanted in the policies that govern market competition, intellectual property, and life on the Internet.[1] Faced with the Great Value Shift, mass-media and entertainment corporations are not eager to surrender their historic market franchises to newcomers without a fight; they are resisting competition from open business models and the commons.

In the United States, cable broadcast operators and telephone carriers are threatening the very future of the Internet as a commons infrastructure. They wish to assert greater control over Web access and traffic, and so are staunchly resisting "net neutrality" rules that would require them to act as nondiscriminatory common carriers. They would like to leverage their roles as oligopolistic gatekeepers to the Internet, and boost their revenues, by choosing whose Web sites will receive superior transmission and whose communications may be censored or put in the "slow lane."

At a further extreme, authoritarian countries such as China, Saudi Arabia, Egypt, and Singapore have shown that national governments still retain great powers to censor and control Internet communications.[2] Even the United States government is reportedly engaged in extensive surveillance of Internet traffic, ostensibly for antiterrorism purposes. Meanwhile, many poor nations, especially in Africa and Asia, are struggling simply to get online and create their own digital commons.

These battles are all part of a larger struggle over "the institutional ecology of the digital environment," in Yochai Benkler's words—a struggle that is likely to continue for many years. What powers and capabilities will the commoners and their institutions have relative to business and government, and how will they be able to protect and enhance the value created within the commons?

A New Species of Citizenship

Perhaps the most enduring contribution of the free software, free culture, and other "open movements" has been their invention of a new species of citizenship. Despite significant differences of philosophy and implementation, these commons share some basic values about access, use, and reuse of creative works and information. No matter their special passions, the commoners tend to be improvisational, resourceful, self-directed, collaborative, and committed to democratic ideals. They celebrate a diversity of aesthetics, viewpoints, and cultures. They are egalitarian in spirit yet respectful of talent and achievement. There is a strong predilection to share because the accrual of digital contributions (code, content, metatags) will lead to a greater good for all and perhaps even democratic change. But there is no hostility to commercial activity—indeed, there is a lively admiration for entrepreneurialism—so long as it does not violate basic creative and civic freedoms or core principles of the Internet (openness, interoperability, sharing). The disagreements that do exist center on how best to achieve those goals.

As this book has shown, the Internet is enabling a new species of citizenship in modern life. It is not just a "nice thing." It is a powerful force for change. The new technologies have been instrumental in helping the commoners imagine and build a digital republic of their own. Over the long term, this citizenship and the culture that it is fostering are likely to be a politically transformative force. They just might help real-world democracies restore a measure of their waning legitimacy and competence.[3]

David R. Johnson, a lawyer and scholar, describes the citizen of the Internet—the "netizen"—as a significant historical development because he or she can potentially compete with government as a source of binding rule sets. In a brilliant essay, "The Life of the Law Online," Johnson writes that "we haven't had a real competition for survival among rule sets. The competition is only between the rule of (our one) law and, presumably, anarchy. So the tendency of all rule sets to become more complicated over time, especially when written by people considering only parts of the system in analytical isolation, has not been checked by evolutionary forces."[4] Government has an unchecked monopoly on lawmaking even though its relationship to the governed, whose consent is vital, is now greatly attenuated.

One evolutionary "competitor" to government-made law and to markets is the netizen—or, in my terms, the commoner. For the most part, members of a commons generate and maintain the rules that govern their collective. By Johnson's reckoning, the commons must be considered a new social metabolism for creating law; it is a new type of "legal organism." It is, in Johnson's words, "a self-causing legal order composed of systems that adopt goals that serve the values of those they regulate, without excessively imposing those goals on others."

A commons is a kind of biological entity operating in a complex cultural ecosystem. It has its own internal systems for managing its affairs, interacting with its environment, repairing itself, and defining its own persistent identity. It is a force by which ordinary people can express their deepest interests and passions, directly and without institutional mediation, on a global stage. This is an unprecedented capacity in communications, culture, and, indeed, human history.

To understand why the commoner represents a great leap forward in citizenship, it helps to consider the history of citizenship in the oldest democracy in the world, the United States. In his book *The Good Citizen*, sociologist Michael Schudson describes the

evolution of three distinct types of citizenship over the past three
centuries:

> When the nation was founded, being a citizen meant little
> more than for property-owning white males to delegate au-
> thority to a local gentleman—and accept his complimentary
> glass of rum on election day. This "politics of assent" gave
> way early in the nineteenth century to a "politics of parties."
> Parties conducted elaborate campaigns of torchlight proces-
> sions and monster meetings; voting day was filled with ban-
> ter, banners, fighting and drinking. . . . The third model of
> citizenship, ushered in by Progressive reformers, was a "poli-
> tics of information." Campaigning became less emotional
> and more educational. Voting was by secret ballot.[5]

We are heirs to the "politics of information," a model of citizenship that presumes, as economics does, that we are rational actors
who, if armed with sufficient quantities of high-quality information, will make educated decisions and optimize civic outcomes.
But as Walter Lippmann noted and Schudson echoes, "if democracy
requires omnicompetence and omniscience from its citizens, it is a
lost cause."[6] Life is too busy, fast, and complex. A new type of citizenship is needed. Schudson offers a fairly weak prescription—the
"monitorial citizen," a watchdog who vigilantly monitors the behavior of power.

But it is precisely here that the Internet is offering up a new,
more muscular model of citizenship. I call it *history-making citizenship*. The rise of the blogosphere over the past ten years is emblem-
atic of this new paradigm of citizenship. So is citizen-journalism,
free software, Wikipedia, the Open Educational Resources movement, open business models like Jamendo and Flickr, and the Creative Commons and iCommons communities. In one sense, the
citizenship that these groups practice is "monitorial" in that their
members spend a great deal of time watching and discussing. But
"monitoring" barely begins to describe their activities. The commoners have the ability—rare in pre-Internet civic life—to publish

and incite others to action, and then organize and follow through, using a growing variety of powerful tools. With the advent of blogs, meetups, social networking, text messaging, and many other digital systems, citizens are able to communicate, coordinate, organize, and take timely action on a wide range of matters, including matters of public and political concern.

I call the new sorts of citizen behaviors "history-making" because ordinary people are able to assert moral agency and participate in making change.[7] This capacity is not reserved chiefly to large, impersonal institutions such as corporations, government agencies, and other bureaucracies. It is not a mere "participatory citizenship" in which people can volunteer their energies to a larger a more influential leader, political party, or institution in order to help out. It is a citizenship in which *the commoners themselves* choose projects that suit their talents and passions. Dispersed, unorganized groups of strangers can build their own platforms and social norms for pursuing their goals; instigate public action that would not otherwise occur (and that may clash with the practices of existing institutions); and push forward their own distinctive agenda.

These behaviors exist in some measure in offline realms, of course, but they are a growing norm in the digital republic. A few examples will suffice to make the point. The Web helped create and propel a handful of cause-oriented candidacies—Howard Dean, Ron Paul, Ned Lamont*—who rapidly raised enormous sums of money, galvanized large numbers of passionate supporters, and altered mainstream political discourse. Although none prevailed in their races, Barack Obama made a quantum leap in online organizing in 2008, raising $50 million in a single month from supporters via the Internet. Obama's candidacy was buoyed by the rise of the "netroots"—Web activists with a progressive political agenda—whose size and credibility enable them to sway votes in Congress, raise significant amounts of campaign funds, and influence local

---

* Lamont was an insurgent candidate for U.S. Senate from Connecticut challenging Senator Joseph Lieberman in a campaign that helped culturally validate opposition to the U.S. war in Iraq.

activism. The stories are now legion about blogs affecting political life—from the resignation of Senate majority leader Trent Lott after he praised the racist past of Senator Strom Thurmond at his hundredth birthday party, to the electoral defeat of Senate candidate George Allen after his uttering of an ethnic slur, *macaca,* was posted on YouTube.

Citizens are now able to initiate their own policy initiatives without first persuading the mainstream media or political parties to validate them as worthy. For example, a handful of citizens troubled by evidence of "hackable" electronic voting machines exposed the defects of the Diebold machines and the company's efforts to thwart public scrutiny and reforms.[8] (The effort has led to a nationwide citizen effort, www.blackboxvoting.org, to expose security problems with voting machines and vote counting.) An ad hoc group of activists, lawyers, academics, and journalists spontaneously formed around a public wiki dealing with the lethal side effects of a best-selling antipsychotic drug Zyprexa, and the manufacturer's allegedly illegal conduct in suppressing evidence of the drug's risks. (Prosecutors later sought a $1 billion fine against Eli Lilly.)[9]

The Web is giving individuals extra-institutional public platforms for articulating their own facts and interpretations of culture. It is enabling them to go far beyond voting and citizen vigilance, to mount citizen-led interventions in politics and governance. History-making citizens can compete with the mass media as an arbiter of cultural and political reality. They can expose the factual errors and lack of independence of *New York Times* reporters; reveal the editorial biases of the "MSM"—mainstream media—by offering their own videotape snippets on YouTube; they can even be pacesetters for the MSM, as the blog Firedoglake did in its relentless reporting of the "Scooter" Libby trial (Libby, one of Vice President Cheney's top aides, was convicted of obstruction of justice and perjury in connection with press leaks about CIA agent Valerie Plame.) Citizen-journalists, amateur videographers, genuine experts who have created their own Web platforms, parodists, dirty tricksters, and countless others are challenging elite control of the news agenda. It is no wonder that commercial journalism is suffering an identity crisis. Institutional authority is being trumped by the "social warranting" of online communities, many of which function as a kind of participatory meritocracy.

History-making citizenship is not without its deficiencies. Rumors, misinformation, and polarized debate are common in this more open, unmediated environment. Its crowning virtue is its potential ability to mobilize the energies and creativity of huge numbers of people. GNU/Linux improbably drew upon the talents of tens of thousands of programmers; certainly our contemporary world with its countless problems could use some of this elixir— platforms that can elicit distributed creativity, specialized talent, passionate commitment, and social legitimacy. In 2005 Joi Ito, then chairman of the board of the Creative Commons, wrote: "Traditional forms of representative democracy can barely manage the scale, complexity and speed of the issues in the world today. Representatives of sovereign nations negotiating with each other in global dialog are limited in their ability to solve global issues. The monolithic media and its increasingly simplistic representation of the world cannot provide the competition of ideas necessary to reach informed, viable consensus."[10] Ito concluded that a new, not-yet-understood model of "emergent democracy" is likely to materialize as the digital revolution proceeds. A civic order consisting of "intentional blog communities, ad hoc advocacy coalitions and activist networks" could begin to tackle many urgent problems.

Clearly, the first imperative in developing a new framework to host representative democracy is to ensure that the electronic commons be allowed to exist in the first place. Without net neutrality, citizens could very well be stifled in their ability to participate on their own terms, in their own voices. If proprietary policies or technologies are allowed to override citizen interests (Verizon Wireless in 2007 prevented the transmission of abortion rights messages on its text-messaging system, for example[11]), then any hope for history-making citizenship will be stillborn.

Beyond such near-term concerns, however, the emerging digital republic is embroiled in a much larger structural tension with –terrestrial "real world" governments. The commoner is likely to regard the rules forged in online commons as more legitimate and appropriate than those mandated by government. Again, David R. Johnson:

> The goals of a successful legal organism must be agreed upon by those who live within it, because a legal system is nothing more than a collective conversation about shared values. When it ceases to be that kind of internally entailed organism, the law becomes mere power, social "order" becomes tyranny, and the only option, over the long term at least, is war.
>
> Organisms can't be repaired from the outside. But, with reference to interactions that take place primarily online, among willing participants who seek primarily to regulate their own affairs, that's exactly where existing governments are situated—outside the vibrant, self-regulating online spaces they seek to regulate. Their efforts to engineer the Internet as if it were a mechanism are not only fundamentally illegitimate but doomed by the very nature of the thing they seek to regulate. They are trying to create social order, of course. But they have not recognized . . . that order in complex systems creates itself.[12]

After all, he or she is likely to have had a more meaningful personal role in crafting those rules. Now, of course, people live their lives in both online and terrestrial environments; there is no strict division between the two. That said, as people's lives become more implicated in Internet spaces, citizens are likely to prefer the freedoms and affordances of the open-networked environment to the stunted correlates of offline politics, governance, and law.

Indeed, this may be why so many activists and idealists are attracted to online venues. There is a richer sense of possibility. Contemporary politics and government have been captured by big money, professionals, and concentrated power. By contrast, in the digital republic, the ethic of transparency deals harshly with institutional manipulations, deceptions, and bad faith. They literally become part of your "permanent record," forever available via a Google search. More fundamentally, the digital republic has a basic respect for everyone's ability to contribute. It respects the principle of open access for all. The "consent of the governed" really matters. How sobering it is, then, to return to the "real world" of the American polity—or most other national governments—and realize that "money talks and bullshit walks." How depressing to realize that the system is highly resistant to ordinary citizen action, such is the mismatch of resources.

The growing dissonance between the American system of governance, as practiced, and the more open, meritocratic online world was surely a factor in Lessig's decision in 2007 to step down as CEO of Creative Commons, a move that eventually took place in April 2008. Lessig's crushing responsibilities as the leader of Creative Commons—the international travel, the fund-raising, the strategic planning, the public events and movement obligations—had surely taken its toll. Feeling a personal need for new challenges as well as a responsibility to let new leaders emerge within the CC world, Lessig announced an ambitious new agenda for himself—tackling the "systemic corruption" of the democratic process in Congress. He joined with Joe Trippi, the campaign manager for Howard Dean's 2004 presidential run, to launch a new organization, Change Congress, which seeks to ban special-interest campaign contributions, secure public financing for campaigns, and bring greater transparency to congressional proceedings. In a shuffle of roles, longtime board member James Boyle—who had been especially active on science and education initiatives—became the new chairman of Creative Commons. Board member Joi Ito, who had been chairman for a brief period, became CEO.

If Lessig is going to succeed in using the tools of the digital republic to reform and rejuvenate the American polity (and perhaps inspire other governments as well), he will have to confront the rather deeply rooted premises of the official constitutional order. The fast-paced, commons-based governance of the digital republic is naturally going to clash with a system of governance that revolves around bureaucratic hierarchies, a slow-moving system of law, archaic types of political intermediaries, and electoral principles de-signed for eighteenth-century life. Can the two be reconciled? The structural tensions are likely to be a significant and persistent issue for many, many years.

A Long-Term Power Shift?

It is hard to get a fix on this long-term transformation because the struggles to actualize an emergent democracy, as envisioned by Ito, are strangely apolitical and intensely political at the same time. They are apolitical in the sense that commoners are chiefly focused on the pragmatic technical challenges of their individual projects; they are not usually involved in official policymaking in legislatures or be-fore courts and government agencies. Yet free software and free cul-ture projects are highly political in the sense that commons projects, taken together over time, represent a profound challenge to the con-ventional market order and political culture. For example, Wiki-travel, Jamendo, and open-access journals arguably provide better value than the commercial alternatives. The success of free software punctures the foundational assumptions of copyright law, making it easier to challenge new expansions of copyright law. Participatory commons are diverting viewer "eyeballs" away from commercial media and its genres of culture, spurring the growth of new hybrid forms of user-generated content. These kinds of effects, which ad-vance project by project, month by month, are likely to have a long-term transformational impact. A new social ethic is taking root.

Free culture, though culturally progressive, is fairly nonjudg-mental about ideological politics. When American conservatives decided they wanted to start Conservapedia because they found Wikipedia too liberal, Wikipedia founder Jimmy Wales was happy to bless it: "Free culture knows no bounds . . . We welcome the reuse of our work to build variants. That's directly in line with our mission."[13] Anthropology professor E. Gabriella Coleman has found a similar ecumenicism in the free software movement, which is ag-nostic about conventional politics but adamant about its own polity of freedom.[14] Thus, the FOSS movement has no position with respect to social justice or globalization issues, but it does demand a strict commitment to the "four freedoms" of software development. Johan Söderberg makes much the same case in his book *Hacking Capitalism*.[15]

As projects like GNU/Linux, Wikipedia, open courseware, open-access journals, open databases, municipal Wi-Fi, collections of CC-licensed content, and other commons begin to cross-link and coalesce, the commons paradigm is migrating from the margins of culture to the center. The viral spiral, after years of building its infrastructure and social networks, may be approaching a Cambrian explosion, an evolutionary leap.

History suggests that any new style of politics and polity will arrive through models developed *from within* the edifice of existing law, markets, and culture. A revolutionary coup or showdown with existing institutions will not be necessary. Superior working models—running code and a healthy commons—will trump polemics and exhortation.

Ideological activists and political professionals are likely to scoff at this scenario. After all, they are suspicious of distributed political power, if not hostile to it. They prefer the levers of consolidated power (laws, court rulings, police powers) that are within their sphere of influence to the dispersed, sovereign powers of an online multitude. The latter is highly resistant to capture and control, and in that sense, profoundly threatening to the traditional configurations of political power. We have already seen how the mandarins of journalism, politics, and business are quick to lash out at the noncredentialed masses who dare to put forward their own interpretations of the world.

However necessary it is to engage in the official governance of a nation, corrupted though it may be, the commoners have shown that building their own functioning commons can be a powerful force for change as well. A commons of technical standards for the Web—how mundane!—can achieve more than most antitrust lawsuits. A common pool of information can prevent a company from reaping easy monopoly rents from the control of a public good. Instead, the company must "move upstream" to provide more specialized forms of value (for example, sophisticated graphing of the information or data analysis). A commons may also be affirmatively helpful to businesses, as Eric von Hippel has shown, by aggregating a body of aficionados into a social community that can articulate customer needs and preferences in highly efficient ways: the commons as a cheap form of R & D and marketing.

In either case, the rise of a commons can be disruptive not just because it changes how market power is exercised, but because it may disperse power to a broader community of participants. Recall Johnson's observation that a commons is a "self-causing legal order" that competes with other legal orders. Individuals who affiliate with an online community may acquire the ability to manage their own social relationships and group identity.

This is not just a form of marketplace power, it is a form of *political* power. In effect, a group may be able to neutralize the power of corporations to use brands to organize their identities. By developing its own discourse and identity, an online community can reject their treatment as a demographic cohort of consumers. They can assert their broader, nonmarket concerns. As a group of commoners, they are less susceptible to propaganda, ideology, and commercial journalism as tools for organizing their political allegiances. They have greater civic sovereignty.

"Free cooperation aims at distributing power," argues Geert Lovink, a Dutch media theorist:

> I am not saying that power as such disappears, but there is certainly a shift, away from the formal into the informal, from accountable structures towards a voluntary and temporal connection. We have to reconcile with the fact that these structures undermine the establishment, but not through recognizable forms of resistance. The "anti" element often misses. This is what makes traditional, unreconstructed lefties so suspicious, as these networks just do their thing and do not fit into this or that ideology, be it neoliberal or autonomous Marxist. Their vagueness escapes any attempt to deconstruct their intention either as proto-capitalist or subversive.[16]

This can be disorienting. Energies are not focused on resisting an oppressor, but rather on building innovative, positive alternatives. In Buckminster Fuller's terms, free culture is mostly about building new models that make the existing models obsolete. Instead of forging an identity in relation to an adversary, the movement has built an identity around an affirmative vision and the challenge of *becoming*. People feel fairly comfortable with a certain level of ambiguity because the whole environment is so protean, diverse, evolving, and dynamic.

The GPL and the CC licenses are ingenious hacks because they navigate this indeterminate ideological space with legally enforceable tools, while looking to informal social practice and norms to provide stable governance. ("Order without law," in law professor Robert Ellickson's formulation.)[17] The licenses use the existing legal order to achieve their goals (the sharing of tools and content), and so the strategies are not seen as politically provocative. Yet the licenses are nonetheless politically transformative because they help new communities of practice to organize themselves and do work that may question core premises of copyright law, conventional economics, and government policy in general.

The beauty of this "ideological straddle" is that it enables a diverse array of players into the same tent without inciting sectarian acrimony. (There is some, of course, but mostly at the margins.) Ecumenical tolerance is the norm because orthodoxies cannot take root at the periphery where innovation is constantly being incubated. In any case, there is a widespread realization in the networked world that shared goals are likely to require variable implementations, depending on specific needs and contexts.

It may appear that the free software hacker, blogger, tech entrepreneur, celebrity musician, college professor, and biological researcher have nothing in common. In truth, each is participating in social practices that are incrementally and collectively bringing into being a new sort of democratic polity. French sociologist Bruno Latour calls it the "pixellation of politics,"[18] which conjures up a pointillist painting slowly materializing. The new polity is more open, participatory, dynamically responsive, and morally respected by "the governed" than the nominal democracies of nation-states. The bureaucratic state tends to be too large and remote to be responsive to local circumstances and complex issues; it is ridiculed and endured. But who dares to aspire to transcend it?

Sooner or later, history-making citizenship is likely to take up such a challenge. It already has. What is the digital republic, after all, but a federation of self-organized communities, each seeking to fulfill its members' dreams by developing its own indigenous set of tools, rules, and ethics? The power of the commons stems from its role as an organizing template, and not an ideology. Because it is able to host a diverse and robust ecosystem of talent without squeezing it into an ideological straitjacket, the commons is flexible and resilient. It is based on people's sincerest passions, not on remote institutional imperatives or ideological shibboleths. It therefore has a foundational support and energy that can outperform "mainstream" institutions.

This, truly, is the animating force of the viral spiral: the capacity to build one's own world and participate on a public stage. (Cicero: "Freedom is participation in power.") When such energies are let loose in an open, networked environment, all sorts of new and interesting innovations emerge. Since an online commons does not have the burden of turning a profit or supporting huge overhead, it can wait for serendipity, passion, and idiosyncratic brilliance to surface, and then rely on the Internet to propagate the fruits virally.

Oddly enough, entrenched commercial interests do not seem to be alarmed by the disruptive long-term implications of free culture. If the users of CC licenses genuflect before the altar of copyright law, it would appear, that is sufficient. Due respect is being shown. Meanwhile, at the level of social practice, the commoners are gradually building a very different moral economy that converges, from different paths, on a new type of civic order. In *Code*, Lessig called it "freedom without anarchy, control without government, consensus without power."

It is not entirely clear how the special capacities of bottom-up networks—a "non-totalizing system of structure that nonetheless acts as a whole," in Mark Taylor's words—can be integrated with conventional government and institutions of power. It is easy to imagine a future confrontation in the political culture, however, as the citizens of the digital republic confront the stodgy bureaucratic state (corporate and governmental). The latter will have the advantages of constitutional authority and state and economic power, but the former are likely to have the advantages of social legitimacy, superior on-the-ground information, and creative energy. How the digital republic will confront the old regime, or supplant it gradually as archaic institutions collapse over time, is the stuff of future history.

Theory has its limits. The building of the digital republic was in many ways animated by theory, of course, chiefly the rejection of certain theories of copyright law and the invention of new narratives about creativity and the commons. But this project has not been an intellectual, theory-driven enterprise so much as a vast, collective enterprise of history-making citizenship. Using the affordances of digital technologies, individuals have stepped out of their customary or assigned roles to invent entirely new vehicles for creativity, social life, business, politics, science, and education. Individuals have come together to make some remarkable new tools and institutions to serve their needs and preferences.

The story of the commons is, in this sense, the story of a series of public-spirited individuals who are determined to build new vehicles for protecting shared wealth and social energies. It is the story of Richard Stallman fighting the privatization of software and the disenfranchisement of the hacker community. It is the story of Eric Eldred's determination to go to jail if necessary to defend his ability to build a Web site for great American literature. The viral spiral, as I have called it, truly gained momentum when Lawrence Lessig, as a boundary-breaking law professor, decided to mount a constitutional test case and then to assemble a larger effort to imagine and build a new licensing scheme for sharing.

The viral spiral then spins off in dozens of directions as newly empowered people discover the freedoms and satisfactions that can accrue to them through this ancient yet now rediscovered and refurbished social vessel. Taken together, countless commons projects are validating some new models of human aspiration. Instead of presuming that a society must revolve around competitive individuals seeking private, material gain (the height of "rationality," economists tell us), the commons affirms a broader, more complex, and more enlightened paradigm of human self-interest. If the Invisible Hand presumes to align private interest and the public good, the commons has shown that cooperation and sharing can also serve this goal with great versatility and sophistication.

Over the long term, the real meaning of the viral spiral may lie in our discovery that the new platforms that we use to create and organize knowledge, and relate to one another, is changing how we think and how we conceptualize our place in the world. John Seely Brown, the former director of Xerox PARC, has said, "From my perspective, a key property of participatory cultures is that they help to create both a culture of learning and a culture of doing. The social basis of doing (e.g. networked communities of interest/practice) that you see emerging here actually form reflective practicum(s). This, in turn, ends up grounding epistemology—ways of knowing—and provides a pathway back to a kind of pragmatism that Dewey first talked about that is situated between realism and idealism. This *is* the pathway to creating a learning society and a culture that can embrace change by unleashing and affording productive inquiry in powerful and exciting ways."[19]

By empowering us to "step into history" and take greater responsibility for more aspects of our lives, it is no exaggeration to say that the commons encourages us to become more integrated human beings. We learn to integrate our production with our consumption, our learning with our doing, and our ideals with practical realities. This is surely why the viral spiral has been so powerfully transformative. It has helped bring our personal needs and interests into a closer, more congenial alignment with the institutions that serve us. We may be caught in a messy transition, and there remains much to negotiate and debate, but we should count our blessings. Few generations are as fortunate in being able to imagine and build a new commons sector of such liberating potential.

NOTES

Introduction

1. Cited by John Seely Brown, former chief scientist, Xerox Palo Alto Research Center, at Open Educational Resources conference, Houston, Texas, March 29, 2007.
2. Keith Aoki, James Boyle, Jennifer Jenkins, *Down by Law!* at http://www.duke.edu/cspd/comics.
3. "Social production" and "peer production" are associated with the work of Yale law professor Yochai Benkler, especially in his 2006 book, *The Wealth of Networks.* "Smart mobs" is a coinage of Howard Rheingold, author of a 2003 book by the same name. "Crowdsourcing" is the name of a blog run by Jeff Howe and the title of a June 2006 *Wired* article on the topic. "Wisdom of crowds" is a term coined by James Surowiecki and used as the title of his 2004 book.
4. http://www.librivox.org.
5. http://faulkes-telescope.com.
6. http://bugscope.beckman.uiuc.edu.
7. http://www.interplast.org and http://creativecommons.org/press-releases/2007/04/%E2%80%9Ca-story-of-healing%E2%80%9D-becomes-first-academy-award%C2%AE-winning-film-released-under-a-creative-commons-license.
8. http://www.scoopt.com.
9. http://www.twotonshoe.com/news.html.
10. See Doctorow's preface to the second release of the book, February 12, 2004, Tor Books. See also his blog Craphound.com, September 9, 2006, at http://www.craphound.com/?=p=1681.
11. James F. Moore, "The Second Superpower Rears its Beautiful Head," March 31, 2003, available at http://cyber.law.harvard.edu/people/jmoore/secondsuperpower.html.
12. Lawrence Lessig, *Code and Other Laws of Cyberspace* (New York: Basic Books, 1999), p. 4.
13. The effect of the elimination of formal registration in copyright law is cogently discussed by Lessig in *Free Culture* (New York: Penguin, 2004), pp. 170–73, and pp. 248–53.
14. Lawrence Lessig, "The Read-Write Society," delivered at the Wizards of OS4 conference in Berlin, Germany, on September 5, 2006. Available at http://www.wizards-of-os.org/programm/panels/authorship_amp_culture/keynote_the_read_write_society/the_read_write_society.html.
15. See, e.g., Joanna Demers, *Steal This Music: How Intellectual Property Law Affects Musical Creativity* (Athens: University of Georgia Press, 2006); Kelefa Sanneh, "Mixtapes Mix in Marketing," *New York Times,* July 20, 2006.
16. Steve Lohr, "IBM to Give Free Access to 500 Patents, *New York Times,* July 11, 2005. See also Steven Weber, *The Success of Open Source Software* (Cambridge,

Mass.: Harvard University Press, 2004), pp. 202–3. See also Pamela Samuelson, "IBM's Pragmatic Embrace of Open Source," *Communications of the ACM* 49, no. 21 (October 2006).

17. Robert D. Hof, "The Power of Us: Mass Collaboration on the Internet Is Shaking Up Business," *BusinessWeek,* June 20, 2005, pp. 73–82.

18. Interview with John Wilbanks, "Science Commons Makes Sharing Easier," *Open Access Now,* December 20, 2004, available at http://www.biomedcen tral.com/openaccess/archive/?page=features&issue=23.

19. See, e.g., Daniel E. Atkins, John Seely Brown, and Allen L. Hammond, "A Review of the Open Educational Resources (OER) Movement: Achievements, Challenges and New Opportunities," February 2007, available at http://www .oerderves.org/?p=23.

20. Interview with Peter Suber, June 28, 2006.

1. In the Beginning Was Free Software

1. Joshua Gray, editor, *Free Software Free Society: Selected Essays of Richard M. Stallman* (Boston: GNU Press, 2002), pp. 190–91.

2. Sam Williams, *Free as in Freedom: Richard Stallman's Crusade for Free Software* (Sebastopol, CA: O'Reilly & Associates 2002), pp. 76–88.

3. Steven Levy, *Hackers: Heroes of the Computer Revolution* (New York: Delta, 1993), pp. 425, 427.

4. Williams, *Free as in Freedom,* p. 127.

5. Stallman at MIT forum, "Copyright and Globalization in the Age of Computer Networks," April 19, 2001, available at http://media-in-transition.mit .edu/forums/copyright/transcript.html.

6. Eben Moglen, "Freeing the Mind: Free Software and the Death of Proprietary Culture," June 29, 2003, available at http://emoglen.law/columbia.edu/publi cations/maine-speech.html.

7. One useful history of Torvalds and Linux is Glyn Moody, *Rebel Code: Inside Linux and the Open Source Revolution* (Cambridge, MA: Perseus, 2001).

8. Eric S. Raymond, "A Brief History of Hackerdom," http://www.catb.org/ ~est/writings/cathedral-bazaar/hacker-history/ar01s06.html.

9. Steven Weber, *The Success of Open Source* (Cambridge, MA: Harvard University Press, 2004), p. 100.

10. Williams, *Free as in Freedom,* p. 100.

11. Torvalds included a brief essay, "Linux kernel management style," dated October 10, 2004, in the files of the Linux source code, with the annotation, "Wisdom passed down the ages on clay tablets." It was included as an epilogue in the book *Open Life: The Philosophy of Open Source,* by Henrik Ingo, and is available at http://www.openlife.cc/node/43.

12. Eric S. Raymond, "The Revenge of the Hackers," in Chris DiBona, Sam Ockman, and Mark Stone, eds., *Open Sources: Voices from the Open Source Revolution* (Sebastopol, CA: O'Reilly & Associates, 1999), p. 212.

13. http://www.opensource.org.

14. Elliot Maxwell, citing Wikipedia entry on "Open Source Movement," in

"Open Standards Open Source and Open Innovation," in *Innovations: Technology, Governance, Globalization* 1, no. 3 (Summer 2006), p. 134, note 56.

15. Richard Stallman has outlined his problems with the "open source" definition of software development in an essay, "Why 'Open Source' Misses the Point of Free Software," http://www.gnu.org/philosophy/open-source-misses-the-point.html.

16. Eric Raymond, "The Cathedral and the Bazaar," available at http://www.catb.org/~esr/writings/cathedral-bazaar/cathedral-bazaar/ar01s11.html.

17. I am grateful to Nicholas Gruen for this insight, taken from his essay "Geeks Bearing Gifts: Open Source Software and Its Enemies," in *Policy* 21, no. 2 (Winter 2005), pp. 39–48.

18. Andrew Leonard, "How Big Blue Fell for Linux," Salon.com, September 12, 2000, available at http://www.salon.com/tech/fsp/2000/09/12/chapter_7_part_one.print.html. The competitive logic behind IBM's moves are explored in Pamela Samuelson, "IBM's Pragmatic Embrace of Open Source," *Communications of the ACM* 49, no. 21 (October 2006), and Robert P. Merges, "A New Dynamism in the Public Domain," *University of Chicago Law Review* 71, no. 183 (Winter 2004).

19. Steve Hamm, "Linux Inc.," *Business Week*, January 31, 2005.

20. Cited by Elliot Maxwell in "Open Standards Open Source and Open Innovation," note 80, Berlecon Research, *Free/Libre Open Source Software: Survey and Study—Firms' Open Source Activities: Motivations and Policy Implications*, FLOSS Final Report, Part 2, at www.berlecon.de/studien/downloads/200207FLOSS_Activities.pdf.

21. Rishab Aiyer Ghosh, "Cooking Pot Markets and Balanced Value Flows," in Rishab Aiyer Ghosh, ed., *CODE: Collaborative Ownership and the Digital Economy* (Cambridge, MA: MIT Press, 2005), pp. 153–68.

22. See, e.g., Benkler, "Coase's Penguin, or Linux and the Nature of the Firm," *Yale Law Journal* 112, no. 369 (2002); Benkler, " 'Sharing Nicely': On Shareable Goods and the Emergence of Sharing as a Modality of Economic Production," *Yale Law Journal* 114, no. 273 (2004).

23. Open Source Yoga Unity, http://www.yogaunity.org; open-source cola, http://alfredo.octavio.net/soft_drink_formula.pdf; open-source beer, Vores OI (Danish for "Our Beer"), http://en.wikipedia.org/wiki/Vores_%C3%98l. See also http://freebeer.org/blog and http://www.project21.ch/freebeer.

24. Interview with Richard Stallman, January 21, 2008.

2. The Discovery of the Public Domain

1. Jack Valenti, "A Plea for Keeping Alive the U.S. Film Industry's Competitive Energy," testimony on behalf of the Motion Picture Association of America to extend the term of copyright protection, Senate Judiciary Committee, September 20, 1995, at http://instructors.cwrl.utexas.edu/~martin/Valenti.pdf.

2. Julie E. Cohen, "Copyright, Commodification and Culture: Locating the Public Domain," in Lucie Guibaut and P. Bernt Hugenholtz eds. *The Future of*

the Public Domain: Identifying the Commons in Information Law (The Netherlands: Kluwer Law International, 2006), pp. 121–66.

3. Pamela Samuelson, "Challenges in Mapping the Public Domain," in Guibault and Hugenholtz, eds. *The Future of the Public Domain*, pp. 7–26.

4. Jessica Litman, *Digital Copyright* (Amherst, NY: Prometheus, 2000), p. 62.

5. Tyler Ochoa, "Origins and Meanings of the Public Domain," *Dayton Law Review* 28, no. 215 (2002).

6. Lawrence Lessig explains the impact of eliminating the copyright registration requirement in Lessig, *Free Culture* (New York: Penguin, 2004), pp. 222–23.

7. Interview with Jessica Litman, November 16, 2006.

8. Ibid.

9. James Boyle, "The Second Enclosure Movement and the Construction of the Public Domain," *Law and Contemporary Problems* 66 (Winter–Spring 2003), pp. 33–74, at http://www.law.duke.edu/shell/cite.pl?66+Law+&+Contemp.+Probs.+ 33+ (WinterSpring+2003).

10. Interview with Peter Jaszi, October 17, 2007.

11. *Sega Enterprises v. Accolade*, 977 F.2d 1510 (9th Cir. 1993).

12. *Harper & Row v. Nation Enterprises*, 471 U.S. 539 (1985).

13. Samuelson, "Digital Information, Digital Networks, and the Public Domain," p. 92.

14. See, e.g., David Bollier, *Brand Name Bullies: The Quest to Own and Control Culture* (New York: Wiley, 2005).

15. Jessica Litman has an excellent historical account of the NII campaign in her book *Digital Copyright* (Amherst, NY: Prometheus, 2000).

16. Litman, *Digital Copyright*, pp. 89–100.

17. Pamela Samuelson, "The Copyright Grab," *Wired*, January 1996.

18. Ibid.

19. Litman, *Digital Copyright*, pp. 144–45.

20. See Wikipedia entry for the Copyright Term Extension Act, at http://en .wikipedia.org/wiki/Sonny_Bono_Copyright_Term_Extension_Act. See also *Eldred v. Ashcroft*, 537 U.S. 186 (2003), F. 3d 849 (2001).

21. Interview with Fred von Lohmann, March 20, 2006.

22. John Perry Barlow, "The Economy of Ideas," *Wired*, March 1994, at http:// www.wired.com/wired/archive/2.03/economy.ideas.html.

23. Ibid.

24. David Lange, "Recognizing the Public Domain," *Law and Contemporary Problems* 44 (Autumn 1981).

25. M. William Krasilovsky, "Observations on the Public Domain," *Bulletin of the Copyright Society* 14, no. 205 (1967).

26. Edward Samuels, "The Public Domain in Copyright Law," *Journal of the Copyright Society* 41, no. 137 (1993), p. 138.

27. Lange, "Recognizing the Public Domain," p. 162.

28. Jessica Litman, "The Public Domain," *Emory Law Journal* 39, no. 965 (Fall 1990).

29. Litman, "The Public Domain," p. 1012.

30. Martha Woodmansee and Peter Jaszi, eds., *The Construction of Authorship: Textual Appropriation in Law and Literature* (Durham, NC: Duke University Press, 1994).

31. Henry Miller writes: "We carry within us so many entities, so many voices, that rare indeed is the man who can say he speaks with his own voice. In the final analysis, is that iota of uniqueness which we boast of as 'ours' really ours? Whatever real or unique contribution we make stems from the same inscrutable source whence everything derives. We contribute nothing but our understanding, which is a way of saying—our acceptance." Miller, *The Books in My Life* (New York: New Directions), p. 198.

32. Rufus Pollock, "The Value of the Public Domain," report for Institute for Public Policy Research, London, July 2006, at http://www.rufuspollock.org/ economics/papers/value_of_public_domain.ippr.pdf.

33. See James Boyle, *Shamans, Software, and Spleens: Law and the Construction of the Information Society* (Cambridge, MA: Harvard University Press, 1995), p. 192.

34. James Boyle, "A Theory of Law and Information: Copyright, Spleens, Blackmail and Insider Trading," *California Law Review* 80, no. 1413 (1992), at http://www.law.duke.edu/boylesite/law&info.htm.

35. These examples can be found in Bollier, *Brand Name Bullies*.

36. Interview with Yochai Benkler, February 7, 2006.

37. James Boyle, "A Politics of Intellectual Property: Environmentalism for the Net," *Duke Law Journal* 47, no. 1 (October 1997), pp. 87–116, at http://www .law.duke.edu/boylesite/Intprop.htm.

3. When Larry Lessig Met Eric Eldred

1. Interview with Eric Eldred, August 1, 2006; Daren Fonda, "Copyright Crusader," *Boston Globe Magazine*, August 29, 1999, available at http://www .boston.com/globe/magazine/8-29/featurestory1.shtml; and Eric Eldred, "Battle of the Books: The Ebook vs. the Antibook," November 15, 1998, at http://www.eldritchpress.org/battle.html.

2. Interview with Eric Eldred, August 1, 2006.

3. Ibid.

4. Richard Poynder interview with Lawrence Lessig, "The Basement Interviews: Free Culture," April 7, 2006, p. 26, available at http://poynder.blogspot.com/ 2006/03/basement-interviews.html. See also Steven Levy, "Lawrence Lessig's Supreme Showdown," *Wired*, October 2002, pp. 140–45, 154–56, available at http://www.wired.com/wired/archive/10.10/lessig.html. Project Gutenberg is at http://wwwgutenberg.org.

5. Wikipedia entry, at http://en.wikipedia.org/wiki/Lessig; Levy, "Lawrence Lessig's Supreme Showdown."

6. Poynder interview with Lessig, April 7, 2006.

7. Levy, "Lawrence Lessig's Supreme Showdown."

8. Lawrence Lessig, "Fidelity in Translation," *Texas Law Review* 71, no. 1165 (May 1993).

9. Lawrence Lessig, "*Erie*-Effects of Volume 110: An Essay on Context in Interpretive Theory," *Harvard Law Review* 110, no. 1785 (1997).

10. Ibid., p. 1809.

11. Julian Dibbell, "A Rape in Cyberspace: How an Evil Clown, a Haitian Trick-

ster Spirit, Two Wizards, and a Cast of Dozens Turns a Database into a Society," *Village Voice*, December 21, 1993, pp. 36–42, reprinted in Mark Stefik, *Internet Dreams: Archetypes, Myths, and Metaphors* (Cambridge, MA: MIT Press, 1997), pp. 293–315, Dibbell quote at p. 296.

12. Interview with Lawrence Lessig, March 20, 2006.
13. Ibid.
14. Lessig, *Code and Other Laws of Cyberspace* (New York: Basic Books, 1999).
15. Esther Dyson, George Gilder, George Keyworth, and Alvin Toffler, "Cyberspace and the American Dream: A Magna Carta for the Knowledge Age," Progress and Freedom Foundation, August 1994, available at http://www.pff .org/issues-pubs/futureinsights/fil.2magnacarta.html.
16. David Hudson, interview with Louis Rossetto, "What Kind of Libertarian," *Rewired* (Macmillan, 1997), p. 255.
17. Steven Levy, "The Great Liberator," *Wired*, October 2002, and Poynder interview with Lessig, April 7, 2006.
18. David Streitfeld, "The Cultural Anarchist vs. the Hollywood Police State," *Los Angeles Times Magazine*, September 22, 2002, p. 32.
19. Lawrence Lessig, "Commons Law," June 24, 1999, posted on www.intellectu alcapital.com/issues/issue251/item5505.asp, and Open Law archive at http:// cyber.law.harvard.edu/openlaw.
20. *Eldred v. Reno* (later, *Eldred v. Ashcroft*), 537 U.S. 186 (2003), affirming 239 F. 3d 372.
21. Lessig, "How I Lost the Big One," *Legal Affairs*, March/April 2004, available at http://www.legalaffairs.org/issues/March-April-2004/story_lessig_marap r04.msp.
22. Lessig interview with Richard Poynder, April 7, 2006, p. 25.
23. "Lawrence Lessig Answers Your Questions," Slashdot.org, December 21, 2001, Question 1, "The question of harm," posted by "caduguid," with Lessig response, available at http://interviews.slashdot.org/article.pl?sid=01/12/21/155221.
24. Lessig response to question 11, Slashdot.org, "Will the extension of copyright continue?" posed by "Artifice_Eternity," available at http://interviews.slash dot.org/article.pl?sid=01/12/21/155221.
25. See http://www.supremecourtus.gov/oral_arguments/argument_transcripts/ 01-618.pdf. See also Lessig, "How I Lost the Big One," and Linda Greenhouse, "Justices Hear Arguments in Challenge to Copyrights," *New York Times*, October 10, 2002. A number of Supreme Court opinions in the *Eldred* case can be found at the Openlaw archive at http://cyber.law.harvard.edu/openlaw/ eldredvreno. The *Loyola Los Angeles Law Review* held a symposium on *Eldred v. Ashcroft*, available at http://llr.lls.edu/volumes/v36-issue1.
26. 537 U.S. 186 (1993). See also "Court Majority Says It Won't Second-Guess Congress," *New York Times*, January 16, 2007, p. A22.
27. Stephen Breyer, "The Uneasy Case for Copyright," *Harvard Law Review* 84, no. 281 (1970).
28. Siva Vaidhyanathan, "After the Copyright Smackdown: What Next?" *Salon*, January 17, 2003, at http://www.salon.com/tech/feature/2003/01/17/copy right.print.html.

29. Interview with Poynder, April 7, 2006, p. 25.
30. Lessig, "How I Lost the Big One." See also Lessig, *Free Culture* (New York: Penguin, 2004), pp. 228–48.
31. Lessig response to Question 11, "Cyberspace Amendment," posed by "kzinti," in Slashdot, available at http://interviews.slashdot.org/article.pl?sid=01/12/21/155221.
32. Interview with Poynder, April 7, 2006, pp. 26–27.
33. Garr Reynolds's blog on professional presentation design, "The 'Lessig Method' of Presentation," October 5, 2005, available at http://presentationzen.blogs.com/presentationzen/2005/10/the_lessig_meth.html.
34. Interview with Aaron Swartz, October 10, 2006.
35. Amy Harmon, "Challenge in Copyright Case May Be Just a Beginning," *New York Times*, October 14, 2002.
36. Interview with Eric Eldred, August 1, 2006.

4. Inventing the Creative Commons

1. Interview with Lawrence Lessig, March 20, 2006.
2. Ibid.
3. Robert S. Boynton, "Righting Copyright: Fair Use and Digital Environmentalism," *Bookforum*, February/March 2005, available at http://www.robertboynton.com/articleDisplay.php?article_id=1.
4. See, e.g., D. T. Max, "The Injustice Collector," *New Yorker*, June 19, 2006, pp. 34ff.
5. The Copyright's Commons Web site is now defunct but can be found at the Internet Archive's Wayback Machine, at http://cyber.law.harvard.edu/cc.
6. Interview with Wendy Seltzer, September 28, 2006.
7. Ross Hanig, "Luring Lessig to Stanford Law School," *Recorder*, October 17, 2001, at http://www.law.com.
8. Wikipedia entry, at http://en.wikipedia.org/wiki/Napster.
9. Interview with Jonathan Zittrain, September 28, 2006.
10. Lawrence Lessig, "Proposal for the Intellectual Property Conservancy," e-mail to ipcommons group, November 12, 2000.
11. Chris Babbitt and Claire Prestel, "Memorandum to Michael Carroll, Wilmer Cutler Pickering, 'IP Conservancy,' " October 24, 2000.
12. E-mail from Richard Stallman to Lessig, September 11, 2000. See also http://www.gnu.org/philosophy/words-to-avoid.html. Stallman suggested calling the project the "Copyright and Patent Conservancy."
13. E-mail from Hal Abelson to Lessig, September 12, 2000.
14. E-mail from Lawrence Lessig to ipcommons group, September 8, 2000.
15. This case, *Stewart v. Abend*, 100 S. Ct. 1750 (1990), required the copyright owners of Alfred Hitchcock's movie *Rear Window* to pay damages to the author of a book upon which the film was based. Saltzman was concerned that the conservancy would be liable for any illicit derivative works. See Daniel A. Saunders, "Copyright Law's Broken Rear Window: An Appraisal of Damage and Estimate of Repair," *California Law Review* 80, no. 1 (January 1992), pp. 179–245.

16. E-mail to ipcommons group, September 18, 2000.

17. E-mail from Lawrence Lessig to ipcommons group, November 12, 2000.

18. E-mail from Lawrence Lessig to ipcommons group, October 11, 2000, which contained e-mail from Laurie Racine to Lessig, October 25, 2000.

19. E-mail from Lawrence Lessig to ipcommons group, November 12, 2000.

20. http://web.archive.org/web/*/http://Openculture.org.

21. Contained in e-mail from Christina Ritchie to ipcommons group, December 15, 2000.

22. Michael Carroll, "Potential Copyright Liability and DMCA Safe Harbor Relief for Creative Commons," appendix to "Briefing Book for Creative Commons Inaugural Meeting," May 7, 2001.

23. E-mail from Eric Saltzman to ipcommons group, January 19, 2001.

24. E-mail from Paul Uhlir and Jerry Reichman, January 30, 2001.

25. E-mails from ipcommons listserv to ipcommons group, January 11, 12, 13, 16, 2001.

26. Dotan Oliar, "Memo on Creative Commons—Towards Formulating a Business Plan," March 19, 2001.

27. Interview with Chris Babbitt, September 14, 2006.

28. The mock-up can be found at http://cyber.law.harvard.edu/creativecommons/site.htm.

29. "Briefing Book for Creative Commons Inaugural Meeting," May 7, 2001, p. 10.

30. Interview with Chris Babbitt, September 14, 2006.

31. Interview with Jonathan Zittrain, September 28, 2006.

32. Oren Bracha and Dotan Oliar, "Memo: May 7th Consensus Regarding the Creative Commons Project," August 20, 2001, p. 1.

33. Interview with Chris Babbitt, September 14, 2006.

34. Laura Bjorkland, "Regarding Creative Commons: Report from the Creative Community," in "Briefing Book for Creative Commons Inaugural Meeting," May 7, 2001, pp. 16–19.

35. Oren Bracha and Dotan Oliar, "Memo: May 7th Consensus Regarding the Creative Commons Project," August 20, 2001, p. 3, note 9.

36. http://politicalhumor.about.com/od/funnypictures/ig/100-Funny-Pictures/Confusing-Florida-Ballot.htm.

37. E-mail from Michael Carroll to Molly Van Houweling and Larry Lessig, October 15, 2001.

38. Interview with Eric Saltzman, April 11, 2006.

39. "Briefing Book," p. 12.

40. Ibid.

41. For background, see "The Semantic Web: An Introduction," at http://infomesh.net/2001/swintro; Aaron Swartz and James Hendler, "The Semantic Web: A Network of Content for the Digital City," at http://blogspace.com/rdf/SwartzHendler; and John Markoff, "Entrepreneurs See a Web Guided by Common Sense," *New York Times*, November 12, 2006.

42. Interview with Lisa Rein, December 20, 2006.

43. Interview with Aaron Swartz, October 10, 2006.

44. Interview with Hal Abelson, April 14, 2007.

45. E-mail from Lawrence Lessig to Hal Abelson, April 22, 2002.
46. Interview with Glenn Otis Brown, June 9, 2006.
47. Oren Bracha and Dotan Oliar, "Memo: Presentation of Two Possible Creative Commons Layer 1 Architectures," October 1, 2001.
48. Interview with Molly Van Houweling, March 21, 2006.
49. Interview with John Brockland, January 5, 2007.
50. Interview with Molly Van Houweling, March 21, 2006.
51. Interview with Glenn Otis Brown, June 9, 2007.
52. The lawyers also wrestled with a host of imponderables that had no obvious answers, such as: What if people started spoofing the licenses by using them in inappropriate ways? Should the Creative Commons establish a central registry for CC-licensed works as a way to ensure the credibility of the project? (After long debate, the idea was ultimately rejected.) Would the Creative Commons be held liable for contributory negligence if someone used a CC license on a copyrighted song? (The CC took its chances.) Would the Creative Commons lose its trademark if it allowed anyone to use its trademarked logo? (Several lawyers warned that CC licensing of its trademark could not be properly policed.) Glenn Otis Brown worried that the board might be sued for facilitating the unauthorized practice of law. "I don't know how long I spent calling up different insurance brokers trying to get a quote," he recalled. "People had no idea what I was talking about. We ended up going all the way to Lloyd's of London to ask them," said Brown, laughing. "They wrote back and said, 'You can't insure that.'"
53. A FAQ at the Creative Commons Web site answers the most frequent user questions about the licenses. It is available at http://wiki.creativecommons.org/.
54. http://creativecommons.org/press-releases/entry/3476.
55. See http://mirrors.creativecommons.org/cc-barlow-valenti.mov.

5. Navigating the Great Value Shift

1. Interview with Glenn Otis Brown, August 10, 2006.
2. Lawrence Lessig, Creative Commons press release, December 19, 2002; "CC in Review: Lawrence Lessig on How It All Began" [weekly e-mail series], October 12, 2005.
3. Interview with Ryan Junell, September 23, 2006.
4. Matthew Haughey, "Blogging in the Public Domain," Creative Commons blog post, February 5, 2003, at http://creativecommons.org/weblog/entry/3601.
5. Susan Butler, "Movement to Share Creative Works Raises Concerns in Music Circles," Billboard, May 28, 2005.
6. John C. Dvorak, "Creative Commons Humbug: This Scheme Doesn't Seem to Benefit the Public," PC Magazine, July 28, 2005.
7. Researchers at the Economic Observatory of the University of Openness, "Commercial Commons," on the online journal Metamute, at http://www.metamute.org/?q=en/Commercial-Commons.
8. Nielsen/Net Ratings estimated 585 million Internet users in 2002; the Interna-

tional Telecommunications Union estimated 665 million. See http://www2
.sims.berkeley.edu/research/proiects/how-much-info-2003/internet.htm.

9. Yochai Benkler, *The Wealth of Networks: How Social Production Transforms Markets and Freedom* (New Haven, CT: Yale University Press, 2006), p. 60.

10. Benkler at the iCommons Summit, Dubrovnik, Croatia, June 15, 2007.

11. An excellent overview of these new spaces is Don Tapscott and Anthony D. Williams, *Wikinomics: How Mass Collaboration Changes Everything* (New York: Portfolio, 2006).

12. Robert D. Hof, "The Power of Us: Mass Collaboration on the Internet Is Shaking Up Business," *BusinessWeek*, June 20, 2005, pp. 73–82.

13. "The Fortune of the Commons," *Economist*, May 8, 2003; Henry Chesbrough, *Open Business Models: How to Thrive in the New Innovation Landscape* (Cambridge, MA: Harvard Business School Press, 2006).

14. I am indebted to my friend John Clippinger for this insight, as explained in his book *A Crowd of One: The Future of Individual Identity* (New York: Public Affairs, 2007), chapter 7, "Transforming Trust: Social Commerce in Renaissance Florence," pp. 97–114.

15. Dan Hunter and F. Gregory Lastowka, "Amateur-to-Amateur," *William and Mary Law Review* 46, no. 951 (December 2004).

16. Tim O'Reilly, "What Is Web 2.0: Design Patterns and Business Models for the Next Generation of Software," O'Reilly Media Web site, September 30, 2005, at http://www.oreilly.com/pub/a/oreilly/tim/news/2005/09/30/what-is-web-20.html.

17. Wikipedia statistics from http://en.wikipedia.org/wiki/Wikipedia:About.

18. David Bollier, "When Push Comes to Pull: The New Economy and Culture of Networking Technology" (Washington, DC: Aspen Institute, 2006), at http://www.aspeninstitute.org/atf/cf/%7BDEB6F227-659B-4EC8-8F84-8DF23CA704F5%7D/2005InfoTechText.pdf.

19. Chris Anderson, "The Long Tail," *Wired*, October 2004, at http://www.wired.com/wired/archive/12.10/tail.html.

20. http://www.openprosthetics.org.

21. Rachel Rosmarin, "Why MySpace Blinked," *Forbes*, April 24, 2007.

6. Creators Take Charge

1. Cory Doctorow, "A Note About This Book," February 12, 2004, and "A Note About This Book," January 9, 2003, in *Down and Out in the Magic Kingdom*, available at http://www.craphound.com/down.

2. Anna Weinberg, "Buying the Cow, Though the Milk Is Free: Why Some Publishers are Digitizing Themselves," June 24, 2005, *Book Standard*, June 24, 2005, available at http://www.thebookstandard.com/bookstandard/news/publisher/article_display.jsp?vnu_content_id=1000968186.

3. Cory Doctorow, "Giving it Away," Forbes.com, December 1, 2006, available at http://www.forbes.com/2006/11/30/cory-doctorow-copyright-tech-media_cz_cd_books06_1201doctorow.html.

4. Smaran, "Alchemist Author Pirates His Own Book," TorrentFreak blog, Janu-

ary 24, 2008, at http://torrentfreak.com/alchemist-author-pirates-own-books-080124.

5. Mia Garlick, "LibriVox," Creative Commons blog, December 5, 2006, at http://creativecommons.org/text/librivox.

6. "Wikitravel Press launches," Creative Commons blog, August 3, 2007, at http://creativecommons.org/weblog/entry/7596. See also Mia Garlick, "Wikitravel," Creative Commons blog, June 20, 2006, at http://creativecommons.org/text/wikitravel.

7. Mia Garlick, "Lulu," Creative Commons blog, May 17, 2006, at http://creativecommons.org/text/lulu.

8. Kevin Kelly, "Scan This Book!" *New York Times Magazine*, May 14, 2006, p. 43.

9. Ibid., p. 45.

10. Mike Shatzkin, "The End of General Trade Publishing Houses: Death or Rebirth in a Niche-by-Niche World," presented to the Book Expo America, New York, May 31, 2007, available at http://www.idealog.com/speeches/endoftrade.htm.

11. Cited in David Bollier, *The Rise of Collective Intelligence: Decentralized Co-creation of Value as a New Paradigm in Commerce and Culture* (Washington, DC: Aspen Institute Communications and Society Program, 2007), p. 27.

12. Matt Haughey, "From LA's Awesometown to New York City's SNL," *Wired News*, October 1, 2005.

13. Samuli Torssonen presentation at iCommons Summit 2007, Dubrovnik, Croatia, June 15, 2007. See also www.starwreck.com.

14. Ton Roosendaal remarks at conference, "Economies of the Commons," De Balie Centre for Culture and Politics, Amsterdam, April 10–12, 2008.

15. The film can be downloaded at http://www.bigbuckbunny.org/index.php/download.

16. Mia Garlick, CC blog, at http://creativecommons.org/weblog/entry/6048; see also "Cafuné breaking the limits for open business models," iCommons blog, at http://www.icommons.org/static/2006/11/22/cafune-breaking-the-limits-for-open-business-models.

17. Harold Feld, "CD Sales Dead? Not for Indies!" blog post on Public Knowledge Web site, March 27, 2007, at http://www.publicknowledge.org/node/890.

18. Donald Clarke, *The Rise and Fall of Popular Music*, chapter 11.

19. Lessig explained his BMI strategy at a speech, "On Free, and the Differences Between Culture and Code," at the 23d Chaos Communications Conference (23C3) in Berlin, Germany, December 30, 2006; video can be watched at http://video.google.com/videoplay?docid=7661663613180520595&q=23c3.

20. From BMI, Inc., Web site, at http://www.bmi.com/genres/entry/533380.

21. Shapiro described his experiences at the "Identity Mashup Conference," June 19–21, 2006, hosted by the Berkman Center for Internet and Society at Harvard Law School, at http://blogs.law.harvard.edu/mediaberkman/2006/06/28/id-mashup-2006-day-two-the-commons-open-apis-meshups-and-mashups. His band's Web site is at http://www.twotonshoe.com.

22. Jon Pareles, "Pay What You Want for This Article," *New York Times*, December 9, 2007.

23. Nimrod Lev, "The Combina Industry," November 16, 2004, at http://law .haifa.ac.il/techlaw/new/try/eng/nimrod.htm.

24. Patti Smith at a panel at the National Conference for Media Reform, St. Louis, sponsored by Free Press, May 14, 2005.

25. A fascinating collision of the Grateful Dead's sharing ethic and the copyright business model occurred in 2005, when the Internet Archive placed a huge cache of fan recordings online, available for free download. When Grateful Dead Merchandising objected, Deadheads accused the band's representatives of betraying the band's long-established sharing ethic. Paradoxically, the band's merchandisers may also have jeopardized the band's commercial appeal by prohibiting the downloads. As music critic Jon Pareles put it, "The Dead had created an anarchy of trust, going not by statute but by instinct and turning fans into co-conspirators, spreading their music and buying tickets, T-shirts and official CDs to show their loyalty. The new approach . . . removes what could crassly be called brand value from the Dead's legacy by reducing them to one more band with products to sell. Will the logic of copyright law be more profitable, in the end, than the logic of sharing? That's the Dead's latest improvisational experiment." Jon Pareles, "The Dead's Gamble: Free Music for Sale," *New York Times*, December 3, 2005.

26. Creative Commons blog, "Musicians Large and Small on Internet Downloading," by Matt Haughey, July 26, 2004.

27. http://news.bbc.co.uk/l/hi/entertainment/3352667.stm.

28. Joanna Demers, *Steal This Music: How Intellectual Property Law Affects Musical Creativity* (Athens: University of Georgia Press, 2006).

29. This story is told by Demers in *Steal This Music*. The court ruling is *Bridgeport v. Dimension Films*, 383 F. 3d 390 (6th Circ. 2004).

30. DJ Danger Mouse's remix received considerable press attention. A good overview is by Chuck Klosterman, "The DJ Auteur," *New York Times Magazine*, June 18, 2006, pp. 40–45.

31. See Negativland's book, *Fair Use: The Story of the Letter U and the Numeral 2* (Concord, CA: Seeland, 1995).

32. Glenn Otis Brown, "Mmm . . . Free Samples (Innovation la)," Creative Commons blog, March 11, 2003, at http://creativecommons.org/weblog/entry/3631.

33. Creative Commons Web site, at http://creativecommons.org/about/sam pling. See also Ethan Smith, "Can Copyright Be Saved?" *Wall Street Journal*, October 20, 2003.

34. See http://wiki.creativecommons.org/ccMixter. Interview with Mike Linksvayer, February 7, 2007, and Neeru Paharia, April 13, 2007.

35. Interview with Neeru Paharia, April 13, 2007.

36. Neeru Paharia, "Opsound's Sal Randolph," Creative Commons blog, October 1, 2005, at http://creativecommons.org/audio/opsound; Mike Linksvayer, "Freesound," Creative Commons blog, October 1, 2005, at http://creative commons.org/audio/freesound; Matt Haughey, "Free Online Music Booms

as SoundClick Offers Creative Commons Licenses," Creative Commons blog, August 11, 2004.

37. Neeru Paharia, "Minus Kelvin Discovered on ccMixter," Creative Commons blog, May 17, 2005, at http://creativecommons.org/weblog/archive/2005/5.

38. Cezary Ostrowski from Poland and Marco Raaphorst from Holland met online at ccMixter and decided to go into business together. They started an online label called DiSfish.

39. Mia Garlick, "Classical Music Goes Digital (& CC)," May 3, 2006, at http://creativecommons.org/weblog/entry/5883.

40. The Enderrock Group, a company that specializes in Catalan music and publishes three popular music magazines, released the two CDs, *Música Lliure and Música Lliure II*, free within the page of its magazines. See Margot Kaminski, "Enderrock," Creative Commons Web site, January 17, 2007, at http://creativecommons.org/audio/enderrock.

41. The group, Gamelan Nyai Saraswait, was blogged about by Matt Haughey on February 1, 2003, at http://creativecommons.org/weblog/entry/3599.

42. Victor Stone, "DJ Vadim Releases Album Tracks Under CC," August 20, 2007, at http://creativecommons.org/weblog/entry/7619.

43. Thomas Goetz, "Sample the Future," *Wired*, November 2004, pp. 181–83.

44. Glenn Otis Brown, "WIRED Concert and CD: A Study in Collaboration," September 24, 2004, available at http://creativecommons.org/weblog/entry/4415.

45. See, e.g., Wikipedia entry, "Ghosts I-IV," at http://en.wikipedia.org/wiki/Ghosts_I-IV.

46. Gerd Leonhard, "Open Letter to the Independent Music Industry: Music 2.0 and the Future of Music," July 1, 2007, at http://www.gerdleonhard.net/2007/07/gerd-leonhards.html.

47. Dan Hunter and F. Gregory Lastowka, "Amateur-to-Amateur," *William and Mary Law Review* 46, no. 951 (December 2004), pp. 1029–30.

48. Interview with Lawrence Lessig, September 14, 2006.

7. The Machine and the Movement

1. Interview with Glenn Otis Brown, June 9, 2006.

2. Ibid.

3. Lawrence Lessig, *Free Culture* (New York: Penguin, 2004), pp. 275, 287.

4. CC license statistics, on CC wiki page, at http://wiki.creativecommons.org/License_statistics.

5. Interview with Mike Linksvayer, February 7, 2007.

6. Glenn Otis Brown, "Announcing (and explaining) our new 2.0 licenses," CC blog, May 25, 2004, at http://creativecommons.org/weblog/entry/4216.

7. Mia Garlick, "Version 3.0 Launched," CC blog, http://creativecommons.org/weblog/entry/7249.

8. Free Culture Goes Global

1. Interview with Glenn Otis Brown, June 9, 2006.
2. Interview with James Boyle, August 15, 2006.
3. The procedures for porting a CC license to another jurisdiction are outlined in a document, "Welcome to Creative Commons International," undated, at http://wiki.creativecommons.org/Worldwide_Overview.
4. Interview with Jonathan Zittrain, September 28, 2006.
5. The most famous court case involving the CC licenses is *A. Curry v. Audax/Weekend,* in which Adam Curry sued the publishers of a Dutch tabloid magazine and two senior editors for using four photos of his family on his Flickr account that had been licensed under a BY-NC-SA license. See http://creativecommons.org/weblog/entry/5944 and http://creativecommons.org/weblog/entry/5823. A District Court of Amsterdam upheld Curry's usage of the CC licenses in a March 9, 2006, decision; see http://mirrors.creativecommons.org/judgements/Curry-Audax-English.pdf.

   There have been two Spanish cases involving CC licenses. In both cases, a collecting society, the Sociedad General de Autores y Editores (SGAE), sued cafés for playing "free music" licensed under CC licenses; SGAE claimed that it was owed royalties for the public performance of music because artists cannot legally apply a CC license to their work (or even release it online) without the consent of their collecting society. In both instances, the cases turned on evidentiary issues, not on the enforceability of CC licenses. See http://creativecommons.org/weblog/entry/5830 and http://creativecommons.org/weblog/entry/7228.
6. Interview with Yuko Noguchi, September 12, 2007.
7. Wikipedia entry, "Tropicalismo," at http://en.wikipedia.org/wiki/Tropicalismo.
8. For a history of Gil, see his personal Web site at http://www.gilbertogil.com.br/index.php?language=en; the Wikipedia entry on him at http://en.wikipedia.org/wiki/Gilberto_Gil; and Larry Rohter, "Gilberto Gil Hears the Future, Some Rights Reserved," *New York Times,* March 11, 2007.
9. Julian Dibbell, "We Pledge Allegiance to the Penguin," *Wired,* November 2004, at http://www.wired.com/wired/archive/12.11/linux_pr.html.
10. Ibid.
11. E-mail from Hermano Vianna, January 8, 2007.
12. Creative Commons press release, "Brazilian Government First to Adopt New 'CC-GPL,'" December 2, 2003.
13. A ten-minute video of the CC Brazil opening can be seen at http://support.creativecommons.org/videos#brasil.
14. Interview with Glenn Otis Brown, August 10, 2006.
15. Film about CC Brazil launch, at http://support.creativecommons.org/videos#brasil.
16. Interview with Ronaldo Lemos da Silva, September 15, 2006.
17. The *tecnobrega* scene is described by Ronaldo Lemos in "From Legal Commons to Social Commons: Developing Countries and the Cultural Industry in

the 21st Century," http://icommons.org/banco/from-legal-commons-to-social-commons-brazil-and-the-cultural-industry-1.

18. Ibid.
19. http://www.ccmixter.co.za.
20. http://www.scielo.br.
21. http://www.portacurtas.comb.br.
22. http://www.overmundo.com.br
23. http://tramavirtual.uol.com.br.
24. Ronaldo Lemos, "From Legal Commons to Social Commons: Developing Countries and the Cultural Industry in the 21st Century," http://icommons.org/banco/from-legal-commons-to-social-commons-brazil-and-the-cultural-industry-1.
25. Gil remarks at New York University, September 19, 2004, at http://www.nyu.edu/fas/NewsEvents/Events/Minister_Gil_speech.pdf.
26. Ibid.
27. Ibid.
28. Interview with Tomislav Medak, CC Croatia, June 25, 2006.
29. Ibid.
30. Ibid.
31. Interview with Andrés Guadamuz of CC Scotland, December 19, 2006.
32. See http://news.bbc.co.uk/2/hi/help/4527506.stm, and interview with Paula Le Dieu, joint director of the BBC Creative Archive project, May 28, 2004, at http://digital-lifestyles.info/2004/05/28/exclusive-providing-the-fuel-for-a-creative-nation-an-interview-with-paula-le-dieu-joint-director-on-the-bbc-creative-archive.
33. Intrallect Ltd and AHRC Research Centre for Studies in Intellectual Property and Technology Law, University of Edinburgh, "The Common Information Environment and Creative Commons," October 10, 2005, at http://www.intrallect.com/index.php/intrallect/content/download/632/2631/file/CIE_CC_Final_Report.pdf.
34. iCommons annual report, 2007, http://www.icommons.org/annual07.
35. Michael Geist, "Push for Open Access to Research, BBC News, February 28, 2007, at http://news.bbc.co.uk/go/pr/fr/~/2/hi/technology/6404429.
36. Creative Commons blog, Alex Roberts, March 8, 2006, at http://creativecommons.org/text/sip.
37. Interview with Juan Carlos de Martin, CC Italy, July 17, 2007.
38. iCommons '06 conference booklet, p. 77.
39. Giorgos Cheliotis, Warren Chik, Ankit Guglani, and Girl Kumar Tayi, "Taking Stock of the Creative Commons Experiment: Monitoring the Use of Creative Commons Licenses and Evaluating Its Implications for the Future of Creative Commons and for Copyright Law," paper presented at 35th Research Conference on Communication, Information and Internet Policy (TPRC), September 28–30, 2007. Paper dated August 15, 2007.
40. Cheliotis, "Taking Stock," pp. 20–22.
41. The French book is Danièle Bourcier and Mélanie Dulong de Rosnay, eds., *International Commons at the Digital Age* (Paris: Romillat, 2004), at http://fr

.creativecommons.org/icommons_book.htm. The Finnish book is Herkko Hietanen et al., *Community Created Content: Law, Business and Policy* (Turre Publishing, 2007), at http://www.turre.com/images/stories/books/webkirja_koko_optimoitu2.pdf. The Australian book is Brian Fitzgerald, *Open Content Licensing: Cultivating the Creative Commons* (Sydney: Sydney University Press, 2007).

42. Creative Commons Netherlands press release, "Buma/Stemra and Creative Commons Netherlands Launch a Pilot," August 23, 2007; e-mail by Paul Keller, CC Netherlands, to CC International listserv, August 23, 2007.

43. Interview with James P. Love, June 13, 2006.

44. Creative Commons blog, Kathryn Frankel, "Commoners: Architecture for Humanity," June 30, 2006, at http://creativecommons.org/education/architecture.

45. See Lessig on Creative Commons blog, December 7, 2005, at http://creativecommons.org/weblog/archive/2005/12/page/3.

46. Interview with James Love, June 13, 2006.

47. Creative Commons "retired licenses page," at http://creativecommons.org/retiredlicenses.

48. Lawrence Lessig, "Retiring standalone DevNations and One Sampling License," message to CC International listserv, June 4, 2007.

49. Interview with Lawrence Lessig, March 20, 2006.

50. http://icommons.org/isummit05.

51. http://icommons.org/isummit06.

52. iCommons Summit '06 program.

53. David Berry, "The iCommons Lab Report," sent to UK FreeCulture listserv, November 9, 2006.

54. Becky Hogge, "What Moves a Movement," OpenDemocracy.org, June 27, 2006, at www.opendemocracy.net/media-commons/movement_3686.jsp.

9. The Many Faces of the Commons

1. Ibid.

2. Interview with Lawrence Lessig, October 23, 2007.

3. Ibid.

4. Niva Elkin-Koren, "Exploring Creative Commons: A Skeptical View of a Worthy Pursuit," chapter XIV in Lucie Guibault and P. Bernt Hugenholtz, editors, *The Future of the Public Domain: Identifying the Commons in Information Law* (Alphen aan den Rijn, Netherlands: Kluwer Law International BV, 2006).

5. Interview with Yochai Benkler, February 7, 2006.

6. David Berry and Giles Moss, "On the 'Creative Commons': A Critique of the Commons without Commonality," *Free Software Magazine*, July 15, 2005, at http://www.freesoftwaremagazine.com/articles/commons_without_commonality.

7. Based on Yahoo queries, June 13, 2006, at http://wiki.creativecommons.org/License_Statistics.

8. Eric Muller, "The Case for Free Use: Reasons Not to Use a Creative Commons–NC License," at http://freedomdefined.org/Licenses/NC.

9. Niva Elkin-Koren, "Exploring Creative Commons: A Skeptical View of a

Worthy Pursuit," chapter 14 in Lucie Guibault and P. Bernt Hugenholtz, editors, *The Future of the Public Domain: Identifying the Commons in Information Law* (The Netherlands: Kluwer Law International BV, 2006), p. 326.

10. Interview with Niva Elkin-Koren, January 30, 2007.
11. Interview with Lawrence Lessig, October 23, 2007.
12. Richard Stallman, "Fireworks in Montreal," at http://www.fsf.org/blogs/rms/entry-20050920.html.
13. Benjamin Mako Hill, "Towards a Standard of Freedom: Creative Commons and the Free Software Movement," *Advogato*, July 29, 2005, at http://www.advogato.org/article/851.html.
14. Interview with Benjamin Mako Hill, June 1, 2007.
15. Ibid. See also Hill, "Freedom's Standard Advanced?" *Mute*, November 23, 2005, at http://www.metamute.org/en/node/5597.
16. Joichi Ito, message on iCommons listserv, June 1, 2007.
17. Interview with Niva Elkin-Koren, January 30, 2007.
18. Wikipedia entry on GNU Free Documentation license, at http://en.wikipedia.org/wiki/GNU_Free_Documentation_License.
19. Michael Fitzgerald, "Copyleft Hits a Snag," *Technology Review*, December 21, 2005.
20. Lessig post to CC International listserv, June 4, 2007. More about the CC's retired licenses can be seen at http://creativecommons.org/retiredlicenses.
21. Interview with Lawrence Lessig, October 23, 2007.
22. David Berry and Giles Moss, "On the 'Creative Commons': A Critique of the Commons Without Commonality," *Free Software Magazine*, July 15, 2005, at http://www.freesoftwaremagagine.com/articles/commons_without_commonality
23. Anna Nimus, "Copyright, Copyleft and the Creative Anti-Commons," at http://subsol.c3.hu/subsol_2/contributors0/nimustext.html.
24. Anupam Chander and Madhavi Sunder, "The Romance of the Public Domain," *California Law Review* 92, no. 1131 (2004), p. 1341.
25. Ibid., p. 1343.
26. "A Letter to the Commons, from the participants of the 'Shades of the Commons Workshop,' " in *In the Shade of the Commons: Towards a Culture of Open Networks* (Amsterdam, Netherlands: Waag Society, 2006), at http://www3.fis.utoronto.ca/research/iprp/cracin/publications/pdfs/final/werbin_InTheShade.pdf.
27. Center for Social Media, at http://www.centerforsocialmedia.org/fairuse. See also Pat Aufderheide and Peter Jaszi, "Fair Use and Best Practices: Surprising Success," *Intellectual Property Today*, October 2007, at http://www.iptoday.com/articles/2007-10-aufderheide.asp; and Peter Jaszi, "Copyright, Fair Use and Motion Pictures," *Utah Law Review* 3, no. 715 (2007), and which also appeared in R. Kolker, ed., *Oxford Handbook of Film and Media Studies* (2007), at http://www.centerforsocialmedia.org/files/pdf/fairuse_motionpictures.pdf.
28. Aufderheide and Jaszi, *Intellectual Property Today*, October 2007, at http://www.iptoday.com/articles/2007-10-aufderheide.asp.
29. Interview with Lawrence Lessig, October 23, 2007.

30. Interview with Yochai Benkler, February 7, 2006.
31. Cory Doctorow, iCommons listserv [thread, "Andrew Orlowski Attacks Lessig], June 1, 2007.

10. The New Open Business Models

1. John Buckman presentation at iCommons Summit, Dubrovnik, Croatia, June 15, 2007.
2. John Buckman entry in Wikipedia, at http://en.wikipedia.org/wiki/John_Buckman.
3. John Buckman at Magnatune home page, at http://www.magnatune.com/info/why.
4. John Buckman, interview with Matthew Magee of Out-Law.com, radio podcast, September 13, 2007, at http://www.out-law.com/page-8468.
5. John Buckman at iCommons, June 15, 2007. For an extensive profile of Buckman and Magnatune, see http://www.openrightsgroup.org/creative business/index.php/John_Buckman:_Magnatune.
6. John Buckman, interview with Matthew Magee, September 13, 2007.
7. See, e.g., Walter S. Mossberg, "Free My Phone," *Wall Street Journal*, October 22, 2007, p. R1.
8. Steve Lohr, "Free the Avatars," *New York Times,* October 15, 2007.
9. See Elliot E. Maxwell, "Open Standards, Open Source, and Open Innovation: Harnessing the Benefits of Openness," *Innovations: Technology, Governance, Globalization* 1, no. 3 (Summer 2006), at http://www.emaxwell.net.
10. Eric Raymond, "The Cathedral and the Bazaar," May 1997, at http://www.catb.org/~esr/writings/cathedral-bazaar. The essay has been translated into nineteen languages to date.
11. Yochai Benkler, "Coase's Penguin, or, Linux and the Nature of the Firm," *Yale Law Journal* 112, no. 369 (2002), at http://www.benkler.org/CoasesPen guin.html.
12. Richard Pérez-Peña, "Times to Stop Charging for Parts of Its Web Site," *New York Times*, September 18, 2007.
13. Frank Ahrens, "Web Sites, Tear Down That Wall," *Washington Post*, November 16, 2007, p. D1. See also Farhad Manjoo, "The Wall Street Journal's Website Is Already (Secretly) Free," *Salon*, March 21, 2008, at http://machinist.salon .com/blog/2008/03/21/wsj/index.html.
14. David P. Reed, "The Sneaky Exponential—Beyond Metcalfe's Law to the Power of Community Building," at http://www.reed.com/Papers/GFN/reedslaw.html.
15. See, e.g., Paula Lehman, "MySpace Plays Chicken with Users," BusinessWeek Online, April 12, 2007.
16. Henry Chesbrough, *Open Business Models: How to Thrive in the New Innovation Landscape* (Cambridge, MA: Harvard Business School Press, 2006).
17. http://www.openbusiness.org.
18. From blog of Professor Karim Lakhani, Harvard Business School, April 27, 2007.
19. Joe Wilcox and Stephen Shankland, "Why Microsoft is wary of open source,"

CNET, June 18, 2001; and Lea, Graham, "MS' Ballmer: Linux is communism," *Register* (U.K.), July 31, 2000.

20. Yochai Benkler, *The Wealth of Networks* (Yale University Press, 2006), Figure 2.1 on p. 47.

21. "Open Source: Now It's an Ecosystem," BusinessWeek Online, October 3, 2005.

22. Microsoft's Shared Source Licenses, at http://www.microsoft.com/resources/sharedsource/licensingbasics/sharedsourcelicenses.mspx; see also Lessig blog, "Microsoft Releases Under ShareAlike," June 24, 2005, at http://lessig.org/blog/2005/06/microsoft_releases_under_share.html.

23. Vauhini Vara, "Facebook Gets Help from Its Friends," *Wall Street Journal*, June 22, 2007. See also Riva Richmond, "Why So Many Want to Create Facebook Applications," *Wall Street Journal*, September 4, 2007.

24. Joshua Davis, "The Secret World of Lonelygirl," *Wired*, December 2006, at http://www.wired.com/wired/archive/14.12/lonelygirl.html.

25. Elizabeth Holmes, "Famous, Online," *Wall Street Journal*, August 8, 2006.

26. Revver entry at Wikipedia, at http://en.wikipedia.org/wiki/Revver.

27. Interview with Steven Starr, "Is Web TV a Threat to TV?" *Wall Street Journal*, August 7, 2007, at http://online.wsj.com/article/SB118530221391976425.html.

28. Lessig blog post, "The Ethics of Web 2.0," October 20, 2006, at http://www.lessig.org/blog/archives/003570.shtml.

29. Nicholas G. Carr, "Web 2.0lier than Thou," Rough Type blog, October 23, 2006. Joichi Ito has a thoughtful response in his blog, "Is YouTube Web 2.0?" October 22, 2006, at http://joi.ito.com/archives/2006/10/22/is_youtube_web_20.html; and Lessig responded to Carr in his blog, at http://lessig.org/blog/2006/10/stuck_in_the_20th_century_or_t.html. The "communism discourse" persists, and not just among critics of free culture. Lawrence Liang of CC India used this epigraph in a book on open-content licenses: "There is a specter haunting cultural production, the specter of open content licensing." which he attributes to "Karl Marx (reworked for the digital era)." From Liang, *Guide to Open Content Licenses* (Rotterdam, Netherlands: Piet Zwart Institute, Institute for Postgraduate Studies and Research, Willem de Kooning Academy Hogeschool, 2004).

30. Interview with Ronaldo Lemos, September 15, 2006.

31. Ronaldo Lemos, "From Legal Commons to Social Commons: Developing Countries and the Cultural Industry in the 21st Century," 2006, at http://www.icommons.org/resources/from-legal-commons-to-social-commons-brazil-and-the-cultural-industry-1. See Paula Martini post on iCommons blog, "Over the Top: The New (and Bigger) Cultural Industry in Brazil," September 28, 2007, at http://www.icommons.org/articles/over-the-top-the-new-and-bigger-cultural-industry-in-brazil.

32. Ibid.

33. Interview with Ronaldo Lemos, November 6, 2006.

34. Sylvain Zimmer of Jamendo, presentation at iCommons Summit, Dubrovnik, Croatia, June 15, 2007.

35. Don Tapscott and Anthony D. Williams, *Wikinomics: How Mass Collaboration Changes Everything* (New York Portfolio, 2006), chapter 5, "The Prosumers."

36. David Bollier, *The Rise of Collective Intelligence: Decentralized Co-creation of Value as a New Paradigm of Commerce and Culture* (Washington, DC: Aspen Institute Communications and Society Program, 2008).

37. Elliot Maxwell, "Open Standards, Open Source, and Open Innovation: Harnessing the Benefits of Openness," *Innovations: Technology, Governance, Globalization* 1, no. 3 (Summer 2006), at http://www.emaxwell.net, p. 150.

38. Elliot E. Maxwell drew my attention to these examples in his excellent essay "Open Standards, Open Source, and Open Innovation."

39. Wikipedia entry, IMDB, at http://en.wikipedia.org/wiki/Internet_Movie_Database.

40. Wikipedia entry, CDDB, at http://en.wikipedia.org/wiki/CDDB.

41. Eric von Hippel, *Democratizing Innovation* (Cambridge, MA: MIT Press, 2005), available at http://mitpress.mit.edu/democratizing_innovation_pdf.

42. Ibid., p. 1

43. Tapscott and Williams, *Wikinomics*, pp. 130–31.

44. Brendan I. Koerner, "Geeks in Toyland," *Wired*, February 2006.

45. Karim R. Lakhani and Jill A. Panetta, "The Principles of Distributed Innovation," Research Publication No. 2007-7, Berkman Center for Internet & Society, Harvard Law School, October 2007, at http://papers.ssrn.com/abstract_id=1021034. See also Darren Dahl, "Nice Threads," *Southwest Airlines Spirit*, December 2006.

46. Evan Prodromou presentation, "Commercialization of Wikis: Open Community that Pays the Bills," South by Southwest Interactive conference, March 10, 2007.

47. William J. Bulkeley, "Got a Better Letter Opener?" *Wall Street Journal*, July 13, 2006.

48. http://www.sellaband.com.

49. William Booth, "His Fans Greenlight the Project," *Washington Post*, August 20, 2006.

11. Science as a Commons

1. Derek Lowe, "Neat! Wish It Were True!" *In the Pipeline* [blog], November 29, 2007, at http://pipeline.corante.com. See also, Donna Wentworth, "Why We Need to Figure Out What We Already Know," Science Commons blog, January 4, 2008, at http://sciencecommons.org/weblog/archives/2008/01/04/why-we-need-to-figure-out-what-we-already-know.

2. James Boyle, "The Irony of a Web Without Science," *Financial Times*, September 4, 2007, at http://www.ft.com/cms/s/2/39166e30-5a7f-11dc-9bcd-0000779fd2ac.html.

3. John Wilbanks, director of the Science Commons, introduced me to this term.

4. See, e.g., Jennifer Washburn, *University Inc.: The Corporate Corruption of Higher Education* (New York: Basic Books, 2005); Derek Bok, *Universities in the Mar-*

ketplace: The Commercialization of Higher Education (Princeton, NJ: Princeton University Press, 2003); Sheldon Krimsky, *Science in the Private Interest: Has the Lure of Profits Corrupted Biomedical Research* (New York: Rowman & Littlefield, 2003); and Corynne McSherry, *Who Owns Academic Work? Battling for Control of Intellectual Property* (Cambridge, MA: Harvard University Press, 2001).

5. John Seely Brown and Paul Duguid, *The Social Life of Information* (Cambridge, MA: Harvard Business School Pulishing, 2000). See also, e.g., Jane E. Fountain, "Social Capital: Its Relationship to Innovation in Science and Technology," *Science and Public Policy* 25, no. 2 (April 1998), pp. 103–15.

6. Committee for Economic Development, *Harnessing Openness to Transform American Health Care* (Washington, DC: CED, 2008).

7. See, e.g., Rockefeller Foundation, "2005 Bellagio Meeting on Open Source Models of Collaborative Innovation in the Life Sciences" [report], Bellagio, Italy, September 2005. See also Janet Elizabeth Hope, "Open Source Biotechnology," Ph.D. diss., Australian National University, December 2004.

8. Interview with Richard Jefferson, September 7, 2006. See also http://www.cambia.org.

9. Robert Merton, "Science and Democratic Social Structure," in *Social Theory and Social Structure*, 3d ed. (New York: Free Press, 1968), pp. 604–15.

10. Richard R. Nelson, "The Market Economy and the Scientific Commons," *Research Policy* 33, no. 3 (April 2004), pp. 455–71. See also Karim R. Lakhani et al., "The Value of Openness in Scientific Problem Solving," Harvard Business School Working Paper 07-050, January 2007, at http://www.hbs.edu/research/pdf/07-050.pdf.

11. Robert Merges, "Property Rights Theory and the Commons: The Case of Scientific Research," *Social Philosophy and Policy* 13, no. 2 (Summer 1996), pp. 145–61.

12. John Willinsky, "The Unacknowledged Convergence of Open Source, Open Access and Open Science," *First Monday* 10, no. 8 (August 2005), at http://firstmonday.org/issues/issue10_8/willinsky/index.html.

13. Interview with James Boyle, August 15, 2006.

14. Jean-Claude Guédon, "In Oldenburg's Long Shadow: Librarians, Research Scientists, Publishers and the Control of Scientific Publishing," at http://www.arl.org/resources/pubs/mmproceedings/138guedon.shtml.

15. http://www.earlham.edu/~peters/fos/fosblog.html.

16. Willinsky, "The Unacknowledged Convergence."

17. Interview with Peter Suber, June 28, 2006.

18. Association of Research Libraries, *ARL Statistics 2005–06,* at http://www.arl.org/stats/annualsurveys/ar/stats/arlstats06.shtml.

19. Peter Suber, "Creating an Intellectual Commons through Open Access," in Charlotte Hess and Elinor Ostrom, eds., *Understanding Knowledge as a Commons: From Theory to Practice* (Cambridge, MA: MIT Press, 2007), p. 175.

20. Association of Research Libraries, "Tempe Principles for Emerging Systems of Scholarly Publishing," May 10, 2000, at http://www.arl.org/resources/pubs/tempe/index.shtml.

21. http://www.earlham.edu/~peters/fos/timeline.htm.
22. The Budapest Open Access Initiative can be found at http://www.soros.org/openaccess.
23. http://www.earlham.edu/~peters/fos/overview.htm.
24. Peter Suber has an excellent account of the final OA legislation in *SPARC Open Access Newsletter*, no. 17, January 2, 2008, at http://www.earlham.edu/~peters/fos/newsletter/01-02-08.htm.
25. Science Commons brochure [undated].
26. Science Commons, "Scholar's Copyright Project—Background Briefing," at http://sciencecommons.org/literature/scholars_copyright.html.
27. Interview with John Wilbanks, November 19, 2007.
28. Patricia Cohen, "At Harvard, a Proposal to Publish Free on the Web," *New York Times*, February 12, 2008. See also Peter Suber's coverage of the decision in *Open Access News*, at http://www.earlham.edu/~peters/fos/2008/02/more-on-imminent-oa-mandate-at-harvard.html, and subsequent days.
29. Donna Wentworth blog post, "Ensuring the freedom to integrate—why we need an 'open data' protocol," Science Commons blog, December 20, 2007, at http://sciencecommons.org/weblog/archives/2007/12/20/ensuring-the-freedom-to-integrate.
30. National Research Council, *A Question of Balance: Private Rights and the Public Interest in Scientific and Technical Databases* (Washington, DC: National Academy Press, 1999), p. 14.
31. John Sulston and Georgina Ferry, *The Common Threat: A Story of Science, Politics, Ethics and the Human Genome* (Washington, DC: Joseph Henry Press, 2002), pp. 212–13.
32. http://www.hapmap.org.
33. Andrés Guadamuz González, "Open Science: Open Source Licenses in Scientific Research," *North Carolina Journal of Law & Technology* 7, no. 2 (Spring 2006), pp. 349–50.
34. http://www.hapmap.org/guidelines_hapmap_data.html.en.
35. Interview with John Wilbanks, November 19, 2007.
36. Ibid.
37. Moody and Singh quotations from Donna Wentworth, Science Commons blog post, December 20, 2007.
38. Brian Athey, University of Michigan, presentation at Commons of Science conference, National Academy of Science, Washington, DC, October 3, 2006.
39. Stevan Harnad, "Maximizing Research Impact Through Institutional and National Open-Access Self-Archiving Mandates," *Electronics & Computer Science E-Prints Repository*, May 2006, available at http://eprints.ecs.soron.ac.uk/12093/02/harnad-crisrey.pdf.
40. Interview with Michael Carroll, August 7, 2006.
41. Thinh Nguyen, "Science Commons: Material Transfer Agreement Project," *Innovations*, Summer 2007, pp. 137–43, at http://www.mitpressjournals.org/doi/pdf/10.1162/itgg.2007.2.3.137.
42. Ibid.

12. Open Education and Learning

1. Interview with Richard Baraniuk, January 21, 2008.
2. Rice University Press homepage, at http://www.ricepress.rice.edu.
3. http://cccoer.pbwiki.com.
4. MIT press release, "MIT to make nearly all course materials available free on the World Wide Web," April 4, 2001.
5. Carey Goldberg, "Auditing Classes at M.I.T., on the Web and Free," *New York Times*, April 4, 2001, p. 1.
6. Interview with Hal Abelson, "OpenCourseWare and the Mission of MIT," *Academe*, September/October 2002, pp. 25–26.
7. David Diamond, "MIT Everyware," *Wired*, September 2003.
8. Daniel E. Atkins, John Seely Brown, and Allen L. Hammond, "A Review of the Open Educational Resources (OER) Movement: Achievements, Challenges and New Opportunities," February 2007, at http://www.oerderves .org/wp-content/uploads/2007/03/a-review-of-the-open-educational-re sources-oer-movement_final.pdf, p. 23.
9. OpenCourseWare Consortium, at http://www.ocwconsortium.org.
10. Ibid.
11. See, e.g., John Markoff, "For $150, Third-World Laptop Stirs a Big Debate," *New York Times*, November 30, 2006.
12. J. Philipp Schmidt and Mark Surman, "Open Sourcing Education: Learning and Wisdom from the iSummit 2007," September 2, 2007, at http://icommons .org/download_banco/open-sourcing-education-learning-and-wisdom-from -isummit-2007.
13. http://www.capetowndeclaration.org.
14. Schmidt and Surman, "Open Sourcing Education."

Conclusion: The Digital Republic and the Future of Democratic Culture

1. For a nice overview of these policy contests, see Yochai Benkler, *The Wealth of Networks: How Social Production Transforms Markets and Freedom* (New Haven, CT: Yale University Press, 2006), chapter 11, "The Battle Over the Institutional Ecology of the Digital Environment," pp. 383–459.
2. Shanthi Kalathil and Taylor C. Boas, *Open Networks, Closed Regimes: The Impact of the Internet on Authoritarian Rule* (Washington, DC: Carnegie Endowment for International Peace, 2003).
3. David Bollier, *The Rise of Netpolitik: How the Internet Is Changing International Politics and Diplomacy* (Washington, DC: Aspen Institute Communications and Society Program, 2003).
4. David R. Johnson, "The Life of the Law Online," *First Monday* 11, no. 2 (February 2006), at http://firstmonday.org/issues/issue11_2/johnson/index.html.
5. Michael Schudson, *The Good Citizen: A History of American Civic Life* (New York: Free Press, 1998), dust jacket.
6. Ibid., p. 310.

7. I am inspired in this choice of terms by Charles Spinosa, Frnando Flores, and Hubert L. Dreyfus in their book, *Disclosing New Worlds: Entrepreneurship, Democratic Action, and the Cultivation of Solidarity* (Cambridge, MA: MIT Press, 1997).

8. See, e.g., Yochai Benkler, *The Wealth of Networks*, pp. 225–32.

9. Jonah Bossewitch, "The Zyprexa Kills Campaign: Peer Production and the Frontiers of Radical Pedagogy," *Re-public*, at http://www.re-public.gr/en/?p=144.

10. Joichi Ito, "Emergent Democracy," chapter 1 in John Lebkowsky and Mitch Ratcliffe, eds., *Extreme Democracy* (Durham, NC: Lulu.com, 2005), at http://extremedemocracy.com/chapters/Chapter%20One-Ito.pdf.

11. Adam Liptak, "Verizon Reverses Itself on Abortion Messages," *New York Times*, September 27, 2007, at http://www.nytimes.com/2007/09/27/business/27cnd-verizon.html.

12. Johnson, "The Life of the Law Online."

13. Robert Mackey, "Conservapedia: The Word Says it All," *New York Times*, March 8, 2007, at http://thelede.blogs.nytimes.com/2007/03/08/conservapedia-the-word-says-it-all/?scp=1&sq=wales+conservapedia.

14. E. Gabriella Coleman, "The Political Agnosticism of Free and Open Source Software and the Inadvertent Politics of Contrast," *Anthropology Quarterly* 77, no. 3 (Summer 2004), pp. 507–19. See also her Ph.D. dissertation, "The Social Construction of Freedom in Free and Open Source Software: Hackers, Ethics and the Liberal Tradition," abstract at http://healthhacker.org/biella/coleman-abstract.pdf.

15. Johan Söderberg, *Hacking Capitalism: The Free and Open Source Software Movement* (New York: Routledge, 2007).

16. Geert Lovink, "Theses on Wiki Politics," an exchange with Pavlos Hatzopoulos, *Re-public*, at http://www.re-public.gr/en/?p=135.

17. Robert Ellickson, *Order Without Law: How Neighbors Settle Disputes* (Cambridge, MA: Harvard University Press, 2005).

18. Bruno Latour, "We Are All Reactionaries Today," *Re-public*, at http://www.republic.gr/en/?p=129.

19. John Seely Brown, personal communication, January 26, 2008.

INDEX